Journey of the Bard

Celtic Initiatory Magic

by Yvonne Owens

paintings, illustrations and verse
by Miles Lowry

Horned Owl Publishing
Victoria, Canada

Horned Owl Publishing

Victoria, B.C. ███████ Canada

Printed on recycled paper in Winnipeg, Canada.

Canadian Cataloguing in Publication Data

Owens, Yvonne.
  Journey of the bard

  Includes bibliographical references.
  ISBN 0-9696066-2-1

  1. Magic, Celtic. 2. Shamanism. I. Lowry, Miles, 1959- II. Title
BF1622.C45O93 1997   299'.16   C97-910076-3

To my parents, Rose and Arthur Owens,
for their gifts of magic and fairytales.

CONTENTS

Part IV – Gwynned: The Way Back

ACKNOWLEDGEMENTS

I would like to thank the following people for their help and support. The nine priestesses who travelled the realms of the Bard's journey with me in its first form, as a series of musical performances presented over the course of a year and a day, are to be commended for their stamina, dedication, and sense of humour. Thank you Margaret, Lesley, Catherine, Liz, Vanessa, Tracy, Diana — and the two bards who composed all the music for our travels — Naomi Lester and Erynn Marshall. Kathy Phillips must also be thanked for being the first traveller of the journey in its written form. My gratitude goes to Sylvia Skelton for her painstaking proofreading of the manuscript and her editorial suggestions, as well as to Bryony Lake. I will eternally bless my collaborator and friend, Miles Lowry, for being so absolutely excellent in his comprehension and rendering of the bardic arts. Kudos and thanks to my publisher, Rob Von Rudloff, for his endless faith and patience with this project, not to mention his scrupulous care with the manuscript, layout and design. Thanks to my brother, Ian Owens, for timely practical support — also Monika and Jason Smith, and Diana and Don Friesen, for help in times of need. And finally I must express my profound gratitude to Don Brennan, whose assistance greatly aided this magical journey.

Journey of the Bard

Introduction

The Three Worlds of the Tree of Life

Once every people in the world believed that trees were divine and could take a human or grotesque shape and dance among the shadows; and that deer, and ravens, and foxes, and wolves and bears, and clouds and pools, almost all things under the sun and moon, and the sun and moon, were not less divine and change-able. They saw in the rainbow the still bent bow of a god thrown down in negligence; they heard in the thunder the sound of his beaten water jar, or the tumult of his chariot wheels; and when a sudden flight of wild ducks or of crows passed over their heads, they thought they were gazing at the dead has-tening to their rest; while they dreamed of so great a mystery in little things that they believed the waving of a hand, or of a sacred bough, enough to trouble far-off hearts, or hood the moon with darkness.

— William Butler Yeats

Yeats described this way of looking at the world and the elements within it as "the ancient religion." This suggests a mindscape replete with gods, demi-gods, benign and malignant spirits, energetically imbued landmarks and ob-jects, and mysterious realms of the soul that coincide with, and sometimes juxtapose, the "ordinary" world. Such mythic vision is what animates the world-view of primitive societies and underlies our own society and origins as a thinking, feeling, conjecturing kind of animal.

A world saturated with spirit and animate with vital force was the world of our distant (and not-so-distant) ancestors. Their response to such myster-ies was the root of all aboriginal religions, including those of Europe. The Seers, Pythons, Witches, Druids and Bards of antiquity acted as interpreters of the magical realm for their communities. In so doing, they developed a metaphorical language by which the divine could not only be communicated, but experienced. This ritual language became the stock-in-trade of the Bard as well as the repertory of the arts: music, drama, painting, poetry, narrative, and dance. Eventually, with the erosion of indigenous traditions, practition-ers of these arts became the channel through which magico-spiritual teach-ings were passed on. In the words of Caitlin Matthews, "The storyteller was an initiator then — albeit unknowingly as, with the poet, he became the sole guardian of the mystery teachings when the druidic role was taken over by the priest and monk."[1]

In Jodie Forrest's contemporary fairy tale, *The Rhymer and the Ravens,* the Queen of the Fairies says to the main character, Thomas the Bard, "A bard partakes of mysteries, but to win his bread, this mongrel age of yours requires diversion from him. Yet in times not long past and in lands not far away, bards had no enemies, and their persons were sacred . . . rather like priests."[2]

The Old Religion was a mode of celebratory ritual, reverential and pregnant with significance. The sacrosanct quality of all life and the prime movements of the spirit were given predominant respect. The elect, in the world of women and men who inhabited the sacred realm, was (and is still) the shaman, whose purpose it is to reconcile the various levels of reality. For ancient communities, and for primal societies of today, her or his function was that of mediator in the exchanges of mortals with what is eternal and divine. Such individuals, known as the "Wise," served their communities as agents of the kind of ordered chaos which is creativity.

Because of this, the Wise Ones were essential to the ritual life of their societies. The shaman figure is an administrator, of sorts, of divine will or whimsy. She or he invokes, evokes, or conjures "the divine" with an entire technology of chants, incantations, dances, gestures, and visual images, wielding sacred skills and tools, facilitating a magic space in which the realms converge. Mircea Eliade called such individuals "Technicians of the Sacred." The magical/spiritual function of the shaman as orchestrator for the interactions of women and men with sacred consciousness remains of such importance that it continues to be prominent in the folklore of contemporary archaic and technological societies.

As a contact to or ambassador for the Mysteries this character performs a vital role for those who desire ". . . the truly sacred and essential moment, a moment like those throughout history when men's [sic] eyes have been opened to the insubstantiality of the solid-seeming world, and they have found reality — and themselves — transformed. Here for a transfixed instant the two dimensions are in a special relationship; the bright supernatural realm, in sympathy with the doings of humanity, is reaching through the cracks in the visible universe into time and space; and the human community has simultaneously opened itself to wonder, perfectly attuned to the mystery beyond and within the ordinary."[3]

The necessity of this function has made the shamanic figure an indelible imprint upon the collective imagination. It is distillations of the shamanic archetype which surface in disguise, edited and revised, as the strangely gifted herdsmen, coachmen, blacksmiths, heras (heroines), witches, heroes, warriors, and crones of Western folklore. The dimly illuminated shaman is to be found amid the obscurity of tales involving mysterious passengers, magical hitchhikers, awesomely attuned mountain dwellers — in fact, all the odd, inspired, eerily skilled characters of urban myth and apocryphal tales. The shamanic role is present in the legends of civilised, even sophisticated, societies, as well as being plainly present in the life of primal groups. As in the case of Yeats (as a longtime member of the Golden Dawn mystical order, both poet and magician) the primary shaman's role among Celts was, and is still, that of the Bard.

Mircea Eliade has theorised that shamanistic methods migrated from northern central Asia into western Europe, south to Russia, further south to India, and east across the Bering Strait to North America, incorporating indigenous spiritual practices which they encountered. The irregular waves of migration that populated this continent would have brought with them the same basal culture which was simultaneously spreading westward to the British Isles in similar, irregular waves of invasion. It is probable that the shaman's craft proliferated among Celts, Greeks, early Chinese, and among ancient Eurasian populations in general. We know that these practices continue among isolated pockets of the population — in Siberia, the Himalayas, India, and among Druids, Witches, and other neo-Pagans.

It appears that where (what we now call) "rational" patterns of thought became emergent, as in Greece or Persia, or where intellectual/cultural sophistication developed, the shamanic method was transmuted into that of the priest — or fragmented and specialised into the roles of the artist, physician, poet, dramatist, musician, storyteller or seer. Eliade speculates that all of these divergent realms of endeavour evolved from a single, incorporated prototype: the shaman.

A world view that does not see the magnitude of the divine infusing every given thing instead compartmentalises it into sacred and profane elements. The multifarious nature of the universe becomes polarised into opposing realities, severed and separate. A "rational" scientific, supposedly "enlightened" civilisation such as the one we, as a culture, have constructed around ourselves will apparently choose, of these opposing worlds, the least deniable by collective consensus, that being material reality. Religion follows suit and becomes organised and orthodox, subjugated to a supportive role for the societal structure, geared to the task of perpetuating the social order prevailing. No longer religion for ecstasy's sake, it becomes religion for the state, merely another institution.

The edifice of such interlocking institutions we mistake for civilisation feels it cannot afford to harbour individuals in whom such personal authority and personal power is vested. The incorporated role of shaman has been systematically fractured and its power and influence dispersed in programs as deliberate as the Inquisition, and as casual as the erosion of the prestige of artists in this culture. The spiritual function of ritual drama has suffered from the attempts to conventionalise it into that of the priest. In the words of Steven Larsen:

> In almost all orderly, stable societies there has been a preference for the priestly way. The shaman is a much too dangerous character to have around. He is

often a solitary, half-mad creature through whom a god or demon may begin speaking unexpectedly. Or he may suddenly keel over in a trance, leaving his body lifeless and glassy-eyed, only to return from the invisible realm of myth with some outrageous demand, not at all in keeping with the demands of social progress. The shaman's primary allegiance is to the supernatural dimension, not to the society.[4]

Aside from contributing to the reason Witches, alchemists and others with heretical philosophies were executed by the hundreds of thousands (if not millions) in Europe during the Middle Ages, this attitude has served to deprive people of their own, personal approaches to self-realisation. Inspiration, creativity, revelation, religious and artistic experience — knowledge in general, especially ancient or women's knowledge — was considered suspect by the early Church. Yet a pre-Christian culture — such as that of the Celts — can offer us an image of European, shamanic roots of great richness and transformative power. For that reason, this book will focus upon Celtic and other Eurasian (tribal) cultural vestiges and motifs, with a comparison to corresponding universal forms and practices. In every case, common values of world shamanism are perpetuated by the poets, artists, troubadours and Bards of those cultures. The imagistic tools of the Bard's craft provide a way of accessing these earlier attitudes towards the creative (or "transformative") vision.

For all that, it is not the purpose of this book to glamorise Celtic society. Though there were advantages along gender lines, there were definite disadvantages along lines of class structure, distribution of wealth, and warfaring policies. The part of Celtic culture I would like to bring forward is in its magical world-view, the animistic belief that all of nature is conscious, powerful, and intrinsically sacred.

This is the culture base of folk and fairy tales, and the vessel of shamanic lore that survives from the earliest European tribal systems. Mythic correspondences and magical beliefs that can be traced to the Ice Age can be found in what survives of the oral traditions of rural Europe, whether on the continent, the British Isles, or exported to Oceania or the Americas. These basic ideas are ingrained in all languages descended from Indo-European roots. Their images and motifs were codified in the heroic verse, songs, stories and legends of Bards, themselves shamans within the priesthood of the Druids. The old stories, ideological ancestors of modern fairy tales, were told and retold according to certain, magical formulae, revealing a map of the magical world.

Within the mythic landscape of ancient Celts lay a complex, choreographed approach to sacred, personal power. This force was seen as, essentially, creative — the power to make, or change, reality. Within age-old, traditional guidelines, artistic self-expression was achieved through self-knowledge. This is the reason poetic, artistic and musical arts were so highly esteemed by Celts, the highest honours accruing to those who became accomplished as Bardic facilitators of magic.

The Song of Taliesin, The Song of Roland, The Song of Amergin, The Ring Cycle and countless other legends describe the mantic power of inspired utterance. Numinous words and songs were thought to have the ability to conquer alien lands or to restore health and balance in times of blight or famine. Magical arts were believed to create whole, new realities. Life follows art, and modern psychology and medicine have come to recognise the value of creative imaging and verbal "affirmations" in healing.

The magically charged landscape of ancient Celts postulated three "worlds," corresponding to human physiology. The way a Mage came to mantic, magical power was by learning to navigate in these regions of the body consciousness. Trance journeying followed a particular map, one that is recognised by shamanic systems worldwide. This map delineated a particular cosmology, the three "worlds," known universally as The Underworld, The Garden (Earth, or Paradise), and the Celestial Realm (or Heavenly Sphere).

These realms were to be found by traversing the mini-universes contained within the Tree of Life, a symbolic model not only of the universe but also of the human spiritual body, known to Hebraic Cabalistic lore, Siberian shamanism, Scandinavian paganism, Mesopotamian astrological magic, African mythology, and encompassed within folklore as the familiar "bean stalk," or enchanted pear tree of fairy tales. The Tree of Life represents a "microcosm with its three zones — sky, earth, underworld — at the same time that it indicates the means by which the shaman accomplishes the breakthrough from plane to plane and establishes communication with the world above and the world below."[5]

The Oak, Birch, Ash, Rowan, Fig, Elder, Alder, Apple, Pear, and many other trees figure in magical lore worldwide as the bridge to other realms and altered states of consciousness. The reasons for this encompass many levels of interpretation. The simplest reason lies in our physiology. Though primitive people would have been unable to detect this fact except by virtue of trance or heightened perception, the electrical-type activity of the human nervous system describes a familiar pattern. With the legs and feet containing root-like clusters and extensions, the spine containing a densely packed nexus like a trunk, and the cerebral cortex and brain radiating invisible lines of force like a crown, the average human energetic body resembles nothing so much as a tree (figure 1).

Other reasons for the universality of the World Tree, Tree of Life, or Tree of Knowledge motif may lie in our origins as a forest species, or in the simple fact that much of the planet was once covered by forests. Our evolutionary move towards upright mobility probably contributed to our affinity for trees. When the first "humans" began to walk upright, they created an energetic and spiritual axis between earth and sky that has been traced within shamanic and magical traditions ever since. A common form of the sacred Tree symbol is a simple pole or staff, topped with a bird or wings. One of the earliest renderings of this image is a cave painting in France which dates from the Upper Paleolithic period (figures 2). Ancient Sumerian and Hebraic images of the Tree of Life show a serpent coiled around the base, as do Hindu versions.

The Birch axis (tent) pole of Siberian tribes, the seven-tiered ziggurats of Babylon, the seven-storey pagodas of Chinese tradition, and the World Trade Towers in New York City all have one thing in common. They seek to link heaven and earth. According to Eliade, "The Tree connects the three cosmic regions. The Vasyugan Ostyak believe that its branches touch the sky and its roots go down into the underworld."[6] Without hubris, the more primitive versions of the World Tree seek to link head to heart, spirit to matter, body to soul, past and future, foundations to projections, and any and all metaphorical regions in between.

In this book, I propose to map the magical landscape of the ancient, Celtic world-view. This handbook for spirit journeying has value for those who care to approach self-knowledge and creative power in terms of their ancestral or cultural roots in European shamanism. So many of the landmarks in the magical landscape of Celtic lore are familiar to people who have grown up with European folk and fairy tales. They are as ubiquitous as (and in fact include) Mother Goose. There is no reason why these familiar realms and the archetypical characters who dwell in each should not be turned back to the

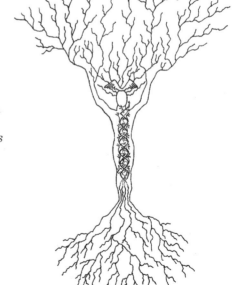

Figure 1: The human energy system as the Sacred Tree.

magical, transformative roles they originally held. They belong to us; they are within our collective psyche, expressing various dimensions of our Self, so we might as well thrive from the association.

It is my belief that knowledge of all dimensions of the personal and collective Self is the key to personal evolution, health and magical (creative) ability. To that end, it is appropriate to enquire who we are as English-speaking people within a European tradition of thought and to pursue self-knowledge within that context. What traditions underlie our current Judeo-Christian-based mishmash of ethnic cultures? One common thread, and the thread from which the tradition of Bardic magic derives, is from the fabric of Celtic mythology. The Journey of the Bard explores this terrain, in the context of initiatory magic and world shamanism.

THE CELTIC CULTURAL MATRIX

The Celts have been described as a loose confederation of European tribes who shared some common bloodlines, mythic and artistic traditions and linguistic patterns. The culture matrix conservatively defined as "Celtic" existed

Figure 2: The Sacred Tree, as represented by a pole topped with a bird. Left: from Upper Paleolithic cave painting, Lascaux, France. Right: twentieth century grave marker from Bella Coola, British Columbia, Canada.

from about 700 B.C.E. (Before Current Era) to 400 C.E., throughout much of Europe north and west of the Alps. Essentially they were descendants of early Neolithic agricultural peoples and the warrior bands who swept over the continent in waves of westward migration from about 4000 B.C.E. until about 500 B.C.E.

At the turn of the century, Charles Squire described the genesis of British Celtic culture in his book, *Celtic Myth and Legend*, as follows:

> The ancient inhabitants of Britain — the Gaelic and British Celts — have been already described as forming a branch of what are roughly called the "Aryans." This name has, however, little reference to race, and really signifies the speakers of a group of languages, which can be all shown to be connected, and to descend remotely from a single source — a hypothetical people which we term "Aryan," or more correctly, "Indo-European." This primeval speech, evolved, probably, upon some part of the great plain which stretches from the mountains of Central Europe to the mountains of Central Asia, has spread, superseding, or amalgamating with the tongues of other races, until branches of it are spoken over almost the whole of Europe and a great portion of Asia. All the various Latin, Greek, Slavic, Teutonic, and Celtic languages are "Aryan," as well as Persian and other Asiatic dialects derived from the ancient "Zend," and the numerous Indian languages which trace their origin to Sanskrit.[7]

This theory of common linguistic roots is out of fashion now, having been rendered obsolete by more recent findings. It is now felt that there was a greater diversity among language groups, even in prehistoric times. Nevertheless, certain word/concept similarities are the foundations for common mythic motifs, symbols and themes. Identical, primary meanings are in evidence across Eurasia, from India to Persia to the British Isles.

For example, *duir*, thought to be the Indo-European root for both "Druid" and "door," has similar meanings to the Sanskrit word *duir*, which means "door." The Celtic lunar calendar of trees names the Oak tree, sacred to Druids, "Duir," known in folk culture as the "Druids' Door." Oak month (or "moon") stands at the halfway mark in the Celtic lunar year, directly across the year-wheel from Samhain or All Hallows, marking the portal from the "dark half" to the "light half" of the year.

Besides the diffusion of ideas through the dispersal of languages, there was also far more actual contact among far-flung regions and their inhabitants, due to trade and exploration, than is generally supposed. Scandinavian words have prefixes, suffixes and roots in common with the language of the ancient Hindu Vedas and Welsh Gaelic. Baltic amber has been found in jewellery and talismans from Asia Minor to North Africa, and British tin has turned up in Italy and the Middle East. The bronze figurine of the Celtic sky-god at Le Châtelet (Haute-Marne) holds a thunderbolt identical to that of the ancient Persian god, Zervan Akarana.[8] This thunderbolt was originally the *vajra*

(Sanskrit for "thunderbolt") of Vedic Mitra-Varuna (figure 3).[9]

Charles Squire pointed out that, "While the Aryan speech survived, though greatly modified, the Aryan blood might well have disappeared, diluted beyond recognition by crossing with the other races whom the Aryans conquered, or among whom they more or less peaceably settled. . . . There are no European nations . . . which are not made up of the most diverse elements. Aryan and non-Aryan long ago blended inextricably, to form by their fusion new peoples."[10] In current terminology, that is as much as to say that Indo-European tribal groupings evolved from an ideological and genetic mixture of westward-migrating, proto-Indo-European cultures and non-Indo-European indigenous cultures. New tribal cultures would have developed, along with new clan structures and caste delineations.

Among these "new peoples" were the Celts. Tall, fair-skinned, with red or blonde hair, they have much in common with the "People of Odin" — tribes who migrated north and west from east/central Europe to Scandinavia to become the Norse. According to one legend, these tribes followed Odin and left a trail of mythologies concerning Valkyries, heavenly warriors, doomsday wolves, Valhalla, and the Tree of Life, or sacred Ash. They can be compared to the Scythians, originating north of the Black Sea, and who invaded south into Anatolia, the Middle East and the Caucasus. Their ancestors were anciently

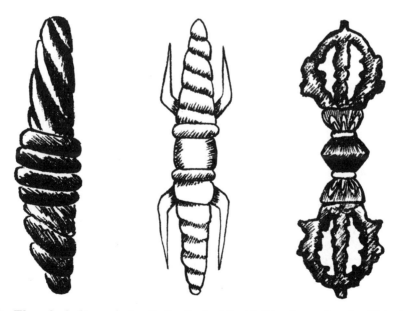

Figure 3: Thunderbolt symbols. Left: that of the Celtic sky-god at Le Châtelet, Haute-Marne, France. Centre: that of the Persian god Zervan Akarana ("Boundless Time") at Roman temple of Mithra, Ostia. Right: Tibetan Dorje *("Diamond Sceptre") or Sanskrit* Vajra *("diamond" or "thunderbolt").*

called "the Medes," a name given to the early Persians, ancestors of modern Iranians, Turks, and Kurds.

The conquering cultural complex of the proto-Indo-Europeans incubated for centuries in the high, desert-like grazing lands north of Afghanistan, between the Pamir mountains and the Aral Sea, before its relatively sudden dispersal in every direction starting about 4000 B.C.E. Ethnically, ancient Celts can be compared, in some respects, to modern day Kurds, Serbs, Magyars, Tartars, Prussians, and Afghanis. Brilliantly dyed wool clothing and soft, leather boots were typical attire of these semi-nomadic, pastoralist tribes. Such clothing was prized by ancient Celts, and indicated status and wealth. Mummified burials of "Caucasians" dating from as early as 4000 B.C.E. disclose an identical style of clothing as far east as Beijing.

Such a wide diffusion of influences is to be considered natural, as human boundaries are constantly being expanded on every level, as normal expression of human inquisitiveness. Joseph Campbell has underscored the affinities not only of East Indian mythic motifs with the Celtic, but of the similarities of certain North American Indian concepts with Celtic thought.[11] In the words of Charles Squire:

> . . . just as the Aryan speech influenced the new languages, and the Aryan customs the new civilisations, so we can still discern in the religions of the Aryan-speaking nations similar ideas and expressions pointing to an original source of mythological conceptions. Hence, whether we investigate the mythology of the Hindus, the Greeks, the Teutons, or the Celts, we find the same mythological groundwork. In each, we see the powers of nature personified, and endowed with human form and attributes, though bearing, with few exceptions, different names. Like the Vedic brahmans, the Greek and Latin Poets, and the Norse scalds, the Celtic bards — whether Gaels or Britons — imagined the sky, the sun, the moon, the earth, the sea, and the dark underworld, as well as the mountains, the streams, and the woods . . . every passion, as War and Love, and every art, as Poetry and Smith craft, [ruled by] its divine founder, teacher and exponent . . . [around which] they wove the poetical and allegorical romances . . .[12]

The Celts' society was stratified according to a caste system, similar to that of their relatives to the East, who invaded the Indian subcontinent via the mountain passes of Kashmir. The primary ranking system had five basic levels. These were the priestly caste (druids, shamans, bards, and artists), the warrior caste (kings, queens, knights and "gentry"), the merchant caste (traders, manufacturers of "mundane" goods), the farmer caste (landed or indentured peasantry), and serfs. Serfs had no status or rank, but were considered the slaves, property or chattel of the upper castes. For the most part, the serf caste was made-up of the indigenous populations of lands conquered by the tribal hierarchy.

The social systems of all countries of the Indo-European language group still reflect the elitism of this class structure. In fact, European class distinctions (especially in Britain) are maintained by the ranking codes still inherent within language itself. For example, a B.B.C. production of the Robin Hood myth, popular in the 1980's, put Oxford accents in the mouths of any and all figures of authority, such as Maid Marion, the village headman, or Robin Hood himself. Any and all "follower" characters are given the accents of the British lower classes. Apparently, British audiences in 1988 simply could not buy the idea of a noble leader-type speaking the patois of the streets, factories, or fields. The outlawing of native speech was a favourite instrument of political domination by both Norman and Anglo-Saxon ruling elites: aboriginal languages were suppressed by British conquerors in North America, just as Gaelic was suppressed as a Celtic cultural vestige in Wales, Scotland and Ireland up until the last century.[13]

The Celts' own spirituality reflected this cultural hierarchy of values, but with vestiges of their own, proto-Indo-European, matriarchal origins still present. In addition to the matricist values from their own history, the earth-based, Goddess-centred beliefs of the otherwise invisible serfs (indigenous, Neolithic Europeans) rubbed-off on their conquerors, as did those of their cousins in India upon their Vedic ("Aryan") overlords. This is in part due to the fact that the Mother Goddess spirituality of indigenous, aboriginal Europeans closely resembled the belief structure that proto-Indo-Europeans themselves once held sacrosanct.

Previous to the patriarchal revolution in their thinking that spurred their warfaring policies of expansion, conquest and invasion, proto-Celtic peoples had also been matriarchal. Ancient belief in the "Nine Clan Mothers" has survived to this day as the mythologies of the Ennead, the Nine Muses, the Nine Ladies of the Lake, the Nine Clan Mothers, the Nine Swan Sisters, The Nine Witches of Gloucester, and other female complements of nine.[14]

Among early Celts in Europe, the struggle between patricist and matricist values struck an intriguing balance. With the caste-system already in place, the highest caste of shamans gradually became an elite priesthood of Druids and the Druid-appointed "royal" war-band chief evolved with his subdominant, warrior elite into a proto-aristocracy. But there was an island of time when matricist and patricist values maintained a delicate equilibrium. Both men and women could hold and control property. Male children inherited from their fathers and female children inherited from their mothers. Partners in a marriage (or any other kind of legal contract or bond) held and retained their own, independent rights, authority and property. Roles were not determined by gender, only by rank. Women could rule, wage war, be Druidic priestess-shamans, artisans, landholders or Bards. Though war with other tribes was waged almost as a sacred duty, there was no evidence of a war between the sexes, beyond the common themes of love, fealty and betrayal.

Male or female serfs were abused equally by higher-ranking Celts, without undue consideration of sex.

The clash of cultures that occurred across Europe from the invasions of proto-Celts produced a dynamic blend of shamanism and Goddess-worship which we recognise today in the culture base of Witchcraft and modern Druidism. The incipient patriarchy of the Celtic expansion found its full expression in the latter days of primary Druidism, as recorded by Roman historians. But Goddess traditions remained intact within Witchcraft, the craft of the "Wise," the appellation for which derives from Anglo-Saxon *wiccacræft*. This is possibly due to a difference in Muses, or guiding principles. Druidism, though originating as a lunar-based philosophy, became a primarily "solar" religion, ultimately focusing on the solar symbol in their pantheon (and calendar) of trees — the Oak.[15] Witches, meanwhile, remained primarily inspired by seasonal "lunar" energies, evoked by the lunar tree of the ancient calendar and pantheon, the Willow (symbolised by the Moon Hare, the magical Crane-woman, Cerridwen as the lunar boar, or by the shape-shifting Goddess, Rhiannon, as a rabbit — among many other symbols).

The linguistic root for the related concepts of bendability, shape-shifting, "lunar" (menstrual) wisdom, and Willow Bentwood (or Wicker) is *wic*, pronounced "wi'ch"; this is also the probable origin of the word "Witch." The term confers the ideas of magical flux and transformative power. It refers to both the bendable qualities of Willow wood and the "wicker" made from its supple branches historically used for sacred offering baskets. The word also refers to the "shape-shifting" abilities attributed to devotees of the "lunar" (menstrual) Willow tree, and so the word and its derivatives also mean "wise."

All of proto-Indo-European culture was once lunar-oriented, which is to say matrilineal and observant of lunar (menstrual) time. The original standard for time measurement and agricultural phases was the moon cycle, associated with the monthly ("moonth-ly") fertility cycle of women. The originators of human and agricultural fertility calendars, in the Paleolithic and Neolithic periods respectively, based their systems upon the changing shape of the moon. They thereby structured the ritual observance of Time, the seasons and cyclical stages of growth. Shamanistic lore of this type became the magic of lunar priests and priestesses of early cultures the world over, not just among Druids. Ancient Sumerian, Babylonian, Canaanite, Egyptian, Aztec and Mayan priesthoods were versed in astronomy and seasonal, celestial movements.

The first calendars were moon calendars, not just among Celtic tribes, but among aboriginal peoples the world over. The Celtic lunar calendar named each of the thirteen moons, or "months," for a tree of the sacred grove of the Moon Goddess. Because of the association of women and the moon, anything that came under the auspices of "women's magic" was construed as lunar in nature. These areas of association included motifs of fertility, agriculture, birth, maturation and death, growth, nurture, fate, evolution, change, transformation, lunar or seasonal ritual observance, auspicious timing of events, and countless other themes of the life-cycle. Common symbols for these and other "lunar" ideas include any and all magical vessels, hearth fires, rivers, streams, caves, clefts in the earth, water-loving trees (and, indeed — due to lunar/agricultural growth cycles — all trees), wells, springs, most (but especially water-dwelling) birds, boars, cauldrons (as womb symbols), butterflies, double-axes, triple Goddesses, any and all crescent shapes, the countless stone carvings of moon-phases in Celtic art, and scores of other images.

The Celtic mindset was subtle, poetic or metaphoric in its mystical symbolisations. It was based upon imagistic associations of sympathetic traits, like shapes, colours or functions. The crescent shaped tusks of the boar made it an image of the death-dealing, chthonic, lunar Goddesses, including Cerridwen and Diana. Images of lunar associations were not direct, obvious, or literal. They were not necessarily anthropomorphic symbols of divinity, like those of the "rational" or "left-brain" philosophies of Classical Greece or Rome. Celtic lunar symbols did not necessarily consist of Goddesses (like Diana) with crescent moons on their heads. They were more subtle, ubiquitous and all-encompassing, even after Romanisation.

For the most part, ancient Celts, being animists, found sacrality everywhere — in every aspect of the environment itself. According to Celtic scholar Miranda Green, "The free Celtic traditions of open-air worship and aniconic perceptions of the gods — which allowed the Celtic king Brennus to scoff at anthropomorphic representations of Greek deities at Delphi — changed and developed in the Roman phase. Roman cults were accepted and absorbed into the Celtic religious system, but Celtic perceptions of the divine world remained fundamentally the same."[16]

A good example of how this essentially Bardic, or poetic, system of multiple, mythic association works is through the icon of the "Crane Bag." The Crane Bag is the magical, shamanic "mojo-bag" of Irish/Welsh Manannan, the Sea God. In it is everything of magical import in the mytho-poetic lore of the Welsh and Irish Celts, the collected "treasure" of their spiritualised culture. A list of the contents of the Crane Bag is a run-down of magical objects, poems, songs, images and words from the repertoire of Bardic stories, songs, and initiatory magic. The tale itself is too complex to recount here, but salient points include the following correspondences: The crane bag is made from the skin of a magical woman who shape-shifts into Crane form — the contents of the Crane Bag are therefore to be construed as the magic and lore of women as birth givers and soul couriers. The Crane Bag's "treasures" are poured forth and made available when the tide is high and the moon is full — the "treasures" are therefore to be construed as being lunar in nature.

Manannan is associated with all water-oriented trees but especially the Hazel, which grows over the stream where the Salmon of Wisdom, Fintan, lives. Fintan becomes a compendium of knowledge similar to the Crane Bag by eating nine hazelnuts which fall into the stream — nine being the number of the moon, a triple compound of its three phases of waxing, full and waning, being therefore the esoteric number of completion, and the number of (lunar) months of human gestation. Without knowing the correspondences encoded within the magical lore itself, these references are difficult to access, for they are not literal or overt. They are the esoteric magical property of a specific culture complex, with resonances (if not exact correlations) within related, shamanic cultures throughout Eurasia.

The Crane was a primary lunar symbol due to its association with wetlands, rivers, streams, and shoreline. It is traditionally shown with the Willow or Elder tree, as the Crane — as avatar of menstrual magic — is a psychopomp or soul-courier. It is still associated in folklore as "bringing babies," but the real reason for this is that cranes (storks, ibises, and other long-legged water birds) are "soul birds." They usher souls into life at birth, and so are depicted with the tree which signifies fertility and conception, the Willow, and they come to convey the soul at death, and so are associated with the Elder, the tree of death and rebirth. Many Celtic carvings pair the crane with the lunar bull. This ties in with imagistic traditions across Europe and the Near East, dating back to earliest times.

Lunar observation was used to calculate the passage of time, weather, and the fertility cycles of plants, animals and humans. Gradually values shifted, however, and came to focus more upon the movement of the sun. The megalith builders reflected this shift by building solar clocks in the form of Stonehenge and other monumental sundials. Some of the megalithic stone circles are lunar clocks. Other, more recently built structures are exclusively solar, but some combine lunar and solar time calculation in their function.

This dynamic lunar/solar orientation was the richest expression of Celtic spirituality, and the one we will explore through the "Journey of the Bard." It is this fertile blend of imagery which informs a wealth of myth and lore, fairy tales and romances. "East of the Sun and West of the Moon," a traditional Scandinavian version of the myth of Psyche and Eros, reflects this potent magical symbiosis. Lyrics of traditional English ballads include images such as setting "sail of silver to steer towards the sun." Celtic society reflected a balance in terms of sexual equality largely due to this tradition of thought. The Mabinogion, the "Crane Bag" lore of ancient Druids, the "Great Rite" traditions of the Witches, the "Sacred Marriage" of mediaeval alchemists, and Arthurian sword and grail tales owe much to this marriage of magical concepts.

In Celtic magic and spirituality all things are considered to be spirit. Spirit may be expressed as matter, water, fire or air. In its native form it is "ether" (spirit) but in whatever form it assumes it is alive with consciousness and will. This is an essentially animistic world-view, common to shamanic belief-systems all over the world.

The first of the three worlds of Celtic cosmology is the Underworld, or Abred. Charles Squire, in *Celtic Myth and Legend*, underscored the Celtic belief that everything of value came from the Underworld. Practising Druids, Shamans, Magicians, Witches, Jungians, or Artists will instantly know what this means. The journey within, to subconscious realms of the Self, is what bears fruit in terms of personal riches. The ability to transform, to "shape-shift," depends upon a foray into the personal subconscious or, even more ter-rifyingly, into the collective unconscious. In esoteric lore, the Greek god Pluto is the radical transformer of souls. Lord of Hades, he is also called "Lord of Riches"; his name is from *plouton*, which means "riches" or "giver of riches." It is in this Underworld realm, called Annwyn by the ancient Welsh and Abred by Britons, where the gifts of transfiguration and renewal are to be found, in the form of the Hallows.

The Hallows are the thirteen magical objects of ancient British myth, which the solar god, Arthur, brought out of the Underworld. All reduce to four primary symbols, these being the magical cauldron (or Grail), the magical sword, the plate of plenty (or disk, or coin), and the magical spear (or Wand). Witches and magicians may recognise the symbols of the four directions and the four elements associated with them (water, air, earth, and fire). They are symbols of the magical properties of the earthly realm and also of the powers, or riches, of Abred, the Underworld.

There is a story common to both Ireland and Wales of four men who ar-rived in crystal boats from their homes in the world "below waves." They were credited with bringing magic to the land. They came bearing four magical objects from their respective realms. These were a sword, a chalice, a stone (or pentacle), and a spear (or stave). Their castles were called Gorias, Finias (or Findias), Murias, and Falias. The paradoxical mystery of this story is that their oceanic homelands were thought to be among the stars. This suggests that penetration within will eventually emerge to the collective experience of universal consciousness. The image is of sailing the cosmic ocean in a crystal boat, which is intriguing for a number of reasons.

The Tuatha Dé Danaan, which means "people of the Goddess Danu," are associated with this myth also, arriving in just the same way, and bringing with them identical emblems. Charles Squire says, "What is probably the ear-liest account tells us that they came from the sky. Later versions, however, give them a habitation upon earth — some say in the north, others 'in the southern isles of the world.' They had dwelt in four mythical cities called Finias, Gorias, Murias, and Falias, where they had learned poetry and magic — to the primitive mind (and to this author's) two not very dissimilar things — and whence they brought Ireland their four chief treasures."[17]

It is legendary that British magic came to "Claes Myrddin," or "Merlin's Enclosure" (meaning the British Isles) from the Pleiades. The descendants of these "star people" were known to classical geographers as the "Hyperboreans."

They were said to have brought their magical wisdom into Britain, setting up hermetic mystery schools and founding the fairy traditions of the Hollow Hills, or Underworld. It is they who are reputed to have brought the Triple Spiral pattern as a kind of star map, showing the tri-cosmos and the magical nature of the universe. This is even the same pattern which has appeared in crop circles in recent years.

The Triple Spiral diagram shows three circular, dynamic "worlds" which are linked energetically by lines of movement. The three worlds have different natures, but are connected at the core. This is but one example of how the early Celtic mysticism of the three worlds has been depicted.

The four magical objects brought in the crystal boats not only represent the four elements of the physical realm, but also the four earth realms on the Celtic Tree of Life. Throughout Celtic settled lands there are traditions surrounding the Tree of Life. Shamanic practices of Siberia, Mongolia, India, the Levant, Scandinavia, and the British Isles as well as the Americas, North Africa, Oceania and Indonesia echo these traditional beliefs concerning the Tree of Life. The universality of this archetype is at least partly due to the fact that it is a symbol for the human neural network of the brain, pineal, spinal column, coccyx, and nervous system.

In the countless folk and fairy tales where the magical Tree towers as a test that only the brave and pure of heart can undertake, the hera or hero thus challenged undergoes an otherworldly ordeal within the magical realms of the tree. She or he will often make an underworld descent, a celestial ascent, or both. As well as harking back to the initiatory scaling of the sacred Birch

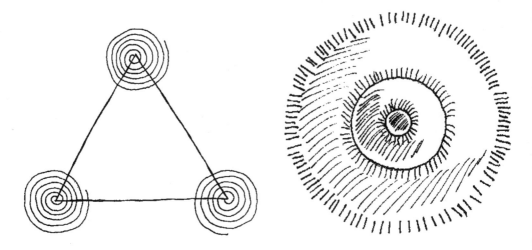

Figure 4: The Triple Spiral symbol.

Figure 5: Irish Triple Circle pictograph of Celtic tri-cosmos.

performed by Siberian shamanist neophytes, this imagery recalls the mythic World Tree, another version of the Tree of Life. The World Tree is a symbol of the planetary heavens and plays an essential role in Central Asian and Siberian shamanism. According to Mircea Eliade, "The Cosmic Tree, expressing the sacrality of the world, its fecundity and perenniality, is related to the ideas of creation, fertility, initiation, and finally, to the idea of absolute reality and immortality. Thus the World Tree becomes a Tree of Life and Immortality as well. Enriched by innumerable mythical doublets and complementary symbols (Woman, the Wellspring, Milk, Animals, Fruits, etc.) the Cosmic Tree always presents itself as the very reservoir of life and the author of destinies."[18]

The Tantric images of the Tree of Life place the moon above the crown as its guiding genius or Muse. A serpentine form ascends the trunk of the tree. The serpent image is a diagram for the spiralling, electro-chemical neural energy in the spine and nervous system we recognise as consciousness, sentience, or "knowledge." It is this dynamic which is illustrated by the caduceus or "Staff of Hermes," the Cabalistic Tree of Life's "Path of the Lightening Bolt," and even by the serpent encircled "Tree of knowledge" in the Garden of Eden. This kinetic awareness flows in a serpentine motion up and down the spinal

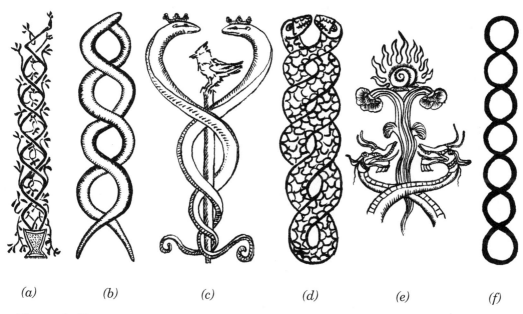

| (a) | (b) | (c) | (d) | (e) | (f) |

Figure 6: Various serpentine spirals. (a) Celtic Tree of Life illumination; (b) Akkadian seal of serpent god Ningizzida ("Lord of the Tree of Truth"), 2350 - 2150 B.C.E.; (c) Caduceus from medieval illustration by Hans Holbein the Younger; (d) Sumerian caduceus from Lagash, c. 2025 B.C.E.; (e) ornament from crown, Liao Dynasty, China, 907 - 1125 C.E.; (f) ancient Egyptian hieroglyph for "Self."

column constantly, through the nerve clusters and neural centres, creating the interrelated whorls of energy we identify as "Life." Visual images for this dynamic are similar in many cultures, dating as far back as the Paleolithic period. The Celtic Tree of Life in the illuminated manuscripts of Mediaeval monks and those carved into Gaelic and Pictish stelae are nearly identical to the ancient Egyptian symbol for this dynamic, which served also as the hieroglyph for "Self."

This is the mythic tree of folk and fairy tale, the ascent of which takes the hero or hera on a magical journey to strange, new realms. Usually she or he will bring home some kind of treasure from these forays. The journey may also lead the traveller on a descent down a well, tunnel, labyrinth, or spiral staircase, to an underworld realm where an old woman or wise hermit offers still greater gifts. One particularly poetic instance of Cosmic Tree imagery comes to us from the central Asian (Altaic) Goldi tribe. According to this motif, human souls sit like birds on the branches, waiting to be brought down to earth and be reborn as infants. This is an extraordinary image of the Tree of Life as the source of immortality and perennial fecundity.

A Hungarian tale tells of "The Tree That Reached Up to the Sky." In this tale, the hero aspires to ascend an enormous tree in order to bring down some of its mysterious fruit to the king (in front of whose window it grows) so that the king might know what kind of tree it is. The lowest branches spread beyond the clouds, so no one has ever been able to see the fruit. Scaling the tree is easier said than done, of course, and the hero has many trials and adventures. At last, the hero succeeds in wresting some fruit from the fairies that perch in the branches and guard it (bringing to mind the Goldi's unborn souls). The hero brings some of the fruit back down to Earth. The king eats it and is rejuvenated. He is transformed into a young man, fulfilling the themes of renewal, resurrection and immortality.

This renewing power, or fecundity, is commonly symbolised by the idea of fruit, especially pears. "The Maiden Without Hands," of fairy tale, was reaching up (with her neck) to take a bite out of a pear hanging down from the king's tree when the king "espies" her, soon to marry and impregnate her. Cinderella, in one of the many versions of that story, leaps up into a pear tree to escape detection by the prince, a tactic in which she succeeds, which would seem rather unlikely except when we discover:

> Shamans and medicine men, to say nothing of certain types of mystics, are able to fly like birds and perch on the branches of trees. The Hungarian shaman (Taltos) could jump up in a Willow tree and sit on a branch that would have been too weak for a bird. The Iranian saint, Qutb ud-din Haydar, was frequently to be seen in the tops of trees. St. Joseph of Cupertino flew into a tree and remained half an hour on a branch that was seen to sway as if a bird had perched on it.[19]

Journey of the Bard

Like the Chinese and Siberian "Soul Tree," the shamanic Birch pole of initiation, or the Djet pillar of ancient Egyptian initiation, this is the World Tree as a primary symbol for shamanic trance journeying. The Asherah of ancient Semites, the Moon Tree of the Assyrians, as well as Yggdrasill (the sacred Ash, also called the "horse," of Odin) are all versions of this primal spiritual map. Odin hung suspended, in a posture of sacrifice, for nine days and nights, until he was granted enlightenment in the form of the Runic oracle by the fairy Norns who dwell at the roots of the tree.

The Tree initiation symbolises the gaining of the shaman's "perfect body," also called the "crystal body," or "light body." What this actually signifies is that the initiate ceases to identify with his or her mortal, finite expression and begins to identify with the conscious, mobile dynamic (spirit or "soul") of the body, which is newly perceived to be unlimited and eternal. This does not mean that the physical body is discounted. It simply means that the physical body ceases to be the only reference point, for the energetic, causal body is discovered to be just as "real."

The shaman's ability to make a celestial ascent to astral conscious levels, and an underworld descent to primordial, ancestral memory relies on her or his ability to traverse the realms of the Tree of Life. This is the reason why nearly every prophet of the Old Testament, of Ahura Mazda (Zoroaster), and of

Figure 7: Yggdrasill, the Norse World Tree, from Finnur Magnusson's eighteenth century edition of The Elder Edda.

Allah (Mohammed) have laid claim to having made both an ascent to heaven and a foray into hell.

The main character of the New Testament, Jesus Christ, was credited with having visited heaven and harrowed hell by his chroniclers after his death, and Dante put his hero in a position to tour both the infernal regions as well as the sublime realms in search of the divine Beatrice. These dualistic, polarised visions of the Underworld and the celestial dome reflect an animosity towards the Underworld that evolved during the reign of the sky gods, Jehovah, Ahura Mazda, Zeus, Allah, and finally, Christ. Nevertheless, though the Underworld was now called Hell and no longer considered a nice place to go, every prophet and magus of note felt the need to post their credentials as veterans of both the descent and the ascent.

The prophets of the later, orthodox religions would have had absolutely no spiritual authority without having this particular magical journey on their resume, though the accounts are transparently similar. Their visits to their respective sky gods upheld their claims to power within their respective power structures. In actual fact, the energy of every living human being traverses the so-called seven heavens (or more archaic, nine heavens) of the Tree constantly. This is the condition of being alive; its cessation means prompt and certain death. It is the degree to which this energy makes the transit consciously which makes all the difference in the world.

The Seven Heavens refers to the seven major hubs of energy in the spine. In each of these centres, a nexus of nerve tissue feeds synaptic responses into the corresponding organs, tissues and muscles. For instance, the nerve cluster in the region of the spine that relates to the air element feeds the energy centre of the upper back. This centre governs the automatic processes of the lungs and heart, which have to do with processing air into oxygen-bearing blood cells for the nourishment of the entire body. Each nerve centre, or "heaven," governs the activities of the organs, tissues and glands within its mandate and purview. The fire element centre heating up the solar plexus governs the volatile chemistry of digestion, and so on.

Francis Huxley discusses the correspondences of the spine and the World Tree in his accounting of the shamanic significance of bones:

> Of all the bones, those of the spinal column are the most important. They represent the ridgepole or the central house-post, and as such are equated with the World Tree. Throughout Siberia it is held that shamans are hatched in nests lodged in the branches of this tree — a great shaman takes three years to come out of the shell, a mere conjurer only one. The eagle, bird of the sun, perches at the summit. To interiorize the light of this sun, the shaman must climb the tree, branch by branch, heaven by heaven, bone by bone. It is a journey during which he meets various personages and adventures, and which he recounts to his audience in great detail. He impersonates all the characters of this other world, and acts out his own laborious efforts. Often he goes

by horseback, the horse symbolised by horsestaves; when the horse tires he mounts a gander, on which he wings his airy way to the heavenly throne where he makes his requests.[20]

Each of the seven centres of the Tree/spine is a realm unto itself, constantly communicating energy and information to all other centres. Each centre has its own kind of wisdom and function essential to life. All these functions, in turn, correspond to universal, collective, or divine functions. They are the personal, bodily representations of aspects of the divine whole. We are perfect in that we are complete, with all divine aspects present and accounted for. We are made in a divine image insomuch as we are complete and in harmonious proportions, not insomuch as we resemble a large, humanoid, bipedal deity of any particular gender. It is more accurate to say that we are divinely complete in our conception and design, formulated (at a certain level) to our own specifications as expressions of the collective planetary soul.

This design contains keys to corresponding parts of the planetary (and even the cosmic) self-concept. These keys correspond to their equivalent realms, and their related functions, throughout time and space, giving access to all regions of mind, body and spirit, in whatever form one desires to encounter this information. The divine whole can be perceived through any individual entity, male or female, human or other, living or inert. To the world-view of Celtic magic, everything that exists reflects this interrelated harmonic.

Traversing the various regions of the divine whole via the Tree of Life can feel, when fully conscious or lucid, like a visionary journey. It is the basic model for the Hero or Hera's journey or vision quest. The landscapes of visions and dreams, with their inhabitants, conforms to certain basic archetypes. There is the silk meadow that augers a shift in awareness, the sense of the garden that tells you you've arrived at magic, the crystal mountain, the glass castle, the magic well. There is the iron fortress, the mist-covered island in the centre of an enchanted lake, the cave entrance to the Underworld, the undersea kingdom, the island of women, the castle of the muses, and the castle above the clouds at the top of the magical tree. There is also the journey through the stars on the magic carpet, magic horse, or dragon, the talking animal, the ally, and many others, each conforming to a characteristic realm of the Tree of Life.

One of Starhawk's frequently-used maxims is "you can not move from where you're not."[21] She employs this bit of wisdom in discussing the magic and power of honestly evaluating where you actually stand at any given moment. Another way to say this would be to say that you can only go "there" from "here," whatever that set of conditions consists of. Unless you are fully present in your life in the moment, aware of yourself, with information from your senses and surroundings focused and centred in your own immediate experience, you are not occupying your centre of power.

If you desire change, it is only by acknowledging dissatisfaction with your current, present reality that you will have the power to change it. Denial, living in the past, future or escape fantasy drains the energy required to make change, though fantasy, memory, and willed projection are essential to manifest change. The trick is to make these forays in consciousness, and to then successfully bring all realisations gained, like treasure, into the present moment of decision and choice.

In the Celtic tri-cosmos, these realms of past, present and future projection overlap upon the tree of life. This is the meaning behind various images of the Celtic Cross, where three circles are nested at the centre, or stacked upon the central column. The Underworld conforms to the past, where events, memories, traumas and experiences have concretised into conditioned beliefs about reality. Abred must be accessed before its treasures of stored and accumulated memory can be released as transformative energy.

The future is accessed in the present as possible combinations of trajectories of choice inherent in each moment. Although the future is a constantly changing projection, contingent on these choices, it is available to our knowledge by a focus of awareness in the present moment. Probable outcomes are the results of the momentum of events already begun and are subject to change, once we become aware of them. These probable eventualities are all here, and

Figure 8: Trecastle prehistoric stone pictograph from Wales, showing the Three Realms.

now. Being here and now is, paradoxically, the way to any and all other states of being, including the realms of conditioned beliefs or enlightened projections, past or future.

The Celestial Sphere, corresponding to *Ceugant* of the Celtic tri-cosmos, conforms to the sum total of all possibility, the future, and expanded projections. It is Ain on the Cabalistic tree of Life. Gwynedd, the Shining Realm, conforms to the present moment of our everyday reality when it becomes potentiated and transformed by conscious, magical choice. It is this world, the Garden, called "blessed" and "pure" by ancient Celts, that is the doorway to any and all other realms. It is the experience of life in the body in the true and immediate sense.

The worldly experience here has none of the calumny attached to "worldliness" in patriarchal Judeo-Christian thought. There is nothing base or foul about the mundane plane in the Celtic tri-cosmos. It is instead considered intrinsically innocent, sacred by its very nature. It is the gift of life in the body on Earth, as a bridge to any and all other realities. As such, it is savoured fully as a fleeting, precious and ephemeral channel — a portal or doorway that will never open in quite the same way again.

How to Use This Book

This book can be read as an entertainment, a cultural history, or as an initiatory process. If the latter approach is your choice, one suggestion is to read the book slowly. This will give time for the chapters (each of which ushers in a different realm of the Tree of Life journey) to exert a subliminal influence upon your imagination. Leaving at least two weeks between each of the narrative chapters, but no longer than one month, will probably provide the best results. If the process is centred within the traditional "year and a day" of magical initiation, the eleven chapters (plus this Introduction and the Conclusion) will slot nicely into this time frame.

With this method, you will find your own subconscious mind and intuitive creativity readily supplying imagery and allegory. Expanded perceptions will occur as your experience of life begins to synchronistically reflect the rhythms and passages of the archetypical Bard's journey. Added dimensions to everyday life, multiple dimensions of reality and deeper layers of meaning will unfold. In short, your life itself will take on the quality of magic which is the nature of any path to self-realisation and creative power.

Part I

Gwynedd: The Way There

Chapter I

The Garden

Long known in the language
of hands
Hands like branches of a
tale
A tale told in a clearing
in a forest
A forest unfolding into
glass
Glass rising in spires and
castle walls
Walls surrounding yet revealing
more
More than the simple music
of a well
A wellspring flowing and changing
form
Form that gives way to a grove
of wands
Wands as wide as they
are long
Long known in the language
of hands

THE GLASS CASTLE

The Bard entered the sacred grove. All the holy trees were here, whose names made up the secret alphabet of the Druids. Here were the thirteen trees which stood as guardians for the sacred round, the wheel of the year, whose names served as consonants for the magical script. And here also were the five whose names served as vowels, all with their separate natures. There were also the Apple and Blackthorn, whose separate natures gave both beauty and strife to the passage of time.

The Bard was privy to the secret language of the trees, as were all Bards. The grove told a story of wholeness and completion. Here, all things assumed their own true shape and perfection. The leaves expressed their essence as the trees' organs of breath. They fluttered, wing-like, in the light breeze. The ferns unfurled their delicate lives in the shade of sheltering Oaks. The stones gave form to the land itself, and thought in patterns even older than those of the trees. Butterflies flitted through the emerald shadows, alighting upon flowers still more brilliant than themselves. Bees droned in their missions of nectar-gathering and pollen scattering. Millions of micro-particles of life conducted epic migrations in the grove, which was also a forest.

Many centuries of these minuscule events had rendered the forest into an exquisitely balanced community of life-forms. The shapes and patterns assumed by the shrubs and bushes, the trees and brambles, the stones and grasses proved this. The Bard instantly saw that this was a place of extreme grace, yet it was merely a wood like any other. Everything shone with its own softly pulsing halo. The Bard knew that one of those extraordinary moments had come when a door, a kind of portal, would open onto another realm and its mysteries be revealed.

There was often pain, like that of growth, connected to the Bard's journey. But the joys of wisdom and knowledge were as freedom and flight compared to the bondage of habit and ignorance. The Bard knew there was no other acceptable choice but to continue the journey.

The trees abruptly thinned out and the Bard entered a grassy clearing. There, in the centre of the glade, was a wondrous sight. It was a fine castle made of glass. Its battlements soared skyward, flying pennants of brave colours. Rainbows of light danced in the air around the turrets and, as the

Bard approached, the sun flashed and winked upon the planes and surfaces of the glass palace.

The Bard approached the outer wall of the castle, seeing shapes moving behind the glass, and crossed over the drawbridge. Inside the castle wall was a beautiful garden, at the centre of which was a crystal well. Lights of different colours emerged from the well and strains of a lovely music. Wraith forms floated up from the well and formed and transformed before the Bard's eyes. Then, suddenly, someone spoke.

"Draw some water from the well," said the voice, "and you shall see what you shall see."

The Bard glanced around in an attempt to spot the owner of the voice. There was a large crow on the ground. It stared steadily at the Bard, shiny eyes unblinking.

"Aye, it is me who speaks and no other," said the bird. "You must drink from the well or go no further on this journey."

Knowing a magical cue when it came, the Bard stepped forth and drew some water from the well. When the bucket came to the top of the well, it was brimming with crystal clear water. The Bard drank deeply, then let the bucket descend into the cool depths. When the Bard again looked at the castle everything had changed. The glass castle still shone in the sun, but superimposed upon its flying turrets was an enormous, towering tree. The crow soared aloft and vanished into its lofty branches.

The base was as wide as the entire castle, the mighty roots coiling into the earth like massive serpents. High, high above, the tree stretched out its arms to the sky. The lower branches scraped the clouds; the top branches were lost to view, disappearing in the blue distance. It was impossible to tell which was the more real, the castle or the tree. They were both equally visible, two realities which occupied the same space. The entrance to the castle hall coincided with a pair of great, double doors in the trunk of the tree. And so the Bard advanced toward the threshold.

The doors opened to admit entry, revealing a castle interior like a hall of mirrors. The Bard approached doorways only to find they were walls. Walls, on the other hand, turned out to be doorways. Here and there, the image of the tree bled in, so that it appeared this was really the interior of the woody tree-trunk. And so the Bard proceeded, never quite sure of direction, with no certainty of passage, never knowing what awaited. As the Bard penetrated further and further into the heart of the castle, a strange music began to fill the air. It was the same sound as that given off by the well in the garden. The Bard began to follow it, knowing it for a guide of some kind. There was a message in the music, something elusive and tantalising. It was as if it spoke a secret, something intimate and magical, something from deep within the soul of the Bard.

The music grew and grew. Soon it filled the Bard's ears with its haunting beauty and caused the Bard's heart to ache with longing. There was no way to name this longing. It was too deep for words, too personal and sensate. It was like a long forgotten flavour or a familiar smell — reminiscent of some childhood event that can not be recalled though the emotions that attend it are still clear and distinct. Such were the thoughts of the Bard as the music grew louder, leading into the heart of the castle.

Down a long, shimmering glass corridor, the Bard came to an oaken door. The door swung open, revealing a hall of surpassing beauty. The floor was of smooth, polished emerald of gemlike clarity and depths. The walls were of rose-hued marble, with lofty columns and arches. The ceiling was of finest alabaster, veined with pink, with soaring vaults and domes. Around about the hall were seven alcoves, and from each emerged a maiden. Each held a marvel in her hands. One held a magic pentacle, another a shining chalice. A fiery-haired maiden wore a tunic embroidered with a winding spiral and held a flame-tipped wand, another bore a wondrous sword. A lady in blue held a sphere of light; it gave a sweet sound and flashed like a star. Her sister held a fiery all-seeing eye, and the last lady bore a jewel-studded crown made for a sovereign.

The maidens encircled the Bard. One said, "You must choose one of us as your ambassador, for we are the Emissaries. We represent the seven realms of the Tree of Life. One of us will be your guide for the next stage of your journey. Whom will you choose?"

The Bard was hesitant, for the objects the maidens held were equally marvellous. But the wand in the hands of the flame-haired maiden beckoned, and so the choice was made.

Sacred perception (or perception of the sacred) is a mildly ecstatic state of awareness, in which one is acutely aware of the complex beauty of the world. The ecology and mythic correspondences, the significance and layers of meaning represented in every set of relationships and in every form becomes apparent, inspiring reverence and awe. This altered state of awareness serves as a bridge to any and all other states of consciousness and, as such, is the portal.

In folk and fairy tales, this moment of heightened awareness, foreshadowing a magical twist of plot, is often cued in the reader with formulaic passages such as, "Then Hans beheld a silken meadow, where the edge of every blade of grass glowed as gold, and the grass rippled in the wind like waves of the sea." A passage like this is specific about the fine detail of each blade of grass, even while it invokes the sum effect of rippling silk. It perfectly recalls the acute perceptions of a state of ecstatic trance, when magic, in the form of transformative vision, is about to occur. It is the moment when the traveller perceives the whole, or complete, forest, despite (and including) the trees.

The sacred groves of the Witches, Druids, and other communities of the "Wise," were "complete" in that they were natural forests. A wild forest is varied and balanced; it will include a full complement of trees, supporting an almost infinitely varied system of biological life, from plants to insects to fungi to bacteria to mammals, large and small. In this sense, an ecosystem reflects the harmony of the cosmos; it is an organic whole, viable and perfect.

The abstract language of the Bards was that of all initiates of Celtic, shamanic lore: the language of trees. The initials of tree names made up the alphabet, and also a sign language known only to initiates. Abstract language itself was considered magically creative. Knowledge of written or gestural language was thought to be quasi-divine. Poetic utterance, storytelling, theatre and song were the stock-in-trade of shamans' "technology of the sacred." Folk and fairy tales are full of references to the mythological significance of trees. The image of a tree near a well or sacred spring is a common motif of Brigid, the Irish Goddess whose February festival betokens initiation into the mysteries.

"Bile" is one of the ancient Celtic names for the Sacred Tree, corresponding to the ancestral god "Bel," "Belenos," or "Beli," from whom Celtic tribes considered themselves descended, and whose roots extended far back into time. The belief was that all magic and sacred talismans, poetry, songs, dances, and other treasures belonging to the tribes had issued from Bile. They, like the God Himself, were thought to have issued from the Underworld, just as the sun, with which He was cognate, emerged from the underworld realms of night, winter, and death. The day of His arrival in Ireland, with His retinue of twenty-four women and twenty-four men, is preserved as "Beltaine" and celebrated with a "Maypole," the symbol for Bile/Beli's aspect as the Sacred Tree. He was married to the great queen, Dana, Danu, Anu, or Ana, the ancestral goddess of the Tuatha dé Danaan. She was also symbolised as a tree, as well as by rocks, streams, rivers (such as the Danube), oceans, mountains, in short, the earth itself — an expression of Gaia.

Later variants of the Tree motif paint St. Brendan travelling westward across the Atlantic to find the otherworldly "promised land." He and his followers discover the "Paradise of Birds," an island full of flowers and trees, "where there was a tall tree beside a well." According to Joseph Campbell, "This is a characteristically Irish vision of the mythological Cosmic Tree . . . the Tree of Life in the middle of the Garden."[22]

The legends and myth-cycles of particular Goddesses, Gods, Heroes, Heras and Warriors are associated with particular trees, and these also denoted particular seasons and cycles of the moon. Gods from many cultures are depicted entering a tree as a symbol of the death/rebirth initiation of shamans and divine personae. Attis, Adonis, Dionysus, Osiris, Hermes/Aphrodite (Hermaphrodite), Odin, and Christ were all interred within or sacrificed upon a tree symbol. In each case, the "mystical death" tree initiation precipitated a shamanic journey to both the Underworld and the heavens, culminating with the resurrection and rebirth of the god at the spring festival. Irish hero, Finn Mac Cumhall, was hidden in a tree-trunk in infancy (or in a magical enclosure of trees), so as to grow to adulthood in safety.[23]

Our words "wicker" and "wise," magically associated with the Willow tree, may derive from the proto-Indo-European root *wic*, or *weik*, expanding on the ideas of flexibility and shape-shifting that are the nature of Willow wood. Our words "strife" and "strafe" derive from Gaelic *Sstraif* or *Ztraif,* the ancient name of the Blackthorn tree, commonly used to make shillelaghs (which do double duty as weapons). The Blackthorn's esoteric meaning is "strife," or necessary hardship. "Birth" relates to the Celtic lunar tree-month Beth (or Bieth) which means both "birth" and "Birch." Birch is the first moon of the tree-calendar, auguring the ancient Celtic New Year, occurring after Samhain, otherwise known as All Hallows Eve. As well as representing a kind of rebirth of the lunar calendar, Birch's esoteric meaning is initiatory rebirth and new beginnings. The Finnish sauna is traditionally made of Birch wood, and used to serve as a birthing room. Many words and concepts from the ancient, sacred grove are still with us in story and myth, as well as in current usage in our speech.

One of the first clues the Bard gets that something beyond the ordinary is happening is that an animal starts talking. Not only that, but the Bard can understand the creature's speech. Understanding animals' speech is a traditional shamanic attribute, and the definitive sign that one has entered into the realm of magic. It is associated with powers of prophecy and esoteric knowledge, as well as a direct communication with nature and the Otherworld. "Learning their language, imitating their voice, is equivalent to the ability to communicate with the beyond and the heavens."[24]

The shaman/Bard, in order to be found equal to the challenges of magical transformation, must display an understanding of animals' speech, implying understanding of the messages that animals, spirit-helpers, totems, allies, and guardians will bring along the way. "Imitating animal voices, using this secret language during seance, is yet another sign that the shaman can move freely through the three cosmic zones: underworld, earth, sky. This is as much to say that he [sic] can make his way safely where only the dead or the gods have access."[25]

The animal who talks to the Bard is a crow. This tells us something about the tone and style this particular shamanic journey will assume. The crow is a totem for several related magical lineages, including those of Owein, Morgan la Fay, Bran the Blessed, and other archetypes with characteristic Underworld colouration.

Owein (Yvain in Mediaeval French romance) was the Welsh "gatherer of souls." Wherever he went he was accompanied by a "murder" of crows, who were thought to be his legions. The crow has ever been the messenger of radical transformation. When a crow starts talking it is certain that an otherworldly, Underworld experience is at hand. It also gives a clue to the nature of our inner hero and of the heroic journey about to begin, as does the spiral sigil embroidered on the flame-haired maiden's tunic.

> Within the Mabinogion, totems have a deeper mystery significance. The totem beast is an Otherworldly helper whose resonance is with the ancestral source of wisdom: the adoption of such a totem is a powerful link with the Otherworld, conveying not only the virtues and qualities of that beast to the person under its aegis but also contact with ancestral levels. The totem beast is not to be confused with an animal of the same species which can be hunted or eaten for food: it is a beast of the Platonic realms, having archetypal reality. The appearance of talking beasts in folkstory denotes a shift of emphasis to a deeper level of awareness: such beasts are not anthropomorphic animals, but archetypal forms. They may mask enchanted human beings but more often they are the ancestral resonances or even aliases for the characters within that story.[26]

The ancient Celtic name of a hero-figure of this type is "Mabon." Mabon is related to "Maponus," worshipped by Roman legions in Europe, who in turn is closely related to, and partly derived from, Apollo. Mabon is the "Wondrous Youth" imprisoned in the Underworld of the deeper aspect of Self, the subconscious realms of hidden memory and emotional layers and beliefs. His name means "son." The story of Culwch and Olwen recounts how he is abducted from Modron, his mother, in infancy and incarcerated in Anwynn, the Welsh Underworld. Arthur and his men "search for, find and liberate him from his prison, so that he is enabled to find the hidden treasures of Anwynn."[27]

This story is a glyph for the search for the inner child within the deeper psychological and emotional regions, and the reclamation of creativity and spontaneity, the "treasures" liberated by integrating these aspects of Self. When the crow starts to speak in the Journey of the Bard, we can be assured that this signifies the challenge of an Underworld descent, where this particular search takes place.

> Always we must be sensitive to the way each character interacts with its totemic beast. The association of people with archetypal animals points to an interaction of this world with the Otherworld. One of the important symbolic

keys to finding and releasing Mabon is the Initiation of the Totems, by which his liberators descend the tree of tradition with the help of totemic animals, each of whom stands as guardian to a cyclic age, back to the beginning of the world where Mabon is imprisoned.[28]

The Bard is immediately ushered into an association with many legendary heroic bards when the bird begins to speak. Countless precedents for this initiation exist. For example, "Only Gwydion . . . can coax the eagle from his perch because he is a poet who speaks the language of the birds. Traditionally, to 'speak the language of the birds' was to be possessed of prophecy and inner knowledge. *The Colloquy* or *Battle of the Birds* is a strong motif in Celtic lore, and . . . the hawk, crow, raven, or eagle was one of the oldest birds."[29] The talking bird is closely associated with the idea of the sacred tree, and *The Battle of the Trees* corresponds in significance to *The Battle of the Birds* in British myth. Both motifs show up to confront our Bard in the sacred grove or garden of Gwynedd.

Gwynedd is not only a grove but a walled garden, a sacred well, a glass castle and many other archetypical, heightened perceptions. Gwynedd is, itself, a state of heightened perception or clarity. Through it, the world is changed, and a realm glimpsed which is parallel to and coincides with this one. It is the power of magical sight, an altered vision of the seemingly mundane, "common" world. As Campbell put it, "I am told that in Ireland, one may walk around and right past a fairy hill without seeing it. One seems to be walking a straight line, but actually is curving past an invisible fairy hill of glass, which is right there, but hidden — like the Hidden Truth."[30]

The spiral image betokens an impending, deep, inner journey, approachable only from the walled garden of Gwynedd:

> The spiral or labyrinth, depicted in ancient tombs, implies a death and re-entry into the womb of the earth, necessary before the spirit can be reborn in the land of the dead. But death and rebirth also mean the continuous transformation and purification of the spirit throughout life; the alchemists use the word VITRIOL to stand for *Visita interiora terrae rectificando invenies occultum lapidem*. "Visit the interior of the earth; through purification thou wilt find the hidden stone." Such a descent into the underworld (the kingdom of Pluto) is the theme of most initiation rituals, and is comparable to the passage through the wilderness, or the "dark night of the soul," which is experienced by mystics on their path. It is furthermore nearly always symbolised by the spiral.[31]

Gwynedd is the "heart" of each, successive moment — the still and present centre, and the only true "place of power." The way "below" into stored memory, the past, and subconscious riches is to be found in Gwynedd. Likewise, the way "above" to the more ethereal regions is through Gwynedd. The abstract thought centres of the brain are arrived at by conscious, energetic "ascent." The mysterious gland in a small hollow between the left and right lobes of the brain, the pineal, is like the apple in the Tree of Knowledge. It is thought by some to be the seat of telepathy due to the high frequencies of synapses occurring in this neural nexus during highly lucid "Alpha" states of creative perception.

In the immediacy of the present moment there is a portal, a doorway, a tunnel, or a stair. It appears in stories as the well down which the hero or hera falls to find another world below, or it may turn up as an oaken door which suddenly appears in the trunk of a giant tree. Penetration into the essence of this moment's perception may reveal a fountain, a floating island, a revolving castle, a piercing sound, a silver staircase, a city of light, a glittering mountain, or many other symbolic cues that the transformative journey has begun.

This is the moment of shamanic initiation in the Celtic pattern. The sensation of travelling may consist of the sensation of falling (perhaps down a tunnel), riding a swift and magical steed, or of soaring in flight. Journeys in consciousness are to be gained by a penetration of Self, experienced in the symbolic imagination as the Tree of Life. There are no realms closed to this mode of entry. The entire spectrum of the universal continuum is available through the metaphoric imagery of human physiology. It is from shamanic traditions which have evolved this process that the legends of Avalon, Summerland, The Island of Women, Glastonbury, Camelot, the Hall of the Fisher King, the Castle of Riches, and countless other mythic images originate.

All of these mythical locations represent the mystical "Centre." The Centre signifies, simultaneously, the centre of Self, the centre of the Cosmos, the omphalos — "navel of the Earth," or World Centre, and the centre of each moment which is both the perceptive state of, and the perceptions gained through, Gwynedd. "I am Knowledge, the known and the Knower; I am Wisdom, the Wise and Wiseness."

> Just as "each part of the universe whether it be a world or a particular being is always and everywhere analogous to the whole," so "every human individual . . . contains the possibility of making himself [sic] the centre in respect of the total being" (R. Guenon, *Symbolism of the Cross*). In their ritual, the Kwakiutl Indians chant: "I am at the centre of the world." Buddha says: "It is I who am the peak of the world . . . it is I who am the Eldest." . . . The centre is equally the centre of any place, or the centre of any person or being.[32]

A riddle still current in Irish folklore, quoted by a Bard to begin a session of storytelling, is "Where is the middle of the world?" The correct answer is "Here," or "Where you are standing."

> The same question appears in versions of the mediaeval European tale of the "Abbe Sans Souci," including one recorded in Brittany, and to explain the answer a finger is placed on the surface of a ball, showing that a centre is

wherever the finger touches. The riddle is in harmony with the Rg Veda's five points: north, south, east, west, and "here." The directions are orientated around wherever one "is." Similarly, significance is not confined to the great ceremonial centres. Every ritual place or cult object is endowed with what Professor M. Eliade has called "the prestige of the Centre," be it a local meeting-hill, a pillar-stone, an inauguration tree, a sacred well, a grave, or what it may . . .[33]

Gwynedd equates, on the Tree of Life, to the heart. The realm of Gwynedd is accessed, in the spirit of connection and unity, through the breath. It corresponds to the medium and element of Air. It is the nexus of the Celtic Cross where the central circle is depicted and is the place of magical alchemy. It is the junction where the spiritual axis intersects with the material plane. Here, the physical energies meet abstract energies, the earth meets sky.

Gwynedd is the land, the surface of the Earth, and the experience of the world through the five senses. Gwynedd's influence confers healing of body and spirit, and physical beauty. This is the realm of perfect proportions, balance and harmony. Finally, ultimately, Gwynedd is the Garden, emerald green and eternally renewing itself.

Part II

Underworld Descent:
The Four Realms Of Abred

Chapter II

The Shining Realms

Fire and sun and golden
armour I bear
Bear the weight of challenge
in the shining realms
Realms of flame spiralling
white
White chambers fitted with
thrones of gold
Gold chains of flowers in
a field of wheat
Wheat lit by another
sun
Sun gleaming like my head
on fire
Fire and sun and golden
armour I bear

The Hollow Hills

As soon as I had made my choice everything changed once again. The Emissary of the Flame stepped forward and the others faded back into their alcoves about the Emerald Hall. A silver, spiral staircase appeared in the centre of the hall, leading to regions both above and below this central chamber of the Tree. My Emissary took me by the hand, told me we must not hesitate, and led me to the stair.

Down, down, down we stepped — around and around. As we descended, the air changed and grew bright with a vibrant haze of gold. At last we came to another chamber, in which the floor was formed of glowing, golden topaz. We stepped onto it from the silver stair, and a sensation of warmth flooded into my feet and rose in my legs to warm and relax my entire body. I was filled with calm confidence and certainty. I felt as if I could not be stopped, whatever obstacles to my journey may arise.

As I gazed around the golden hall, the Fire Maiden asked me what I saw. In the spaces and ceiling vaults of the chamber, high above the gleaming columns wrought of gold, I saw winged creatures and chimeras flickering in the air. I replied that I saw beasts of wondrous hue, who shimmered as if made of flame, and who gently roared as does a consuming fire. And mounted on the glowing chamber walls were the ceremonial armour of royal warriors, winged breastplate and helm, and all was as if fashioned from the purest gold.

"These are the creatures of Fire," said the Maiden. "Their gifts are of courage and fortitude, the power to act with integrity and creative force. It is important not to fear them, or they will turn and rend you to bits, for they are manifestations of your own strength and will. Do you think you can withstand the scrutiny of the creatures of the flame?"

"Yes," said I, "I have come to this place. I will bear whatever tests may come."

As I said this I was unsure where all this new courage and decisiveness was coming from, but I had no time to puzzle it out for just then one of the marvellous beasts began to manifest into solid form. With feathered wings and clawed feet, bearing the head and tail of a lion and singing with a beautiful voice, it began to approach.

"Be blessed with a shining will," it sang as I gazed at it in wonder. "Why do you journey in my realm?"

"I journey here to gain the courage to act by my convictions," said I, realising for the first time as I said it that this is why I had come. The creature seemed pleased with this response for suddenly the golden breastplate and winged helmet flew down from their places high upon the wall and arrayed themselves upon me. The magical armour imbued me with sensations of robust certainty and calm.

The maiden, the fire creatures and my golden armour began to fade, then, in the yellow light of the hall. I felt the first pangs of alarm I had felt on this journey so far.

"Fear not," said the maiden, reading my thoughts as she disappeared, ". . . and do not despair of seeing me again, for you shall find me many times. You have successfully entered Gorias, the first of the realms of Abred, the Underworld. Here you will gain the fire of inspiration and the creative courage to act by your convictions. You will learn to heed the dictates of your own will in all matters, unfailingly, so long as it harms none. Look around. What do you see?"

Once again everything had changed. The lion-bird had disappeared and the silver stair as well. The golden hall and its songs of fire were dissolving into invisibility. The floor beneath me was no longer the glowing, amber jewel but a hillside of golden, summer's grass. Instead of gold pillars a rolling landscape now lay about me. The sky was clear and cloudless, the sun blazing it its zenith above at high noon. Slowly the sounds of bird song and rustling leaves came to my ears, replacing the strange music of the hall of Fire. I searched the terrain for some landmark by which to gain my bearings and saw a signpost at the junction of two straight roads that intersected across the plain.

I set off towards the crossroads to see where I might be. As I came nearer to the signpost and its message came into view, I read the crest above the pole. "The Four Realms of Abred," it announced.

Beneath it, arrows pointed in all four directions. The one pointing south said, To Gorias," the one to the north, "To Falias." The one pointing west said, "To Murias," and the one to the east, "To Finias."

I recognised the ancient names of the four realms of Abred and realised that I must have entered the Underworld when I descended the silver stair of the Tree. When I looked again at the signpost, the arrow that had formerly read, "To Gorias," had changed its message. It now read, "To the Castle of the Muses."

Nonplussed, I examined the others. They remained the same. Taking this for a sign, I decided to take the road to the Castle of the Muses and headed down the path.

In the magical initiation of the Tree of Life, the past is accessed through the realms of Abred, the Underworld roots of the tree. Here all that has gone before — ancestors, past events, and dreams — are concretised, recorded and stored. It is obvious that the Bard intends to make the descent to the Underworld as soon as he chooses the Fire Maiden as his Emissary, for the fire realm of Gorias is the first to be encountered in the shamanic descent.

The image of a spiral staircase or ladder as a route to such realms is common to visionary perception as a symbol of the descent into the realms of consciousness that are usually veiled, and is also typical of ecstatic perceptions of celestial ascent. It is the image of "Caer Sidi," Arianrhod's "Tower of Glass, the Spiral Castle of Otherworld, where the dead are imprisoned, according to mortal opinion, but where they learn the wisdom of the initiating Goddesses according to esoteric lore,"[34] or the "magical tower of poetic initiation."[35] Biblical Jacob described the spiral staircase he saw in a prophetic trance, upon which angels ascended and descended in a constant stream. Both Dante and William Blake had similar visions, as well as Swedenborg, countless Australian and Siberian shamans, the Initiators of the Egyptian Book of the Dead, Initiators of the Orphic Mysteries, Celtic poets, and Nordic *skáld* ("Bards"). Add to this the countless generations who have venerated Bel or Beli (Bile), the sacred Tree, on the Celtic festival of Bel(taine) on the 1st of May, around a Maypole, with its spiralling ribbons, and you have an ubiquitous archetype.

The spinning sensation that accompanies fainting, or the swirling light-headedness that precedes an "out-of body" experience, is roughly what accounts for this. However, it does not quite account for the exactly detailed descriptions, faithful in many respects to one another, regardless of the miles, or centuries, that separate the visionaries. In the early Welsh poem attributed to the heroic Bard, Taliesin, we hear how Arthur and "three shipburdens" of his warriors "entered the Spiral City" to claim its treasures and the "wonderful youth" (the Bard, Gwydion) held hostage there. "Except seven none returned from Caer Sidi . . . the four-square Caer, four times revolving!"[36]

There is an eastern European tale which recounts how a hero descends inside a magical tree to the Underworld in order to find his beloved, who has died. At first she is reluctant to accompany him back to the world of the living, for she has been transformed into spirit and cannot exist as such upon earth, except as a shade. Eventually she agrees to return with him to the world above, but as he leads her from the magical realm of the tree, she flees inside the open door of a nearby house and disappears. The hero follows, only to find that a woman within the house is in labour, and has just given birth to a baby girl. The hero recognises his love in the infant, and patiently waits twenty years for her to grow up and marry him.

This story has resonances of the Psyche and Eros myth, as well as Demeter's descent to find Persephone, and Inanna's descent to meet Ereshkigal. Many shamanic healings consist of a descent into the Underworld to retrieve the soul of the patient, which is thought to be held hostage there. A contemporary equivalent of this idea is to be found in the role of psycho-therapist, whereby an effort is made to reclaim psychological aspects of Self which are subsumed, repressed, or held in "denial." Shamanic "soul retrieval" is an archaic method of facilitating psychological and spiritual integration which is enjoying a revival, with the renewed interest in shamanic healing techniques.

As well as personal integration, the Underworld descent bestows artistic gifts to those courageous or foolhardy enough to brave the depths of self-knowledge. The warrior/poet/bard, Gwydion, made such a descent, "and endured a long imprisonment. The sufferings he underwent made him a Bard — an ancient Celtic idea which one can still see surviving in the popular tradition that whoever dares to spend the night alone either upon the chair of the Giant Idris (the summit of Cader Idris, in Merionethshire), or under the haunted Black Stone of Arduu, upon the Llanberis side of Snowdon (North Wales), will be found in the morning either inspired or mad."[37]

Despite the dangers, no real personal or creative power can be obtained without undertaking the journey within to the vital, "youthful," psychological regions. These have their life in the lower areas of the body-consciousness (or Sacred Tree). Such aspects of Self are felt somewhere between the heart and the toes, or somewhere between the "trunk" and the "roots" of memory. It is in these regions that the "Wondrous Youth" or "Divine Child" awaits our attention and reclamation. This aspect of personality is the achetypal identity of any artist, any poet, musician or Bard, as John James reveals in *Not For All the Gold in Ireland*, when his character asks: "Who was Taliesin? I did not ask, but Pryderi breathed the answer: 'Mabon.' I should have known. This was indeed the Glorious Youth."

There is a certain urgency to the rescue and acknowledgement of this valuable "Child." Those who would seek the Muse, those who would seek to marry themself to any kind of sovereignty, must make the descent down to the earth's centre, to face their utmost fears, and their most secret anxieties. The "sovereignty" referred to here signifies any kind of authority (mastery, or self-possession) — personal, artistic, or spiritual — for "the descent to the Underworld, or Otherworldly journey which many of the heroes make, is paralleled by the personally transformative journey which the shamanic poet or initiate takes."[38]

The Bard is led to the spiral stair by one of the seven Emissaries who confront him in the Emerald Hall of the Glass Castle. Each of the seven Emissaries is an ambassador for one of the seven realms of the Tree, and carries the insignia of her native country. The idea of the number of regions of the

Sacred Tree, or bodily consciousness, numbering seven is extremely widespread and of very ancient roots. There are seven initiatory "Castles" or "Caers" in the pagan Celtic Otherworld.[39] Eliade recorded an initiatory "ladder (klimax) with seven rungs . . . documented in the Mithraic Mysteries . . . A remarkably similar symbolism is found in Islamic mysticism: to ascend to God, the soul must mount seven successive steps . . . The ladder with seven rungs was also preserved in alchemical tradition. A codex represents alchemical initiation by a seven-runged ladder . . ."[40]

The Sacred Tree and its seven levels is thus an ancient and widespread concept. It occurs in the mythologies of historic tribes across Eurasia and is typical to visionary magic and mysticism. The reason for this is due to the correlations made long ago by Indo-Europeans between the Tree of Life, the seven archetypical levels of awareness, and the spine. As Francis Huxley points out, "The identity of tree and backbone is well known in the theory of Yoga."[41] Yoga has its roots in the Vedic shamanic practices of the Brahmins, which postulates seven energy centres in the spine, correlating to the seven celestial regions of Siberian shamans' Birch pole, the seven Caers, or "castles" of Gaelic Bards, and the seven "heavens" of the Mesopotamian Cosmic Tree.

The seven Emissaries who greet the Bard serve as guides to the seven realms of the body consciousness, or "chakras," that can be roughly described as the vibrational centres of the four elemental energies earth, water, fire, and air, plus the three "astral" vibrational centres of ether, thought, and Cosmic Source. The Emissary who comes forward to greet our Bard is the Maiden of the Fire element, auguring the descent from the realm of Gwynned, at the level of the Heart centre, to the realm of the area of the Will, at the level of the Solar Plexus in the body consciousness.

In Celtic myth and romance, the journey of the heroic Bard truly gets under way when she or he is given a suit of magical armour. Many a fairy tale has the hera adopting male attire, including a Knight's armour and weaponry, for the duration of the tasks she must undergo. The hero, likewise, finds his will, along with a magical steed and a suit of arms, for the magical undertaking of his quest. This represents the basic equipment of courage, fortitude, and necessary aggression (in other words, sheer Will) such an endeavour demands. It is the martial, warrior energy she or he will require to meet the challenges and whatever discouragement that may lie along the way.

In the old Celtic stories, the hero at the advent of such an adventure of the spirit is either wearing or is awarded fiery red armour. "Galahad entered the fellowship of Arthur's Knights of the Round Table on the feast of Pentecost, wearing red armour symbolic of the presence in him of the grace of the Spirit, to which his life and character were to be witness. Parzival, too, began his knightly career in an armour of blazing red."[42]

Parzival, wearing the outfit of a fool given him by his mother in hopes he would renounce the martial life, encounters the infamous Red Knight, who has just seized a golden goblet from Arthur's hall, issuing a challenge to all who would hear that they were welcome to come and try to get it back. A lucky, or "charmed," shot by Parzival fells the knight, who then forfeits his armour to Parzival. Thus, wearing the lustrous, bright red armour of his fallen foe, Parzival rides off on the Red Knight's horse, which he has no idea how to control. He was able to start it galloping in a mad charge, but was entirely unable to stop it. The tableau gives a clear image of the difficulty with which innocence (the Fool) learns to manage the fiery energy of an awakened Will (the horse and armour of the Red Knight).

We are reminded that the sacred Ash of Odin (Yggdrasill) was not only the god's Tree of Enlightenment and Initiation, but was also called "The Horse of Odin." The Tree of Life is a vehicle of the Will as well as a structure of the personal and collective Self. These motifs are late versions of a far older theme, one that we recognise in the "Red Champion" of Witchcraft (a name for the divine, male principle)[43] and in the suits of red or golden armour won by the champions of many a folktale or ballad.

The singing Manticore is an auger of magical transformation, with the special charge of the fiery solar regions. It is a metamorphic beast, combining qualities of Phoenix bird and lion, two favourite animals of Mithraic fire initiation. Robertson Davies featured such a beast in his story about Jungian transformation, *The Manticore*, where the numinous, archetypal quality of the image ushered the protagonist into his own transformative journey. Like all magical journeys once begun, there was little or no way to stop its momentum. The only way through was through in Davies' tale, as with Parzival once he'd mounted the horse of the Red Knight.

Our Bard is in a similar position. Filled with renewed desire, our hero/ poet must continue, to whatever realms destiny has in store. The story shifts into the first-person point of view in this segment of the tale, and will remain there for the duration of the adventure. The journey will be narrated in the personal voice hereafter for the Bard has begun the process of becoming self-aware. The statement and posture of the fire-centre of the personal Will is, "I Am."

Chapter III

The Realm
of
Gorias

Beneath me and above
swirls a lake
of fire
Fire dancing
to the sword edge
where I step
Step from a bridge
to look upon
a wonder
A wonder of music
where there was
only wind
Wind whirling to reveal
the memory
of art
Art of nine torches
blazing in
the weather
Weather rising to fall
on the thirsty world
beneath
Beneath me and above
swirls a lake
of fire

The Castle of the Nine Muses

As I stepped along the path, the sun descended no lower in the sky. Time seemed to be stopped at midday in full summer. I hiked over hill and dale, through valleys of wheat and barley, past fine castles and holdings, following the sign's direction. On and on I trudged and eventually the road crested a small hill.

From the top of this I looked over a vast valley, golden with grain. The road widened out and became a causeway, made for the movement of armies. It led to a gleaming castle on a rise which flashed golden in the sun as if fashioned entirely from the precious metal. I thought that the Muses must be rich indeed, to live in a palace made of gold. Wondering what my reception would be, I continued down the hill along the road, towards the castle.

I was halfway across the plain when I saw a brave sight, both wonderful and terrible. A phalanx of golden chariots burst over the drawbridge of the castle, nine abreast, and rushed towards me like a flock of angry swans. They were in flight formation, as geese fly across the sky, led by a fierce warrior queen.

Her cloak glowed red-gold in the sun, billowing about her like a furious cloud. She drew her horses up, mere inches from my toes. I felt their fiery breath upon my face. Then she jumped down from her chariot onto the ground and strode to meet me on the road.

"Who are you and why have you come?" she asked without preamble.

"I am the Bard, and I have come to gain the gifts of Fire," said I, hoping it was the right thing to say, for her sword was at the ready and poised for my neck. Apparently my statement pleased her for she lowered her sword and smiled graciously.

"I am Calliope," she said, startling me, for I had never bethought myself to meet the Bard's own Muse.

"I confer the art of Heroic Verse, as you know," she said, reading my thoughts. "This gift and more can be yours, should the bridge across the fiery moat accept your passage. You may ride with me to the castle."

So saying, she ushered me into her chariot. I was no sooner perched at the rail than she turned her team of fiery horses about with a flick of the reins and we were off, in a cloud of dust, over the plain. When we came closer to the Castle of the Muses, I saw the nature of the moat that surrounded it. It was filled with a fluid like molten gold. It glowed and bubbled evilly, flaring up from time to time in tongues of fire. I realised anyone who fell in this moat would be immolated instantly. As soon as I thought this, the bridge over it became as slender as a blade of grass. I gazed at the bridge in horror as it swayed and wavered in the wind.

"You must cross the drawbridge," said Calliope in my ear. "The bridge will know if you are worthy of the passage."

There were two choices. The first was to bow out, return the way I had come, and try to find my way back to the Glass Castle and the garden in the grove. The other was to marshal my courage and continue across the bridge. Of course, this being a Heroic Journey and myself being a Bard, I chose to continue on. Taking a deep breath I descended from the chariot and began my slow crossing of the hair-fine bridge.

That short distance over the moat seemed to take a hundred years. Whenever a slight breeze would set the bridge to shivering I saw myself in peril of falling into the fire. Continually I reminded myself that the extreme thinness of the bridge was an illusion meant to discourage me. As long as I kept this thought foremost in my mind I never faltered. If I let the idea slip I was instantly in danger, on the verge of falling to my death in the fiery broth below. At last I gained the other side. I stumbled through the gate into the courtyard and saw, to my surprise, that the yard was indeed paved with gold.

No sooner had I stepped foot inside the courtyard than the nine warrior maidens reappeared from within the castle hall. Without their armour they were all as different as the flowers from each other. But they were all alike in that they shone with inner fire. They looked as if their touch would ignite passion in even the most phlegmatic of travellers. Their eyes burned into my very soul with their smouldering intensity. I felt all manner of vague desires and incentives begin to stir inside me. There was suddenly so much I wanted to do, though I could not name any one thing that drove me.

Sensing my discomfort, one of the maidens reached to take my hand. Her touch seemed to burn, but it was delicious. Reassurance and warmth flowed from her and I relaxed in the sure knowledge there would be a place and time for all that I must do.

"I am Polyhymnia," she said. "I confer the art of sacred song. All my sisters have gifts to bestow but they each require your care and nurture. They are as your own children, and so you must choose only those gifts you can cherish and defend."

Puzzled by these words and confused by the feelings animating me, I uttered my dismay. "But Lady, I am merely a traveller and a Bard. Your gifts are generous but how can I know which I must adopt?"

"Do not worry," she said, smiling. "By the time you leave our castle, you will know your own Will in these matters."

Then she led me to the threshold of the great hall. Inside, the high vaulted ceilings were festooned with banners bearing verses of poetry and songs. Dramatic passages were quoted in full and the names of their authors emblazoned upon them. The walls were hung with gorgeous tapestries, depicting fantasial or historic scenes. Fine paintings there were, and beautifully wrought artifacts of every kind.

"This is the Museum," said my guide. "The gallery of the Muses contains all that has been or will be created."

As I looked around me, I saw that this was indeed so, as the exhibits about the hall continued to change, revealing the eras of art making and music as their milieus marched by. It was as if the sum of the creativity of the ages was recorded here.

"What wonders are these?" I spoke out in amazement, for though I could see clearly, I could not understand how such objects, the conceptions of a miraculous craft, could exist here in such lavish array.

"These are the works of Creative Will. They represent the divine spark in life. Look! There are your own works, of another time and other places."

I watched in fascination as works that were definitely mine and intimately familiar paraded before my eyes. This was the more wondrous as I knew I had not made them yet. They were in my future.

I wanted to stop the stream of images to examine them more closely, but it flowed past and my future works were gone. New sets of fascinating objects and scenes, whole realities, opened up before my eyes and I was swept along with them. At last the flow of wonders ceased. The hall resolved into its original appearance, a museum of precious works.

Again, Polyhymnia led me on, out of the hall of wonders and into a long passageway. This too was hung with rich scenes and fabrics of marvellous hue. We came to a door. It opened onto the central hall of the palace. This hall was empty but for a golden dish of flame which stood upon a tripod in the centre of the room. The nine maidens arrayed themselves around this flame in a circle and each held a wand tipped with fire. Polyhymnia drew me into the circle and told me, "This is the eternal flame. She is called Memory. From her can be lit many fires. By her light many wonders can be remembered and regained. Listen now and choose what gifts you may."

At that each of the Muses stepped forward in turn and addressed me.

"I am Thalia," said the first. "I bestow the gift of Music."

"I am Clio," said the second. "I confer the knowledge of History."

"I am Terpsichore. I confer the gift of Dance," said the third.

"I am Melpomene," said the fourth, "and I am Tragedy."

"Erato is my name," said the fifth. "I bestow the arts of Erotica."

"I am Euterpe, and I inspire the flute and wind instruments," said the sixth.

"I am Urania," intoned the seventh Muse. "I confer the wisdom of the stars."

"And I am Calliope, who you know well," said the warrior who had met me on the road, "for I am the story of your own heroic journey."

I looked at Polyhymnia, who had the gift of sacred songs to bestow, but she stood silent, giving me no sign. I felt unable to choose, despite my great decisiveness and my understanding of the responsibilities attendant upon the acceptance of these gifts. The fact was I wanted them all, in some degree, and I could not know what exactly was my greatest desire.

I stepped forth and said, "Gracious Muses, I cannot choose among you for your gifts are equally precious. Therefore I choose the flame herself, Memory, for my gift, that I may remember my own true calling."

At that the Muses were amused. "Wisely done," said Polyhymnia, "for within Memory lies the possibility of all the rest. You have chosen well."

With that, she took a flame from Memory into her hand and brought it close to my breast. "May you be blessed with the memory of your own true nature. May you remember who you truly are, why you were born, and what you came to do."

She placed her hand over my solar plexus. I felt the flame ignite a sphere of fire within the centre of my body like an inner sun. It flared into life, just as a candle is lit by a taper. Its warmth flooded through me. Already, I was beginning to remember the idea I had been born to express, to bring into creative form.

A feeling of belonging here, of owning my life, of having an innate integrity lent me courage and assurance. I knew what I was doing was right, was all a part of my path, my journey here.

As I stood experiencing these sensations, the Nine Muses began to flicker and change. They turned into single flames, each of which flew into the central fire of Memory. Simultaneously, the warmth in my own centre expanded. I silently thanked them and, feeling the fire of my own being steadily increasing in heat and power, I turned and left the hall.

The drawbridge gave me no challenges as I left the Castle of the Muses, but remained comfortably wide. As I crossed the fields and the road began to climb, I felt the flame inside me growing stronger and stronger. I knew it was eternal, that it had always been there, though not always with my knowledge. It would always remain with me.

I felt as if I had come back to myself after a long abandonment. I knew I would never lose the heat and light of Memory again.

The Bard meets the powerful archetypes of the fire element in the Hall of Inspiration and Desire after choosing the path to the south, leading him into Gorias. The sun remains at its zenith in the sky, as the guiding principle of this particular stage of the journey, for the fire element characterises the personal will, or inner sun, of each individual.

The fire element vibrationally rules certain physiological processes: the chemical fire of digestion, which makes use of caustic fluids to convert nutrients into usable energy for body processes, for instance. The biological fuel of calories is assimilated by cellular conversion into energy, producing strength, the ability to act, and actual warmth in the body. Digestion is a chemically combustive process whereby the entire body, not to mention mental and emotional levels, is powered-up. The processes of digestion, assimilation, passion, action and joy are native to, and ruled by, the element of fire. This is how we know this elemental force in our own beings, as well as through the movement of events by the propulsion of our own wills. This is where we perceive heat and light as a source of life. Through coming to terms with and owning this aspect of power, we obtain creative visibility. In other words, we begin to express ourselves creatively, becoming seen and recognised as who we truly are, displayed by our creative acts and works.

Fire is directly associated, in magical process, with the ability to create. This is true with regard to shamanistic spirituality all over the world. As Eliade points out:

> The "inner heat" or "mystical heat" is creative; it results in a kind of magical power even when not manifested directly as a cosmogony (cf. the myth of Prajapati) [and] "creates" on a lesser cosmic plane; . . . everywhere in the world acquisition of "inner heat" is expressed by a "mastery over fire" and, in the last analysis, by the abrogation of physical laws — which is as much as to say that the duly "heated" magician can perform "miracles," can create new conditions of existence in the cosmos . . .[44]

In Kundalini Yoga, the serpent energy (consciousness) is raised in a spiralling pattern along the trunk of the Tree of Life (spine) to the crown (cerebral cortex and "third eye" centre in middle of forehead). The "Fire Breath" is utilised to facilitate this, by raising mystical heat and magical power in the body. The Fire Breath is practised by a rapid pumping of the diaphragm, creating a surplus of oxygen for the body to burn. Actual heat is created in the solar plexus, and the body's metabolic rate rises. (One can also become quite dizzy and pass out.) The energy thus raised has definite potential for transformation and must be channelled carefully to avoid neural "burnout." Kundalini practitioners traditionally practice Pranayama (breath control) and Hatha Yoga (physical postures) for a period of eight years before attempting to raise the Kundalini.

The Fire element resides in the body at the level of the solar plexus, so named for the fiery processes housed there. The stomach, spleen, gallbladder, liver and other assimilative organs here produce the kinetic dynamism of our physical, mental and emotional selves. This is the centre of the body consciousness which houses the Warrior/Bard and Initiator archetypes, typical of fire-ruled personalities such as Aries, Sagittarians, and Leos. Of the five physical senses, the fire element of this centre rules the perception of light, as the sense of sight. It is supremely conscious of light and heat in the form of the sun, and is experienced as love, anger, creative passion and desire.

The urge to move towards something, the incentive to act, the courage to become visible — for your creative, inner Self to be seen . . . all are enabled from processes which occur from this area of the bodily awareness, and so this is called the home of the Will. Owning and acknowledging this aspect of Self is the first step on the road to personal, magical and creative power. "Such 'fire' and mystical 'heat' are always connected with access to a certain ecstatic state — and the same connection is observed in the most archaic strata of magic and universal religion."[45]

The archetypical landscape experienced in the journey to this realm of the "ecstatic state" is that of wide open, prosperous fields and ordered, settled lands. It is the genius and inspiration behind the solar or centralised rule of feudal holdings and empire. This is where we can perceive the political logic of the queen bee: the experience of vast, organic, organised power. It is hierarchical inasmuch as it is self-willed and self-centred. It is a hegemony of one. The statement of purpose, level of realisation and mandate of this region of spirit is, "I Am," reminiscent of the proclamation of Jehovah to Isaiah and certain stages of "Buddha" consciousness attained through meditation.

When early Britons encountered this degree of centralised organisation in the conquering Romans, they began to build a mythology around the solar, Roman Emperor and various Goddess consorts. The tale of "Macsen Wlledig," a Gaelic adulteration of "Maximillian," and his magical wife, Elaine, is an example of this attempt to explain such overwhelming, regimented force. Though Macsen Wlledig was a hero who, in the story, came from the land of the Gauls (France) and conquered Britain, he did so because he had seen the fair Elaine in a dream and fallen in love with her. The woman-revering British Celts could not conceive of anything happening except on account of their Goddess, so Elaine became the true reason, in their mythology, for the Roman conquest. Eventually, it was Elaine who was credited in the stories for the building of castles, cities, outposts, garrisons and roads. She came to be called "Elaine of the Ways," "Builder of Roads," or "Builder of Cities," like her counterpart in Brittany, the Witch Melusine.

The closest thing ancient Britons had to correspond to the vast, organ-

Journey of the Bard

ised inspiration evident in the Roman takeover was the idea of their Muses, along the lines of Brigid, Elaine, Melusine, Rhiannon (Demeter, Epona) and their like. Already ingrained within pre-Roman Celtic culture was the idea of the Company of Nine, a remnant and vestige of the extremely archaic concept of the Nine Clan Mothers of the lunar Ice Age religion depicted in Paleolithic rock carvings and pictographs. The Nine Muses, the Nine Women of the Island of Women, the Nine Maidens, the Nine Korrigans of Brittany, and many other magical, female contingents of nine owe their lineage to the Nine Clan Mothers, essentially a "hearth deity" complex.

Irish literature abounds with "companies of nine," and in a considerable number of cases it is made clear that the nine consist of a leader and eight others. This is strikingly illustrated in a description of Medb's mode of travel in *Tâin Bô Cuâlnge*: "and nine chariots with her alone, two of these chariots before her, and two behind, and two chariots at either side, and her own chariot in the middle between them." King Loegaire, when setting out to arrest St. Patrick, ordered nine chariots to be joined together "according to the tradition of the gods." Eight swordsmen guarded Bricriu on his way to the feast he had prepared in his nine-chambered hall. Cuchulainn has nine weapons of each kind, eight small ones and one large one. Cathbad the druid had eight disciples and Finn appears with eight Cailtres gathered around him.[46]

The esoteric magical meaning of nine is "completion," and also signified this concept to ancient Bards. To quote Reese, "Nine, like five, symbolised the whole. In Welsh medieval society the ninth generation was the recognised limit of kin relationship, and even the human body had nine principal parts."[47] Ninepins, the traditional British game, and Nine Men's Morris perpetuate this motif, as well as still more clearly Pagan customs such as the Scottish "need-fire," kindled by nine men, or the Beltaine fire. In Scotland, Wales, and parts of Scandinavia the fire was traditionally made with nine sticks from nine different sacred trees.

The idea of female divinities bestowing both warriorlike courage and artistic inspiration is an ancient correlation, evident in the archetypes of Arianrhod, Cerridwen, and Brigid, the Muse of both poetry and smithcraft of weapons. Elaine also evinces these qualities which, in modern times, are thought to be contradictory energies. This was not the case for early Celts. The Poet-Warrior was a unified, integrated archetype, the shaman Bard of innumerable heroic ballads and story cycles. Gwion, Gwyddion, Taliesin, and many other Celtic heroes combined such paradoxical (to our minds) qualities within themselves as they were then thought to be inseparable traits. Their merging of these motifs is due to the Celts' recognition of the core energy of both inspiration and war, that being elemental Fire.

The story of an historic Celtic tribal queen, Boadicea, combines these related themes very well. Boadicea ruled the Iceni of Britain, famed for their metalworking, weaponry, poetry and magic. They, like all Celts, lived by the honour of their word. In other terms, their verbal contracts were honoured absolutely, for it was believed that the magical power of incantation and poetry depended upon the gift not being sullied or abused. When the treachery of the Romans became evident, and she found herself and her people under attack, she turned from being a patron of the arts and became, instead, a fierce and determined warrior. The fire element was a vital source of both courage and inspiration in the hearths of the ancient Iceni.

Cuhulain, The Irish Hero-Bard in *Tâin Bô Cuâlnge*, "emerges so 'heated' from his first exploit (which, as Dumézil has shown, is equivalent to an initiation of the martial type) that three vats of cold water are brought him."[48] These vats are for the purpose of cooling him down before he ignites the countryside. The story has it that, "he was put in the first vat, and he made the water so hot that it broke the staves and the copper hoops of the vat as one cracks a walnut. In the second vat the water made bubbles as big as a fist. In the third vat the heat was of the kind that some men can bear and some cannot. Then the little boy's wrath (ferg) lessened, and they gave him his clothes."[49]

When our Bard arrives at the Castle of the Muses, the second test is posed by a bridge that spans the moat, a molten river of fire. This bridge is magical, and becomes as thin and sharp as a razor blade when the Bard goes to cross it. The "hair-fine" bridge played a major role in the initiatory traditions in western Europe in the Middle Ages.[50] According to a medieval legend, Lancelot had to cross a bridge that became as narrow as a sword edge. Before he started the crossing, he saw two fearsome lions awaiting him on the other side, but when he gets there he sees only a harmless lizard (both types of creatures being fire totems). This is a demonstration of the initiatory nature of the trial in that "successfully undergoing the initiatory ordeal in itself makes the 'danger' disappear."[51]

According to Barbara Walker, the Muses represent the "Ninefold Goddess as the source of 'inspiration,' literally breathing in 'I-deas' or Goddess spirits within. . . . First of them was Mnemosyne, 'Memory,' who made poets able to remember sacred sagas. The seven-tone musical scale was the Muses' invention, supposedly based on their 'music' of the seven spheres."[52] Museums, the store-houses of all manners of creativity, are literally "places of the Muses."

What the Bard learns in the Castle of the Muses is that all creativity resides within each of us, as undifferentiated potential. With the aid of Memory, one's own true nature and purpose can be recalled and actualised as a unique, artistic expression. The personal will is the wand of such an endeavour and, once ignited, must be protected and honoured. When one has successfully undergone the initiation of the Will, magical creativity will thrive and endure. This is the "Eternal Flame," an image of creative fire which has survived from the earliest fires of Vesta, the hearth fires of Hestia, Heartha, and the Nine

Clan Mothers. It can never be destroyed, for it exists at the very centre of our being — hot, brilliant, and undying.

The identity of the domestic hearth with the central one is expressed in the rekindling of its fire from the central fire. For the purposes of this ritual the centre of any locality is the hill or cairn on which the bonfire is lit, and in the house the focus is the hearth.[53]

Ben Jonson's poem, "On Lucy, Countesse of Bedford," extols the pyrotechnical virtues of his personal Muse:

> *This morning, timely rapt with holy fire,*
> > *I thought to forme unto my zealous Muse,*
> *What kinde of creature I could most desire,*
> > *To honour, serve, and love, as Poets use*[54]

William Blake likewise made the fiery quality of his Muse obvious in "The Crystal Cabinet":

> *O, what a smile! A threefold smile*
> > *Filled me that like a flame I burned;*
> *I bent to kiss the lovely maid,*
> > *And found a threefold kiss returned.*
>
> *I strove to seize the inmost form*
> > *With ardour fierce and hands of flame*[55]

However, Robert Herrick made his devotion to the fire of inspiration most clear in this paean to his art, "A Hymn To The Muses":

> *O! you the Virgins nine!*
> *That doe our soules encline*
> *To noble Discipline!*
> *Nod to this vow of mine:*
> *Come then, and now enspire*
> *My violl and my lyre*
> *With your eternall fire:*
> *And make me one entire*
> *Composer in your Quire.*
> *Then I'le your Altars strew*
> *With Roses sweet and true*
> *Acknowledger of you.*[56]

Chapter IV

The Realm of Murias

Signs, portents, lines of birds
pointing the way
The way of lakeland and veils
of smoke without fires

Fires of light riding on the waves
Waves unfolding from the prow
of a coracle

A coracle bound for the
islands of promise
A promise of life renewed
and a gift of sight

Sight beyond my questing vision
Vision of apple boughs
and a sweet choice

Choice within the wisdom of nine
Nine maidens of the cauldron
and the Grail

The Grail whose wisdom follows signs
Signs, portents, lines of birds
pointing the way

THE CASTLE OF THE NINE NEREIDS

As I travelled north along the road I saw that the sun had moved into the west and was now lying low in the sky. This was the only indication of how much time had passed. Days or weeks could have transpired, I could no longer tell. As I trudged along the sun descended no closer to the horizon. Once again it seemed time was suspended and would not progress until I had penetrated another of the realms of Abred. At last the signpost appeared upon the horizon. As the road approached the crossroads I noticed the sign that pointed to the west. It was lit by the rays of the setting sun and was inscribed, "To Murias."

As I watched the words changed to say, "To the Castle of the Nereids." Taking this transmutation of words for my cue as before, I decided to take the road west into the light of the dying sun.

For a time the road continued west across the plain without any pronounced change in the landscape. Then I began to notice my surroundings transform. The ground became more moist and water-loving trees and bushes clustered by the many rivers and streams. Hazel bushes, Elder trees, Alders, Catkins, Willow, Reeds and Bulrushes filled my view, and the sound of water-hunting birds filled my ears. The fresh smell of the river rose to my nostrils. The breeze was cooling, becoming a moist and gentle kiss upon my skin. Though the sun still shone, an orange orb low in a deep blue sky, the first stars were already appearing. A crescent moon hung over the trees.

The road led on and on, through marshy fens and wetlands. To the side of the road pools of clear water winked between the leaves of the overhanging trees and the ground was lush with green growth. Every now and then a fish would leap in the pond or pool I was passing, its silver arc reflecting the setting sun. The road emerged into a deep valley and I looked across it to a scene of great loveliness.

A lake filled this valley. Its banks rose up steeply in wooded hillsides, covered in evergreens and deciduous trees of every kind. In the centre of the lake rose an island crested by a castle made of chalcedony. It glowed like a carnelian in the setting sun. I thought that the Nereids must be rich indeed to live in a castle wrought of a single gem of such magnitude. Encouraged by my success at the Castle of the Muses I sallied forth, feeling brave and expecting great wonders.

The road began to descend into the valley. As I came closer to the lake I realised there was no bridge over the water to the island in its midst. The road led up to the water's edge and just stopped there. There was no causeway, nor even a bridge as inhospitable as the that of the Muse's castle of gold. I stood on the shore and realised that in order to approach the castle of the Nereids I must swim, a prospect that weighed on me, for it was a great distance to the island.

I had just surrendered to the idea when I noticed a small boat pushing off from the beach of the island. A silver sail fluttered then caught the wind and filled. Soon the vessel was steering a course toward me. I made out a figure at the helm, a maiden in a hooded cloak of deep blue. I could not make out her face at all, for it was hidden by the hood. Though she came closer and closer over the waves, she never raised her head to look at me. Even when the small ship glided on the sand and the woman stepped on to the shore, I caught no glimpse of the features of she who had come to ferry me across the water to the island.

A silvery voice emerged from the hood. It said, "Step aboard my vessel, Bard. We have been expecting you. I am Nimue, your guide in Avalon."

When she had spoken these words, the maiden threw back her hood and I beheld the face of the eternal nymph, Nimue. With the appearance of a young girl, she was ancient beyond memory, ever-renewing, immortal. It was she, I knew, for I had seen her face many times in my dreams.

I thanked her for her courtesy and climbed aboard the little boat. It was a graceful craft, with a high prow carved in the likeness of a water dragon. The ship obeyed some silent command from the maiden of the lake and turned its head to the waves. The silver sail fluttered and the maiden called to the wind to fill it. A light wind came obligingly astern and the ship sailed smoothly across the water with a broad reach. Before long we were coming in to shore of the island, Avalon. The hull slid along the snow-white sand and I stepped onto the magical isle.

The road emerged from the water at the shore and led off into the apple grove which surrounded the castle. We walked through the trees, their fruit hanging heavy in the branches. It felt like an evening in late Autumn in the grove, when the apples are ready for harvesting. I could feel the trees watching us as we passed, probing me for my intent, my meaning. The branches parted and the castle appeared, the chalcedony walls rising before me suddenly, glowing in the last light of the sun.

The main gate was open and we walked through the donjon into the castle yard. A large fountain, carved in carnelian, stood in the centre of the courtyard. Its water leapt in the setting sun, describing a graceful arc.

"My sisters await you in the grotto," said the Nymph. "The Castle Murias is built upon the site of an ancient sacred spring; its waters fill this fountain. It is the fountain of renewal so often sought by queens and conquerors. But we must go down, below the castle, to find its source. Follow me."

So saying, the maid led the way within and soon we were walking along the passageway that appeared to have been hewn from the living rock in dim and distant ages past. The passage began to descend, winding around, ever lower into the bowels of the castle. On and on we walked, down and around, until the passage opened up into a huge, underground chamber.

It was a natural cavern, containing a great, underground lake. Its water was clear and fragrant. I looked across its glassy surface and saw a grotto in the rock of the other side. A robust stream of water flowed steadily out from this place. We walked around the shore of the lake and entered the grotto, to find the Nymph's eight sisters waiting there.

"I am Morgan Le Fay," said the one with raven hair. "This is the source of the water of life, but you must pass my test before you may drink of it."

The Fay then produced two apples from within the folds of her night-black robe. She held them out, one in each hand. In her right palm lay an apple of wholesome appearance, blushing with a bright red bloom. In the left palm lay an apple of the most vivid blue.

"One is the apple of knowledge, the other is deadly poison. You must choose the right one or go no further on your journey," said Morgan Le Fay, and waited.

I thought hard. One had the deadly cast of cyanide, yet the other seemed deceptive in its normal appearance. I knew I was in the realm of reflections, where everything could be opposite what it seemed. The red apple emitted a warning to my senses, while the blue apple seemed to say, "pick me."

I took the blue apple from the hand of The Fay and bit into it. The taste was piercingly sweet and I knew I had chosen well.

"You have chosen the apple of vision and clarity," said Morgan Le Fay. "You have the power to see beyond illusion and glamours. Never will you be misled by false projections and delusions. You may travel safely in the watery realm, and you may drink safely of the Grail."

Nimue spoke up then, saying, "You must choose one of us as Grail Maiden, for the cup brings different blessings depending on the bearer."

I looked at each of the Nereids in turn and saw that they were all quite different from each other. Each bore a chalice, of an appearance differing from the others but all equally lovely, some of silver, others of gold or platinum, all studded with precious jewels.

"I am the Initiator," said Nimue. "You know me well for we began this journey together, in your dreams."

"I am Elaine," said a lovely woman in a veil of sheerest sea-foam. "I confer the boon of equal love."

"I am Enid," said the third Nereid. "I bring the gift of joy."

"I am Guinevere," said the one in shining white with the cloak made of flowers. "I confer dominion and felicity."

"I am Igraine," uttered the fifth. "I am balm for grief and bring comfort."

"I am Argante," said the sixth Nereid, a queenly woman in a gown of royal purple. "I give nurture and balance."

"I am Morgan Le Fay," said she of the raven hair. "I bring you growth for I come to challenge you."

"I am Kundry," said a woman shorn of hair like the Priestess of an archaic temple. "I bring ancient knowledge and wisdom."

"And I am Ragnel," said a fay who kept changing from young to old and back again. "I am compassion."

I was indecisive as before in the Castle of the Muses, for it was plain that all the gifts were of great value to the soul. How could I choose between them? It occurred to me then that the gift of Morgan Le Fay would be my choice, for her tests would spur the growth that was timely to my journey.

"I choose you to bear the cup, Morgan Le Fay," said I, and her stern face lit with a rare smile.

"How wise of you to choose the seventh Nereid," said she, "for surely my challenges are most fitting for a Bard."

With that The Fay made a sweeping gesture with her arm and at the centre of the circle of Nereids appeared a huge cauldron. It seethed and bubbled like a volcanic pit, emitting sulphurous fumes and a smell of molten iron. The liquid was as viscous and active as lava, terrifying to behold. Suddenly Morgan Le Fay grew to an enormous size and gripped me, flinging me into the pot. I rolled and tumbled in the boiling, bubbling liquid like a rag. All my flesh melted away until my bones were as bare as an overboiled chicken's. Then she yanked me back out of the pot and stood me up on my bony legs.

Gently, as I stood there, she began to shape and gesture with her hands. I saw that my flesh was reforming, stronger, firmer, better than before. Then she began to intone, "May your feet be sure of their footing and carry you in pathways of your own making. May your belly be strong as a well-formed bowl in which to mix your own creations. May your centre be as powerful as a furnace in which to forge your purpose into will, and your heart be as light as a bird's wing. May your throat give voice to your own true expression, and your brow hold the light of your conscious intent. May you be crowned with the sovereignty of your being."

As The Fay said these words, the flesh and organs of my body were renewed. I found that my new eyes saw with greater clarity and that my new skin was acutely sensitive to the fluctuations of environment. My feet felt firm and solid against the earth and my sense of smell was increased to the degree that I could scent the deer among the apple trees outside the castle. I could hear the tiniest of sounds clearly and could almost taste the quality of the air around me. I had been reborn from the bubbling pot and felt more alive than ever I had.

"You have received the boon of the cauldron of rebirth," said Morgan Le Fay. "You have won your perfect body. All your senses, your purpose and your mind have been renewed. There are now no realms forbidden to you."

I was about to thank her, when I realised she was gone. It was as if she and her sisters had never been there in the cavern at all, except for Nimue, who remained. She stepped forward and took my arm.

"It is time for you to go," she said. "You may return here, to Avalon in Murias, for now you know the way. But your journey awaits your arrival in Falias."

So saying, the Maiden led me back along the passageway to the Castle, then out into the evening air of the apple orchard. As we strolled through the trees, I wondered at the refreshment of my senses and perceptions. The sights, sounds and smells of the orchard seemed more intense. It was as if I were truly noticing them for the first time.

We went back the way we had come, to the boat on the sand. Then Nimue ferried me back to the other shore. She bid me farewell from the boat as I waded ashore, then turned her craft about and was gone. A mist arose and Nimue, boat, castle and island disappeared completely from view. As I set off along the road, I wondered how easy it would ever be to find Avalon in Murias again.

Evening is the time of day associated with the West. The direction of West is where the sun sets, the afterglow creating the transitional period of twilight, associated with mysticism. Twilight is the borderland between two states; it is neither day nor night, and is therefore highly charged with transformational potential. All borders in time and space are considered magical in the transformative trance journey, as the visible cracks in the so-called "normal" world of appearances. Shorelines, rivers, bridges, cliffs and precipices all offer opportunities for transformation. Transitional states and places are thresholds; they allow the more usual perceptions to slip a little, permitting a glimpse "beyond the veil" into the Otherworld.

In western coastal areas, the sun appears to set in the sea, appropriately enough, as the West is also associated with the element of water. In terms of seasonal magic, West is associated with Autumn (in the northern hemisphere), when the sun begins its descent from summer's zenith, to the equinox. Thereafter, the sun's light will visibly diminish daily, until its nadir at the Winter's Solstice (associated with the direction of North). West is the direction where light exists in relation to darkness, where oracular vision may penetrate the darkness of otherwise eclipsed realities. It is the direction associated with intuition, emotion, deep knowing or Gnosis, and dreams.

The Bard walks north from the southerly location of the Castle of the Muses, leaving the realm of fire. The sign at the crossroads directs the Bard to take the road that travels west, into the light of the dying sun. There is a sacrificial tone to the westerly, watery direction. Mystery and veiled wonders are associated with the western, otherworldly regions. "The Western Isles" were the destination of ancient Mediterranean adventurers, "where Cronos lies dreaming."[57] "Summerland," "The Apple Isle," and the paradisiacal Otherworld promised to heroic martyrs were thought to lie in the "Western Sea," mist-shrouded islands awaiting the worthy traveller.

As the Bard travels along the road into Murias, towards the Castle of the Nereids, the landscape changes, exhibiting landmarks and foliage corresponding to the water element. Hazel is the type of wood used for "water-witching," or the divining of water underground. The more subtle qualities of Hazel include the ability to penetrate to the heart of a matter, and to divine the essential truth of any situation. Hazel's affinity for water and for the type of wisdom associated with the Otherworldly West is captured in the myth about "The Salmon of Knowledge."

The Bardic hero, Finn mac Cool, was learning the art of poetry from Finegas, guardian of Fintan, the Salmon of Knowledge, "oldest of creatures." Fintan had absorbed ultimate knowledge by eating a lunar number of hazelnuts — nine of them — which had fallen into the stream. Finn acquired the prophetic wisdom of the ancient fish, seemingly by accident. He, as the apprentice of Finegas, was roasting Fintan for Finegas to eat when juices from the aquatic meal of knowledge spurted onto his thumb. He put the finger to his mouth to cool it and thus gained the stored knowledge of Fintan.

In the account of Taliesin's acquisition of "All Knowledge," he, as Cerridwen's servant, was tending her cauldron. Cerridwen was brewing a potion to make Her son, Morfran, all-wise as compensation for his extreme ugliness. It was necessary for Cerridwen's cauldron to brew for a year and a day in order to perfect the gift of knowledge. But on the final day, the three boiling drops of the liquid containing the magic fell upon Taliesin's fingers, scalding them. He immediately put his fingers to his mouth to soothe the pain, and thereby "accidentally" acquired the initiation of wisdom so long in the making.

Cerridwen, in response to the destruction of her plans for her son, pursued Taliesin in fury. He now had the magical/shamanic abilities of "the Wise," however, so he quickly shape-shifted through a series of manifestations. He transformed himself into thirteen different forms, corresponding to the thirteen lunar months of the historic Celtic "year and a day." Cerridwen finally caught him on the final day (which corresponds to Samhain or All Hallows Eve).

Taliesin had transformed into a seed of grain and Cerridwen, in an act symbolic of the gleaning of the fields associated with Samhain, assumed the form of a hen and gobbled him up. She became pregnant from this seed, however. Nine months later, back in her Goddess form, She gave birth to him as "Taliesin of the Radiant Brow." In his new incarnation, the wisdom of Cerridwen's cauldron survived within him, intact. The number nine is significant in these and other accounts. The Salmon of Knowledge had become wise by virtue of swallowing nine of the Hazel nuts that regularly fell into the stream, nine being the number of the moon, of human gestation, and of the lunar Priesthood.

Elder trees are also associated with the West, as guardians of death and rebirth. It is known as a "Witch Tree." Tree lore included the cautionary tale that Priestesses, Witches, dryads, spirits or fairies took the form of Elders at certain times. For this reason, it was taboo to ever take an axe to an Elder without first obtaining its permission, lest it be a Witch or nymph in disguise.

Alders are associated with water because of their ability to withstand it. Alders were historically used for ships' timbers, and to make the supports and pilings of bridges and other structures spanning water. The use of Alder in supportive structures brought with it the protection and patronage of Alder's corresponding (Welsh) deity: Bran the Blessed. The name "Bran" means "Alder," and also "Raven," as the raven is Bran's totem bird. This is the real reason why ravens have always been kept in the Tower of London, invoking the potent protection and oracular vision of Bran as anti-invasion magic and as a charm to maintain national sovereignty. Alder's appearance in the Bard's magical landscape implies that there will be a test concerning boundaries and inner integrity. Bulrushes and Reeds appear to signal that a choice is upcoming for the Bard, one that will require decisiveness and clarity. Reed's magical qualities are those of swift action and true aim. Motives and agendas, conscious and veiled, come under scrutiny and are put to the test. The Bard, understanding the language of trees, is alerted to the necessity for unhesitating, balanced action. The action of Reed is poised in perfect alignment with the true position of the Self, keeping one's ultimate goal in clear sight.

All these signs are subliminal, for a magical rhythm and cadence has already taken over the Bard's journey, and it is necessary only to trust, and to continue on, heeding the signs given. This is the nature of all Otherworldly travels. As one becomes habituated to liminal, transformative passages, one begins to recognise these signals. Normally insignificant objects and events take on a numinous charge. However, it is the peculiar nature of Westerly experiences in the realm of the water element that one is sometimes not certain if one is on a spiritual quest or merely being delusional. One comforting realisation to hang on to is this: if you are wondering if you're crazy, you're probably not. If you were truly becoming delusional, it would never occur to you to wonder about it. You would probably be quite certain you were a totally realised being, some sort of cross between Cleopatra, Jesus Christ, Mary Magdalene, The Virgin Mary, Buddha, and the Atman. Delusions of grandeur can occur in the Westerly, watery direction. West is the home of reflection, illusion, and projection.

Eventually the Bard arrives at the shore of a large, mysterious lake. An island rises from the centre of the lake. This is, of course, legendary Avalon. It also represents any and all other mythical Western Isles, including "The Island of Women," to which Bran, son of Ferbal, journeyed, and in which he dwelt for many years, thinking it only a year and a day.

Bran son of Ferbal, walking in the gardens of his royal house one day, hears the sound of "sweet music."[58] The music lulls him to sleep and when he wakens he finds a silver branch, crowned with a white blossom, lying on the ground beside him. This is "a branch from the apple tree from Emain Ablach," or the "Apple Isle," also known as the fabled Island of Women.

He takes the branch inside the hall and, before the assembled hosts, "a woman in strange raiment" appears. She sings a lay in which she describes the magical islands of the Western Sea, where "treachery, sorrow and sickness are not known."

She then departs, but the silver branch springs from Bran's hand into hers. Bran follows her, setting sail the very next day, with "three companies of nine, each headed by one of his foster brothers." He encounters the sea god, Manannan, who relates how the sea is, to him, "A Many Flowered Plain of Delight" in a long poem. Bran and his company eventually reach the Island of Women, where they are made welcome and where, "there is a bed for every couple, even thrice nine beds, and the food that is put before them does not diminish."

Again, the theme of nine is important, nine being the number of lunar wisdom and magic, which is to say women's magic. "Thrice nine" is twenty seven, the digits of which, like all multiples of nine, still add up to nine, creating the number of the "fays," or magical company. "Thrice nine" plus a "leader" amounts to twenty eight, the number of nights in the lunar months of the Celtic tree-calendar.

Like Emain Ablach, the Apple Isle of Avalon offers a form of sanctuary, though aspects of it, such as the passing of time, are illusory. Avalon is a "place

Journey of the Bard

that is not a place, and a time that is not a time," meaning it is "out of time" — a twilight realm of mists and wraiths. Avalon is where the soul goes for rest and recuperation between lives, as Arthur's did after his mortal clash with Mordred on Camlan plain. Here, the spirit is rejuvenated and made new. What seems a single day to the incorporeal soul is actually "a hundred years" in the world of mortals. This is an image of the "no-time" of dreams, where an entire narrative sequence that seems to have gone on all night in fact only took a split second to experience during the rapid-eye movement period of sleep. It is an image of visionary experience beyond temporal reality. "Defying definition in space, the Other World also transcends mundane time."[59]

The island is crowned by a castle carved of a single gem, a glowing carnelian. Carnelian (and any orange stone) is the gem of the cauldron, corresponding to the swirling energies at the navel chakra. Vessels of every sort are associated with this place in the body-consciousness, for they represent the emotional containers for the watery element within our own bodies. Ideas of containment and psychological flotation relate to this centre. Mystical ships, or dream vessels, safely sail the dreamer over the ego-less, watery abyss, as with the Jungian "ego-boat" archetype.

The belly is the cauldron of the body, supported by the "pelvic bowl," and (according to magical correspondences) is ruled by the moon. This centre of the body consciousness relates to Yesod of the Kabbalistic Tree of Life. In women, it is the womb centre, and in men, it is the region of the inner chalice, or Grail. It is here, within this realm of the Tree of Knowledge, that the Bard, artist, magician or priest seeks the inner font of inspiration. Ships and vessels signify the definition and conveyance of Self amid the amorphous tides of emotion and unconscious psychic contents.

Countless images of mystical vessels exist from various cultures, including Minoan Crete, Thessaly, Egypt, Macedonia, Phoenicia, Phrygia, Oceania and Asia. K. Esther Harding called them "Moon Boats," in her Jungian treatise, "Women's Mysteries," but these soul vessels also contain images of giant trees, women in worship-mode, birds, animals, and ithyphallic men. They are glyphs for the containment of life itself, traversing the Cosmic ocean, safely navigating the seas of boundless time.

Folk and fairy tales are filled with accounts of mystical ships, with silver sails and crystal hulls, that mysteriously sail themselves. Frequently they abduct the heroes and heras of such tales, over the sea to fairy isles or other magical realms. Here, time will stand still and the adventurer whiles away the time in pleasurable pursuits, unaware that years are slipping away in the "real" world.

The Bard's journey is halted at the edge of the mysterious lake. There is no bridge, and no apparent way to cross the water, except to swim. This is another threshold, on the shore of land and water.

The thin line between opposites has essentially the same significance as the dangerous bridges that lead to the citadels of the Other World, the narrow bridge, the razor-edge bridge, or the see-saw bridge which can only be negotiated by leaping on to its middle. It is the space between the blades that rise from the threshold and those that depend from the lintel of the door to the Giant's castle, it is the middle course between Scylla and Charybdis. Irish poets deemed that the brink of water was always a place where "eicse" — "wisdom," "poetry," "knowledge" — was revealed.[60]

There is no bridge over the water to the beautiful island, but a small ship sets out from the other shore, bearing a cloaked and hooded courier. No glimpse can be gained of the courier's features, for this is the first contact with Mystery itself. Mystery bears no one visage; it is young or old, male or female, ugly or beautiful, human or other in turn — similar to Dionysus, Hermes, or Thoth. The courier turns out to be Nimue, which lets us know that the Bard is facing an important initiation, for Nimue is the Initiator of the transfiguration of Self.

This transfiguration does not imply that the Bard or any other seeker will be alienated from themselves. What "transfiguration" means in this instance is that, by magical, shamanic methods as old as human culture, initiates are transformed in such a way as to more perfectly express who it is they truly are. The body and the outer life are transfigured so as to reflect the inner soul of the seeker through the element of water, or "baptism."

In shamanic initiatory trance, immersal in a cauldron signifies rebirth. The old Self is melted or boiled away, and the essential Self emerges, full of magical, spiritual power. Initiates of many shamanic traditions the world over undergo versions of this visceral, visionary experience. It is an image of the disintegration of the mundane, mortal Self, and a reintegration — or re-membering — of one's true soul-nature, which is immortal. The shamanic initiate is ushered into an "eternal" point of reference, whereby her or his awareness transcends the bounds of the single, mortal lifetime.

The initiate is said to have acquired her or his "perfect" or "crystal" body. This means she or he now identifies with the "essence" or spirit body which survives the individual life, and no longer solely with the physical body. The magical personality perceives itself differently. A shaman's conception of the world shifts accordingly. It is at this moment that the shaman (magician, artist, or Bard) begins to re-sacralise their experience of life. It now begins to be possible to inhabit the Sacred Garden full-time.

In our story, the initiating priestess is Morgan La Fay; in folk and fairy tale it is often a blacksmith, giant, ogre, Goddess or Witch who fulfils the role. To quote Eliade:

Let us note that the myth of renewal by fire, cooking or dismemberment has continued to haunt men [sic] even outside the spiritual horizon of shamanism.

Medeia succeeds in having Pelias murdered by his own daughters by convincing them that she will restore him to life rejuvenated, as she did a ram. And when Tantalos kills his son Pelops and serves him at the banquet of the gods, they resuscitate him by boiling him in a pot; only his shoulder is missing, Demeter having inadvertently eaten it. The myth of rejuvenation by dismemberment and cooking has also been handed down in Siberian, Central Asian, and European folklore, the role of the blacksmith being played by Jesus Christ or certain saints.

... among the Yakut, the Buryat, and other Siberian peoples, shamans are believed to have been killed by the spirits of their ancestors, who, after "cooking" their bodies, counted their bones and replaced them, fastening them together with iron and covering them with new flesh.[61]

These themes can be found in the Mabinogion, the Welsh myth cycle. Effnissien, the baleful brother of ancestral deities Bran and Branwen, engenders war between Bran and the Irish king over an insult to Branwen, whom the Irish king has married and taken to Ireland. She trains a starling and sends it with a message to Bran, her brother, concerning her plight. He then mounts an invasion to rescue Branwen and restore her honour. In the ensuing war, the Irish warriors who fall in battle are continually resuscitated by being thrown into the "Cauldron of Regeneration."

This magical vessel (which came, originally, from the bottom of an Irish lake, borne on the back of a gigantic blacksmith-type deity called Llassar) has the power to bring dead warriors placed within it back to life, lacking only the power of speech. Finally, in an uncharacteristic act of personal sacrifice, Effnissien salvages the situation by diving into the cauldron and breaking it apart from within, disposing of the Irish, magical/military advantage.

The Welsh light God, King Arthur, descended into the Underworld to retrieve a magical cauldron from the Lord of that land. "A Welsh poem, ascribed to the Bard, Taliesin, relates, under the title, 'The Spoiling of Annwn,' an expedition of Arthur and his followers into the very heart of that country, from which he appears to have returned (for the verses are somewhat obscure) with the loss of almost all his men, but in possession of the object of his quest — the magic cauldron of inspiration and poetry."[62]

The verse referred to is:

Is not my song worthily to be heard
In the four-square Caer (Castle), four times revolving!
I draw my knowledge from the famous cauldron,
The breath of nine muses keeps it boiling.
Is not the Head of Annwn's cauldron so shaped;
Ridged with enamel, rimmed with pearl?[63]

The cauldron in this story is just one of the many vessels of rejuvenation and inspiration within the body of Celtic lore:

In the later romances, the Holy Grail is a Christian relic of marvelous potency. It had held the Paschal lamb eaten at the Last Supper; and, after the death of Christ, Joseph of Arimathea had filled it with the Saviour's blood. But before it received this colouring, it had been the magic cauldron of all the Celtic mythologies — the Dagda's "Undry" which fed all who came to it, and from which none went away unsatisfied; Bran's cauldron of Renovation, which brought the dead back to life; the cauldron of Ogryvan the Giant, from which the Muses ascended; the cauldrons captured by Cuchulainn from the king of the Shadowy City, and by Arthur from the chief of Hades . . .[64]

All of these Celtic images, and still more, described magically regenerative vessels. They show a great similarity to images still current within Arctic and Siberian shamanism, as in this dream account recorded by Eliade:

> . . . the candidate came to a desert and saw a distant mountain. After three days' travel he reached it, entering an opening, and came upon a naked man working a bellows. On the fire was a cauldron "as big as half the earth." The naked man saw him and caught him with a huge pair of tongs. The novice had time to think, "I am dead!" The man cut off his head, chopped his body into bits, and put everything in the cauldron. There he boiled his body for three years. There were also three anvils, and the naked man forged the candidate's head on the third, which was the one on which the best shamans were forged. Then he threw the head into one of the three pots that stood there, the one in which the water was the coldest. He now revealed to the candidate that when he was called to cure someone, if the water in the ritual pot was very hot, it would be useless to shamanize, for the man was already lost; if the water was warm, he was sick but would recover; cold water denoted a healthy man.
> The blacksmith then fished the candidate's bones out of a river in which they were floating, put them together, and covered them with flesh again. He counted them and told him that he had three too many; he was therefore to procure three shaman's costumes. He forged his head and taught him how to read the letters that are inside it. He changed his eyes; and that is why, when he shamanizes, he does not see with his bodily eyes but with these mystical eyes. He pierced his ears, making him able to understand the language of plants. Then the candidate found himself on the summit of a mountain, and finally he woke in the yurt, among his family. Now he can sing and shamanise indefinitely, without ever growing tired.[65]

Without an understanding of the spiritual dimensions of such imagery, these themes and motifs can be bewildering to critics of art history or folklore. Despite this, their archetypical quality insures that they continue to emerge, even in contemporary fairytale imagery, such as *Apple Staff and Silver Crown*, by Nancy Lou Patterson:

> She climbed to the top of the tripod and sat upon it, with her shawl wrapped

round her and over her head. And she never knew how long she sat there, for she fell into a stupor at the first full breath of the smoke, and had the last and longest dream of all her Apple Chasm dreaming. The dream she dreamed on the tripod was like this.

She saw three women, clad in blue linen and green wool and red leather, with grey veils covering their faces. Each one bore in her arms a great bronze cauldron. The first held a cauldron of water, and the second a cauldron of burning coals, and the third a cauldron perfectly empty. The first set her cauldron of water on the fire-filled cauldron of the second, until the water began to boil. Then the third set down the empty cauldron, and drew a bronze knife from the folds of her red leather dress, and, coming to where the dreaming Princess sat, she took her by the arm and pulled her down, and cut her throat (still dreaming) so neat and quick that she never felt a thing, but her lifeblood pouring out and filling the empty cauldron.

Then in the manner of dreams she beheld herself cut into pieces entirely, till all that was left was a pile of flesh (which went into the cauldron with the blood), leaving her bare but still alive in her little white skeleton, lighting up herself with her two grey eyes. And she sat down shivering in her bones to see what would happen. The three women put the cauldron of body and blood on top of the water above the fire, to boil until they were done.

Then, with the greatest tenderness, they drew the pieces of her delicate body out, as good as new, and put them onto her bony frame again. Last of all they poured the boiled blood back into the wound at her throat, where she felt it coursing through her veins to her fingers and toes, as if wine had been poured there instead of blood. And she was made all over again, better than before.[66]

In this story, the hera was also endowed with heightened senses, and made "Mistress of talents and skills." Shamanic images such as these are behind the true meaning of the (often misunderstood) image on the well-known Pagan Celtic artifact, the "Gundestrop Cauldron." The narrative relief impressed around the bowl shows a Priest or God figure immersing a youth, or Bardic hero, in a cauldron (figure 9). Many art historical commentaries, or anthropological analyses, describe this image as probably a scene of "human sacrifice." Familiarity with the magical motifs makes it very clear that, to the contrary, the scene depicts shamanic transformation, which is an act of personal, not victim, sacrifice. An early Celtic Christian image parallels the image almost exactly, where an angel dunks a figure in a giant chalice, or Grail, with one hand and holds aloft a holy wafer, or host, in the other (figure 10). Votive wafers of this type inscribed with the equal-armed cross symbolised the sacrificial "Greenman," or vegetation god in most parts of continental Europe for may hundreds of years before the coming of Christianity. In Germanic lands, such a wafer represented Wotan.

The Cauldron is the prototype of the Grail itself: an Otherworldly vessel whose gifts include variously: rebirth, knowledge, spiritual fulfilment, paradisal bliss and magical power, as well as providing physical nourishment. The cauldron is the pagan resonance of the Grail which has been identified with the redemptive symbol of Christ's new covenant. Both Grail and cauldron dispense the draught of salvation, the waters of everlastingness; both are vessels which have an Otherworldly provenance; both are attainable only by people of sovereign power or heroes of daring courage. Death, both physical and spiritual, is written into the scenario of its quest; those who fail are slain; those who win die to the world and are reborn or initiated into a different and Otherworldly condition.[67]

From this rebirth, the soul emerges refreshed and renewed. It is a regeneration at the soul level which puts the seeker back in touch with the eternal, ageless Self. This is as much as to say that, when one drinks at the well of soul memory, one realises one's own immortality. This is an alchemical experience, the marriage of heart and mind, unconsciousness to consciousness, left brain to right, body to soul. The body is recognised as a transitory expression of the ageless and immortal soul; the soul is recognised as eternally renewing itself.

A dream or vision of this sort constitutes an actual experience of the "Fountain of Youth," searched for by many a literalistic explorer besides Vasco de

Figure 9: Pagan Celtic image of dead warriors being inserted into cauldron of rebirth and emerging reborn, from Gundestrup Cauldron.

Figure 10: baptism illustration from the Roda Bible, eleventh century C.E.

Journey of the Bard

Gama during the Age of Discovery. As in so many such misguided quests, the seeker was not aware that the direction of query lay not in the New World, but in the world within. Nimue is a symbol for this understanding. As the youthful, questing aspect of the Lady of the Lake, or the initiatory process, she nevertheless changes her form continually. She can appear young or old at will, for she contains the awareness of both mortal and immortal being.

The journey over water, similar to passage over a bridge, is an immediate sign that a threshold experience is beckoning. In all folk and fairy tales, the crossing of water and arrival at another shore betokens a transformation of consciousness. Psyche crossed the river Styx to reach Eros, captive of the Underworld realm of Hades. The ferryman, Charon, conveyed souls to the "Other Side" in Greek myth. This figure is a fairly ubiquitous one, albeit disguised, found in the characters of countless ferrymen and women, who will convey the soul of the newly dead (or of the magical traveller in the realm of death) for one copper penny. It is for this reason that folk custom in many parts of Europe required that a penny be put in the mouths of the deceased, to "pay the ferryman."

The underground spring that feeds the lake below the Castle of the Nereids is analogous to any and all "source" wells and springs in myth and fairy lore. The aquatic fairy, Melusine, was said to inhabit the "River Source" in her natural form, which included a scaly fish or (in some versions) serpent tail. She inhabited the pool just below the spring that was the source of the river, singing, combing her hair, and interrogating her magic mirror, like many a mermaid of myth and lore. She would also proffer her magical cup of blessing to any in need. The cup would provide food, drink, healing and grace to the needful or afflicted. In this nurturing, healing capacity, she was akin to countless "maidens of the wells" of western European folklore. Their attrition is equated with the desolation of the land, creating the Wasteland of the Fisher King.

> In ancient times Logres was a rich country but it was turned into a Wasteland so that it was worth scarcely a couple of hazelnuts. For the kingdom lost the voices of the wells and the damsels that were in them. The damsels would offer food and drink to wayfarers. A traveller would only have to wish for food and seek out one of the wells and a damsel would appear from out of the well with the food he liked best, a cup of gold in her hand. No wayfarers were excluded from this service.[68]

All of the themes associated with the direction of West and the element of Water come together in the image of the sacred well or spring. To early Celts, these features of the natural landscape were an abiding source of inspiration and spiritual nourishment. To quote Alwynn and Brinley Rees, from *Celtic Heritage*:

. . . the secret well brings to mind the Mysterious Well of Segais, or Connla's Well, which nobody durst visit except Nechtan and his three cup bearers. Like Mimir's Well at the root of the Scandinavian World Tree, this well was the source of inspiration and knowledge. Over it grew the nine hazels of wisdom, "out of which were obtained the feats of the sages." The hazel nut dropped into the well and caused bubbles of mystic inspiration to form on the streams that issued from it. Alternatively, the nuts were eaten by the salmon in the well, or they passed into the River Boyne. Those designated to partake of the nuts or of the salmon obtained the gifts of the seer and the poet. The location of the well is variously described. It is the source of the Boyne, the source of the Shannon, the source of the seven chief rivers of Ireland, and it has its counterpart in The Land of Promise where the five rivers that flow from it are the five senses.[69]

Apple trees, boughs, orchards and fruit are an ubiquitous feature of mythologies the world over, even in areas where Apple trees are not a part of the native flora. Apple trees were probably not native to the British Isles, but are thought to have been imported by Mediterranean mariners in the first millennium B.C.E. The Apple is the fruit of the Tree of Knowledge of Good and Evil in the Biblical Eden. A golden apple is the fruit given to Aphrodite by Paris in the Greek beauty contest myth, though this is a late, Classical interpretation of an ancient image. Earlier accounts would have portrayed Aphrodite and Her divine Sisters awarding the apple to the Hero or Warrior/Poet, as the gift of wisdom.

An Apple falling from a tree is even credited with the inspiration given Newton, whereupon he composed his gravitational theories. But the real reason the Apple is such a primal, widespread symbol for inspired wisdom is that it is an archetype for the fruition of spiritual awareness. In literal terms, the Apple corresponds to the pineal gland, the organ of psychism and genius. It grows at the crown of the Tree of Knowledge, or the spine, in the midbrain. In Yoga it is called "The Cave of Brahma," located where the two lobes of the brain meet. Here, knowledge of the marriage of polarities of all kinds is alchemised as an inexhaustible fountain of inspiration, for it is connected, in consciousness, to all other systems and totalities. Cosmic dynamics are perceived here, as well as the intricate, balanced forces of sex and fertility. The Apple is not merely the "Temptation of Eve." It is more properly understood as the Goddess' invitation to engage the Mystery of Creation, and to ingest the gift of prophetic wisdom.

The snake wound around the Apple tree, proffering the apple from amongst the leafy branches, is more properly understood as the kundalini serpent. The serpent is the ancient symbol for the mercurial energy which makes its home at the root of the tree, or spine, and ascends to the crown, where it is expressed as divine consciousness. It is this energy which is symbolised by the serpents entwined around the Staff of Hermes, or Caduceus, symbol of the healing arts.

One of the ways in which this sacred energy is perceived most clearly is through the practice of Tantric Yoga, the purpose of which is to raise the Kundalini, serpent energy through the measured sacrament of sexual engagement.

Apples were well known to the Celts as otherworldly fruit, and there are numerous stories in which heroes are found sleeping beneath apple trees and are carried off by otherworldly women, or again are offered apples which have the effect of bespelling them so that they waken in fairyland. If we see Nimue-Gwyenddydd as the guardian of such apples, then we are nearer to the idea of her as an otherworldly or faery woman who has the power in her own right to convey people into the Otherworld.[70]

Apple was added to the Celtic sacred grove of Druidic lore, to the Ogham script, and to the lunar calendar of trees, sharing a month with the Hazel tree from (roughly) the middle of June to the middle of July. The magical significance of Apple within this system of divination is called the "choice of beauty." Apple indicates decisiveness and discrimination, and encourages accurate choices based upon "good taste." The Apple choice is made in accordance with knowledge of what is good for you, based upon the sensory cues of attraction and repulsion. The "choice of beauty" is what Joseph Campbell referred to as "following your bliss."[71]

The hero who descends to the Underworld becomes the guardian of the Otherworldy Hallows in the paradise of Avalon. Those who have eaten of the fruit of the apple which grows there can only return as the reborn Mabon, the son of Modron, because that fruit bestows eternal youth with potent restoration of spent strength.[72]

Chapter V

The Realm
of
Falias

First to the crossroads and the
freezing air
Airborn across the chasm
to the sheltering stones
Stones in corridors
to walk upon
Upon a lengthening path
to the mountain
of white

A white owl calling, gliding
to the stairs
Stairs widening to the
feasting hall
Halls where words survive
the descent
Descending the root
to the watery jewel

Jewel of the tree
in its climb to the light
Lighting the memory of those
who came first
First to the crossroads and the
freezing air

THE CASTLE OF THE NINE WHITELADIES

The sun had dropped below the horizon as I walked back to the crossroads. The stars had come out and a full moon shone over the landscape. A pale shape dived out of the starry sky and startled me. It was a great white owl out hunting. Her plumage shone in the moonlight.

After what seemed like hours of walking, I came again to the wide plain where the four roads met. The arrow pointing north read "to Falias." As I watched, the words changed. "To the Castle of the Whiteladies," the sign announced. Taking this for my cue, as before, I took the road north.

The air grew colder and colder. Before long there was a layer of white snow upon the ground. The stars shone hard and brilliant in a clear, black sky and the moon sailed high among them. Time seemed to be standing still again, though my travelling north seemed to bring the winter on. The trees were bare and the air itself seemed to crystallise, like freezing water. White Birches and Rowans stretched their leafless branches towards me like the arms of the fey Whiteladies. I felt a shiver of fear, unlike that I had felt at the approach of the warrior Muses, or at the challenge of Morgan Le Fay. This was a fear more subtle and profound. It crept from a place deep within me, for I knew I was heading into the region of death.

The Whiteladies are the guardians of the grave. They inhabit the Hollow Hills, and protect the hall were Arthur sleeps, awaiting the call for his return. They are the *Bean Sidhe*, the Women of the Mounds, the Shining Ones, the Ninefold Sisterhood, or White Company. Their terrain is that of the spirit's wandering, their riches those to be found deep within the earth were it is perilous, dark and labyrinthine.

From this region it is difficult to return to the daylight world above. Many a time the way out has closed over, swallowing the traveller below, never to reopen. Yet the greatest treasures lie buried there, all that is hallowed, sacred and profane, treasures of the spirit as well as of the Earth. This much I knew, for the Bards of greatest power were those who had journeyed there and returned to tell of it. From this slender thread I took heart, though my fear was still present and becoming more pronounced with every mile.

The weather grew colder and more fierce until a blizzard began to blow, so I looked around for shelter. I was freezing and numb with weariness. My footsteps were getting slower and slower as I fought on through the blinding sleet. The wind dropped suddenly as I came into the shelter of a large rock upon a rise, and I looked out over a magical scene.

Across a vast plain, sparkling in the moonlight, arose a mountain range of awesome height and beauty. The highest peak rose from the midst of these giants, majestic and perfectly formed. Most wondrous of all, its slopes had been carved into the towers and battlements of a formidable castle. High, slitted windows sent shafts of yellow light streaming through the falling snow. I knew this was the Castle of the Whiteladies. Their castle was the mountain itself, the highest mountain in all of the three worlds.

I no longer felt the swirling snow or icy wind. The mountain castle ahead looked like the very home of magic, and wonder gave wings to my frozen feet. I know not how long it took to cross that plain. I know only that the mountain was ever before me, its flanks slipping out of sight behind the foothills in the foreground as I approached. By the time I stood in their shelter only the peak of the Castle of the Whiteladies was visible. The road began to climb into the hills, and then onto the mountain itself, and still I climbed on.

After days or weeks of climbing in the snow, during which the moon grew no lower in the sky as it remained perpetual night, I arrived at the foot of the Castle. High above, the rock jutted out in mighty turrets and crenelated walls. The window slits issued forth yellow light and the promise of warmth through the snowy night. The road wound around, climbing the flanks of the mountain. From every vantage, as I climbed, the rocky stronghold seemed merely to grow more vast. Finally, the road straightened out and I saw the entrance to the fortress ahead.

My heart dropped as I saw that it was on the other side of a crevasse that fell to alarming depths below. As I stood at the edge of the precipice and looked down, I could not even see the bottom, just a dizzying void. There was a drawbridge by which to cross the abyss but it was drawn up and closed to me. I started to feel cold and tired again, but just at that moment I heard a voice.

"What brings you here to the Castle of the Whiteladies?" it asked.

I looked up and saw the snowy-white owl. It was she who addressed me from a rocky outcropping above. She peered down at me from her perch high upon a wall of the castle.

"I come to gain the Bard's greatest power, that given by the Ancestors, though they be long dead," said I, and my answer must have pleased her for, with a groan and a creak, the drawbridge started to descend.

"Enter here from where very few return, and be welcome," said the owl, and flew off into the night.

I crossed over the drawbridge, looking neither to the right nor to the left, as the plummeting depths on either side made me dizzy with fear. Immediately upon entering the castle I felt warmer. A soft light bathed the interior of the castle rock, though I could see no source for this ambient warmth. There was no one about. The hall seemed quite empty and deserted. Despite this, I had the persistent feeling I was being watched, even that an invisible presence walked beside me.

As I roamed the passages I saw that this was a place of surpassing luxury. Opulently furnished chambers opened onto richly appointed halls, one after the other, and drew me on and on into the interior of the mountain. After many twistings and turnings down countless corridors, I rounded a corner and emerged into a great hall. The floor was strewn with deep, soft carpets of intricate design. The walls were hung with lustrous draperies. Columns of red jasper rose to a ceiling festooned with silk and satins like an Arab's tent, and gold-trimmed treasure chests stood about, overflowing with jewels and precious metals. Coins were stacked in small towers and scattered upon the rugs. It was like a treasure house of the richest queen, with items of great value spilling everywhere.

In the centre of the hall upon a raised dais lay a fat, white sow. She was huge, the luxury of her flesh creased in rolls around her neck. One dainty hoof lay extended with a diamond bracelet around it. A diamond necklace lay upon her neck, among the folds of fat, and she reclined on a bed of pearls.

"I am Cerridwen," said she, with a rich, contralto voice. "What brings you to my stronghold?"

"I come to gain the greatest power of a Bard," said I, "which can only be won from the country of death."

"How true, how true," said the sow, sounding slightly bored. How many times had she heard this answer from aspiring Bards, I wondered. Countless candidates for the deepest and most fearful initiations of their craft must have journeyed here, and countless more would come this way, in time.

"In that case," said the sow, "you must meet my sisters. They await you in a chamber far below the earth, beneath the mountain. It does not do to keep them waiting. If they are made to wait too long, they may not give you back."

So saying, the sow smiled a hungry smile, and turned away to a board of magnificent food that awaited her attentions. I realised I was dismissed and should hurry to the chamber far below. But how to get there? Just then I noticed a small ermine who seemed to have materialised at my feet.

"I have been following you," it said. "Now you follow me, and do not be late."

Off it went, scampering toward a curtained archway down the hall. I pushed through the curtain, hurrying after my guide, and fell into a dark tunnel. I was so startled that I screamed. The scream was torn away from my lips as I hurtled into darkness. I was falling down and down, through black, empty space. I continued to fall for what felt like hours. The hole seemed to drop away into the very centre of the earth; it was deep and dark as pitch. Then, abruptly, I landed on something soft but resilient.

A sliding, slithering sound started up. Then my landing place began to move beneath me. A glowing red light began to come from somewhere and by its illumination I saw the thing that had broken my fall. Its head loomed over me and two slitted eyes examined me minutely. These orbs were the source of what light there was in the pit. The massive head wove around, turning so as to look at me with each of its ruby eyes in turn.

It was an enormous serpent, glowing white in the red gloom, the largest I had ever seen or was likely to see. It was undoubtedly the largest serpent that had ever existed, in any of the three worlds. It opened its huge jaws and its tongue flicked out, smelling me. Then it spoke.

"What brings you to my lair, disturbing my winter's sleep?"

For once, words failed me and I spluttered helplessly about ancestors. Without realising it I must have said the right thing, for the Serpent smiled and said, "You have travelled well for I am indeed the Ancestors. I am the ancient mind of the world and the owner of its riches. No one gains anything of value without meeting me in my hall at the root of the Tree of Life."

The hall had become brighter and brighter as the Serpent warmed to its subject and its eyes glowed brighter. I looked up to see that the ceiling of the Serpent's hall was formed of a massive, twisting root - the tap root of the World Tree. I realised the Tree must be the same as that which superimposed the Glass Castle in Gwynedd and that it must also coincide with the castles of the Muses and Nereids. It seemed whenever I arrived at a place of magic, I returned to the great tree. The mountain was just another of its manifestations. I had been here, within the realms of the Tree, all along.

"You are right," said the Serpent, divining my thoughts. Then the monstrous creature transformed, before my eyes, into a shining, white woman.

"I am the sow you met above, as well as the owl and the ermine. My manifestations are many, and I am also triform."

With that statement, she split into three shining women, one young, one mature, one old. Each of these tripled herself, then nine shining women stood before me, their white skin gleaming in the ruddy glow that now filled the hall. Each held a pentacle in her hand, but each of a different precious metal. They stood before me in a half circle. The red glow was increasing steadily, emanating from the walls and ceiling. By this light I gradually determined that this chamber at the root of the Tree was inside a giant gemstone. It had been hollowed out, carved in a thousand, glittering facets, from a single, massive ruby.

The walls shone like claret wine, and the floor was the same. A fount of water issued from an opening high in the chamber and tumbled down to fill a pool inlaid with garnets. From this pool drank the tap root of the great Tree, snaking down from the ceiling coils to immerse its tip in the water.

"I am Ana," said one of the Whiteladies. "I bring the ability to crystallise energy into form. Because of this I bring worldly success."

"I am Danu," said the second. "I give the ability to change form in accordance with your own design."

"I am Boan," said the third. "I confer the joy of manifest works."

"I am Urda," intoned the fourth. "I am worldly power."

"I am Eartha," said the fifth. "I bring health, balance and physical perfection."

"I am Ursa," said the sixth. "I am bounty and charity and collaboration."

"I am Hel," said the seventh. "I bring physical breakthroughs."

"I am Moira," said the eighth. "I empower those who would change their fate."

"And I am Mab," said the ninth. "I bring the aid of the ancestors, riches, and accomplishment."

The gifts and abilities the Whiteladies proffered overwhelmed me, for they were all greatly to be desired. But I remembered that it was really to gain the boon of the ancestors that I had come, so I made my choice.

"I choose the gifts of Mab, that I may inherit the endowments of my lineage, and thus honour my ancestors," was my response.

"A sentiment in the best tradition," said Mab. "The endowments of your genesis and soul's lineage will be yours, as well as the accomplishments of all those who have gone before you on this path, for such things are cumulative. Receive your inheritance and the Blessings of the Old Ones."

The pentacle she held expanded as she said this, then became a cube which encompassed me. I felt protected by a pattern and a momentum I had not suspected was there. I felt that I came into my entitlement as a Bard, for I could feel all the ancestors of my body and my craft, my philosophy and art converge to form a foundation for my work. Their stability and wisdom, their accomplishments and matter supported me. Suddenly I knew all that they had known. I accessed the abilities they had developed in their own lives within myself. I became aware of the magic of how shape becomes form, how patterns accrue matter, designs manifest into realities and ideas become the physical world. I had inherited a virtuosity for magic, which made possible all the rest.

With this realisation, the Whiteladies began to transform. Rapidly, before my eyes, they shifted through myriad shapes and manifestations. In a brief moment, they had become all of the manifest forms of the created world. Indeed, I realised they were the world itself, continually changing, ever being born, ever dying, giving fleeting, concrete form to an ever changing dream. I realised that the world, by its very nature, is miraculous.

Soon the Whiteladies were just patterns, like snowflakes, in the air. One of these resolved into a small pentacle which flew into my hand. It was formed of bronze and studded with rubies. I placed it in my travelling bundle to keep with me always.

Then the Whiteladies were gone and in their place a silver staircase spiralled up into the red gloom of the ceiling. It rose right up into the taproot of the giant Tree, and disappeared from sight in the woody coils. I understood that this was the same stair as that I descended into Gorias, the Fire realm of Abred. And so I began to climb. I climbed and climbed, until I emerged into another realm, higher on the Tree of Life.

As the Bard comes once more to the crossroads, the sun has set and the night has come on. The moon is shining, full and bright, amid a scattering of brilliant stars. In approaching the northerly quadrant of the Otherworldly journey, one encounters the qualities of winter and darkness. While (in the magical landscape) South is associated with midday, summer and the element of fire — and West with evening, autumn and the element of water — North corresponds to night, winter and the element of earth.

The first creature to gain the Bard's attention in this new realm is an owl. We are ushered into the presence of the Owl Goddesses of winter. These powerful archetypes include Greek Athena, Mesopotamian Lilith, Libyan Anath, British Blue Annis, and Welsh Blodeuwedd. Their lineage can be traced to the "Eye Goddesses" of Old Europe.[73] They are associated with night vision, the power to see in the shadows or in the dark, the power to travel in Underworld regions — even into the realm of death. They are archetypes of the primordial feminine wisdom considered to be menstrual, nocturnal, fertile and lunar. "That Blodeuwedd's fingers are 'whiter than the ninth wave of the sea' proves her connection with the moon; nine is the prime Moon-number, the Moon draws the tides, and the ninth wave is traditionally the largest."[74]

In the Welsh myth, Blodeuwedd is wed to the light god, Llew Llaw Gyffes.

She falls in love with a mortal man, however, and contrives to do away with her divine husband. Her father-in-law, the godlike Hero/Bard, Gwydion, turns Blodeuwedd into an Owl because of her attempt to dispose of Llew, but this is a late adaptation of a far older tale. As Graves describes: "When Blodeuwedd has betrayed Llew, she is punished by Gwydion who transmogrifies her into an Owl. This is further patriarchal interference. She has been an Owl thousands of years before Gwydion was born — the same Owl that occurs on the coins of Athens as the symbol of Athena, the Goddess of Wisdom, the same owl that gave its name to Adam's first wife, Lilith, and as Annis the Blue Hag ..."[75] Barbara Walker adds: "Blodeuwedd's totemic form was an owl, the same bird of wisdom and lunar mysteries that accompanied or represented ancient Goddesses like Athena and Lilith. Owls were almost invariably associated with witches in medieval folklore. She was also the ninefold Goddess of the western isles of paradise, otherwise known as Morgan, the Virgin blending into the Crone of death."[76]

Blodeuwedd says, of herself, according to a Medieval tome attributed to the Bard, Taliesin:

> *Not of father nor of mother*
> *was my blood, was my body.*
> *I was spellbound by Gwydion,*
> *Prime enchanter of the Britons,*
> *When he formed me from nine blossoms,*
>   *Nine buds of various kind:*
> *From primrose of the mountain,*
> *Broom, meadow-sweet and cockle,*
>   *Together intertwined,*
> *From the bean in its shade bearing*
> *A white spectral army*
>   *Of earth, of earthly kind,*
> *From blossoms of the nettle,*
> *Oak, thorn and bashful chestnut —*
> *Nine powers of nine flowers,*
>   *Nine powers in me combined,*
>   *Nine buds of plant and tree.*
> *Long and white are my fingers*
>   *As the ninth wave of the sea.*[77]

The long association of the owl with Blodeuwedd has resulted in the folk name, "Flower Face," for owls in Britain. Blodeuwedd means "Flower Face," and refers to the petalled pattern of white on the owl's face. In Scottish Gaelic, the owl is called "calleach," for "old woman." Calleach is also a name of the Goddess, as Crone, from Gaelic tradition. The owl is Her bird, and under Her protection.[78]

The owl leads us into the realm of deepest wisdom — the wisdom of age and of the ancestors. She guides us "north," into wintry reflection, incubation, and introspection. When the owl appears, we are given a sign auguring an inward focus upon the deepest regions of the Self. We know, at that point, that we are contemplating a further "descent" into the inmost structures of "earth." In other words, we can anticipate a period of introversion. We are about to plumb the depths, delving into the very architecture of the beliefs which fabricate our reality.

What this means is that we are about to get a look at the programming which formats our subconscious assumptions. These are the levels of habit and tradition, family legacy and inherited predispositions which actually manifest as the circumstances of our everyday lives. Our subliminal, unquestioned convictions concerning the nature of reality, and of ourselves, are what create the terms of our existence. If these are to significantly change or improve, the transformation must occur at this deep level.

This is the real reason why those who aspire to be magically creative — artists, shamans, magicians or Bards — must make the descent to the tip of the root of the Tree of Life. The root is at the foundation of our existence. Whatever beliefs are held here as subconscious ideas, traumas or convictions are what will manifest in our lives, for here is the formational core of all matter. At the root of the most infinitesimally small, micro-particle there may be naught but a dynamic or momentum around which subatomic particles move, describing a form. At the substratum of all matter, there may merely be pure "shape."

This is as much as to say that the basis of the physical universe is nothing but an abstract construct in space, in other words, an "idea." The "created world" is just that, created from a notion, a collective dream — a thought. Our material existence is fabricated moment to moment — its component parts fitting together like some vast, consensual, three-dimensional jigsaw puzzle. The overall shape of this puzzle, and the picture that it paints, are determined by the balance of beliefs at any given time. These, naturally, have greater determinative effect in one's immediate neighbourhood. For instance, beliefs about oneself most directly effect the Self. They have only an indirect effect on others, and other's beliefs about you will have nowhere near the influence upon your reality as your own assumptions concerning yourself.

Beliefs held in common concerning the global reality will most directly influence the course upon which our world will proceed. Our own, collective beliefs about our planet will have more immediate effects on our combined destinies and that of the ecosphere than overwhelming, seemingly uncontrollable cosmic events. Apparently random occurrences like meteor strikes or solar flares cannot effect us with anything approaching the direct effects of our own ideas. Ultimately, it is our beliefs or expectations concerning such phenomena which draw so-called "random" events into our sphere.

As the legendary realm from which the magical pentacle was brought to Britain, Falias represents the element of earth, as well as the magical interaction of elements, or alchemy, described above. The physical realm issues, "in the round," or in three dimensions, from the fourth, which is shape — or thought. These four elemental dimensions dance within the choreography of the fifth elemental dimension which is a quality of movement, the fluctuations of attraction and repulsion. We could as well call this fifth influence "energy," "consciousness," "intent," the "Chi," "prana," "mana," "spirit," or "ether." They are all words, deriving from different cultures, disciplines or approaches, for the same thing.

We are here, in physical manifestation, on the material plane, within a life, upon the planet. And so we know that, on some level, we have willed it. The existential manifesto, "I think therefore I am," could as well be, "I believe therefore I am," "I intend therefore I am," or even the pronouncement of the Godhead in religious traditions around the globe, which is, simply, "I Am that I Am." Because we each know, with absolute certainty on some level, that we "are," we exist. It is the details — the Who, What, Where, When and How of the event that often require fine-tuning.

Most of us want positive change. Few of us are content with things as they are. This might be due, partly, to the idea that it is not the point, in the earth plane, to be content. It is the point to want to change things — to grow, evolve, tinker with, and improve — to shape, to mould, to expand, enlarge and rework. This, the deepest realm of our personal Underworld, is our opportunity to connect with our God/Goddess nature while in a mortal life. This is the realm where consciousness can be made manifest, the Word made flesh, in form. Physical manifestation (which is to say, incarnation) allows us the opportunity to realize, actualise and manifest transformative change, from consciousness to form, as is our divinely creative birthright.

Though uncomfortable, the opportunity presented by our worldly discontent is the reason we are here. It is the motivation, the impetus, the incentive and trigger of consciously wrought changes. Becoming an artist with the medium of one's own life is the point of having come into a life in the first place.

Creative, evolutionary change is the nature of the universe. It is its genius or muse. It is what the godhead (consciousness, Chi, Tao, energy, ether, all-that-is) does with itself. Creating (and destroying so as to create again) is the cosmic occupation. When we understand, accept and participate in this universal impulse (which is to become divinely, creatively conscious — a shaman or artist), while in a physical expression (incarnation, medium or "life") on earth (our studio, laboratory or theatre of choice), we come into our full inheritance as divine, magical and creative beings.

Life changes dramatically at this point. Though it is not fair to say that

problems disappear overnight, or that life suddenly becomes a state of unremit-
ting bliss, it is certainly fair to say that the joy factor increases in direct proportion to one's creative empowerment. More importantly, you begin to remember
who (and what) you actually are. You entered this journey from the air realm of
the heart, Gwynned. By an act of your will, or fire element, you've embarked
upon this journey. With the fluidity afforded you by an acknowledgement of your
emotive, fluxient, water element, you now know that everything can change, in
accordance with your will. And now, with the grounding and centring influence
of your earth element, you know where and at what level that transformation
must ensue. With the basic four personal elements present and accounted for,
the Self is ready to take on radical transformation or, to give it another name,
sheer magic.

Though it is difficult (for transformation entails the acknowledgement and
release of crystalised pain) it is by now apparent that the result is worth it. For
the result is possession of your Self — your actualised, articulated, realised and
re-membered Self — body and soul. So the Bard continues, in the face of cold,
darkness and sleet, deeper and deeper into the heart of winter in the North, the
ultimate stronghold of the powers of Earth. Birches and Rowans, winter trees,
stretch out their "leafless branches." They appear, to the Bard, as the arms of
the fay "Whiteladies," guardians of the Hollow Hills, abodes of the Fairies, the
long-dead Bean Sidhe and the ancestral Tuatha dé Danaan.

From the Upper Paleolithic cultures of Malta and Siberia to the Bronze Age
and Neolithic villages of Old Europe, a certain form of funerary statuary was
consistently made. Some of the earliest found date from 16,000 to 13,000 B.C.E.
More recent versions of this figurine are well-known to us as the most commonly-
excavated Cycladian artifact (figure 11). In many areas surrounding the Mediterranean and the Aegean (from approximately 6,000 to 1,300 B.C.E.), human
burials included the small, alabaster Goddess figurines known to archeologists
and historians as Stiff White Ladies. The figures are carved from white substances, such as marble, bone, ivory or alabaster. They assume a characteristic
repose, with arms folded tightly across the breast, and knees sometimes bent, as
if wrapped and prepared for burial. They bear a strong resemblance to the figures carved during preceding millennia, across Europe and Siberia, which have
a similar, stylised shape. Both types of figurines are characterised by violin
bodies and elongated heads or necks.[79]

These earlier figures are catalogued by Russian archeologists and art historians as "figures of birds." And this they certainly are. But they are also much
more, for they are inscribed with breasts and pubic triangle, and sometimes with
minimised facial features. They are Goddess figurines, incorporating the at-
tributes of the magical birds anciently thought to be their familiars and shape-
shifting forms. Swans, owls, herons, cranes, geese, ibis and other large, majestic
birds were symbolic of the Goddess as psychopomp, conveying souls to the
Otherworld at death. They were seen as actual souls in flight, winging their way

across the skies, a transmigration of spirits. The "Swan of Tuonela" is a late, Finnish version of this image.

The "Whiteladies" who found their way into Celtic culture have come down to us as the moaning "Banshee," or "Woman of the Mounds." They still haunt the "Hollow Hills" or artificial mounds and burial cairns of Ireland. They are still featured in stories of fairy abductions, usually at Samhain or Beltaine (or "Halloween" and "May Eve"), into beautiful but dangerous regions "inside the hill." Such journeys are deemed perilous because so few travellers return from such jaunts. Most remain in the twilit land of the Fairies forever.

From this complex of images around the death Goddesses, the image of Death as the Bride emerges. She is beautiful and seductive, but her embrace is eternal — unless, of course, one happens to be a Bard (artist, shaman, magician, etc.). In that case, one will make the journey into the Underworld and return, at least once if not many times, with the ultimate magical treasure of the realm, that being the ability to knowingly direct energy into form.

Gwenhwyfar (Guinevere) is one of the Whiteladies. Her name means White Phantom or Shining White. Gwenhwyfar is not only an avatar of Sovereignty. She is symbolic of the ultimate transformer, Death, as posed by the tomb which is also a womb, the land itself. It is She whom the Grail serves.

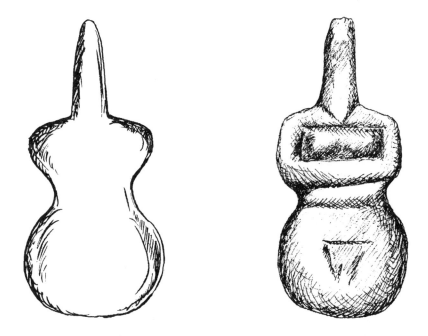

Figure 11: Marble figurines from Cycladic Islands, Greece, c. 2500 B.C.E.

She is the deepest, ultimately manifested sphere on the Kabbalistic Tree of Life, Malkuth: The Kingdom.

She is like Greek Persephone, Sumerian Ereshkigal and Egyptian Nephthys — a Goddess of the deepest realm of the Underworld, and the ultimate transformer of fates. In certain, mortal states of affliction, whether physical, emotional or spiritual pathologies, the soul is a captive of this region. This is the hostage-taking territory of old, no longer viable programs, calcified beliefs and crystalised pain. The shaman, hero, hera or Bard travels into this deepest sphere in order to retrieve the soul held hostage by its own, rigidified, subconscious patterns.

Demeter searched the world of winter for Persephone, Inanna descended into the seven levels of the Underworld to rescue Tammuz — shedding a veil at each threshold, and Isis journeyed in the Wasteland in search of the dismembered Osiris, finding him finally with the help of Nephthys, her dark sister. Also, with the help of Nephthys, Isis then re-membered Osiris, thus healing Him and restoring Him to life.

This is the primordial pattern for shamanic healing. Folk and fairytales perpetuate this theme, in tales of heroic journeys into treacherous otherworldly realms, in search of the lost treasure, realisation, anima, animus, or soul. It is this function that is referred to as the venerable practice of "soul-retrieval," and it is still undertaken by the more effective healers and teachers today, whether they practice as Jungian therapists, Witches, shamans, or artists of other transformative disciplines. The basic model for the heroic journey, or "healing crisis," is the same.

In the Hungarian folk story, "The Tale of a King, a Prince, and a Horse," the hero undertakes a quest to find the comrade of his father's youth.[80] His father is the king, and he had fallen out of contact with his oldest friend, the king of a neighbouring land. For want of a reunion with his comrade, the king has been laughing with one eye, and crying with the other, for years. The hero-Prince embarks on this quest with the help of a magic, talking, flying horse. The magical horse arrives at his splendid, Otherworldly potential after eating a bucket of embers, followed by a bucket of water. This unlikely procedure is repeated three times.

The two fly off with magical speed to cross the first of the three bridges that must be crossed on the journey. There is a crisis of faith between the hero and his magical/spiritual advisor and guide (the horse) immediately before crossing each bridge. In order to successfully cross the bridge, the Prince must decapitate the horse, then put him back together with the aid of healing substances to be found in the horse's ear. The horse comes back to life stronger and more powerful than before each time this is done. He then tells the Prince how the monster that dwells under each bridge must be dealt with.

The ultimate barrier to be traversed is a towering glass mountain, impossible for others to scale. The horse, however, has had the magical foresight to have himself shod in crystalline, diamond shoes which score the mountain to gain a foothold, enabling the passage. The horse carries the prince to the lost comrade, who is held captive in an incessant battle with legions of demons that occupy this enchanted landscape. The hero wages war against these demons who possess the territory and thus releases the comrade from bondage.

After settling the existentialities of the liberated land with the king of those parts, and ensuring his intention to return, the hero brings the old comrade home to the friend from whom he'd been severed so long ago. The king's comrade had also been crying with one eye and laughing with the other simultaneously since the separation. They are both cured of this affliction and rejuvenated upon being reunited by the Prince.

In the skeleton of this tale are innumerable shamanic themes. The quest the Prince undertakes is for the king's soul, the part of the Self he has been severed from. It is the equivalent of the shaman's search for a sick person's lost or captive spirit. The shaman/Prince travels to an afflicted region of the king's spirit to release the soul/Self from the possession of "demons," or pathological patterns of belief, which are in temporary custody of it. The king, or patient, being spiritually disunited or disintegrated, is suffering in confusion and seeming schizophrenic madness. When the shaman/Prince retrieves the lost soul from the demon-infested wasteland, or spiritual ailment, that possesses it, the patient is unified and made whole. His behaviour becomes integrated; he cries and laughs alternately instead of simultaneously. He is rejuvenated and becomes young at heart.

> As soon as they arrived, the prince presented his companion to his father. There was such a great to-do that even the birds in the trees began to weep and laugh for joy. And the two kings felt as young again as in the best days of their youth and were weeping now with both eyes and then laughing merrily so that their eyes too became as clear and young as in the days of their youth.[81]

When the horse ingests the bushels of hot coals, he is obtaining "mystical heat," and also demonstrating his magical/shamanic mastery over the element of fire.[82] In other words, he is stoking his will, his creative initiative, just as the Bard did in the realm of Gorias, at the Castle of the Muses. Then the horse, the magical ally, stand-in and alter ego of the shaman/prince, must undergo dismemberment in the form of decapitation at each threshold.

In shamanic imagery, as mentioned before, dismemberment denotes the disintegration which precedes reintegration in the new, vital or "perfect" body. An emphasis on the head is significant; symbolic decapitation always refers to a renewal of attitudes. A new or different "head" simply means a transformed attitude set. This is necessary to successfully tackle thresholds, challenges, initiatory ordeals or "tests" — both in sacred and mundane undertakings. Beheadings always, in shamanic lore, denote an expansion of potential.

We are empowered to do precisely what we believe to be possible — no more and no less. Seemingly impossible tasks require a redefinition of the word "possible" in relation to the Self. In other words, one must reconfigure one's beliefs concerning one's ability and natural birthright. This is a version of the dismemberment and re-memberment the Bard underwent at the hands of Morgan la Fay in the Cauldron of Rebirth in Murias. The necessary flux of the Water element has been supplied, lending the fluidity and mutability required to change, or to restore, one's concept of Self.

The Prince's horse is a *taltos* horse, which (in the Hungarian Magyar folkloric tradition) means that it is a magical beast, the hero's ally, empowered alter-ego, and guide. When the Prince and his *taltos* horse arrive at the Glass Mountain, we are shown in no uncertain (imagistic) terms that this story is really all about the Self. The mountain, in shamanic imagery, signifies the centred and grounded architecture and integrity of Selfdom. As such, it is the *axis mundi*, the cosmic centre or world hub. It is Mt. Meru of the Himalayas, Mt. Sinai of the Sinai Peninsula, Mt. Ararat of the Anatolian plateau or the perfectly conical mountain in northern Nevada which is the power spot of Navaho shaman Rolling Thunder. It is wherever the Self is, in focus and power, symbolised by countless sacred mountains the world over, and in many cultures.

The World Mountain is an image for the structure of the Self-concept. It is the formation or architecture of one's beliefs about one's Self. As such it is similar to, but just slightly different from, the manner in which the World Tree symbolises the Self. The Tree evokes a sense of an organic, evolving, living structure — while the Mountain evokes the calcified, crystalised foundation of Self.

The mountain signifies the power of the world to give "magical" expression to consciousness. Hardened structures of thought and conditioned beliefs become manifest as matter and reality, one's body and one's lifestyle, self-image and circumstances. There are aspects of the World Mountain which are similar to The Tower trump of the Tarot. Due to the rigidity of formalised beliefs, it is sometimes necessary for the Mountain to move in order to permit creative growth and a change in circumstance. The foundations of reality, which are constructs of belief, must shift. The Mountain of our Self-definition must be renewed and reconstituted, right down to the molecular level. This, by any culture's definition, is an heroic feat.

> Ascending a mountain always signifies a journey to the centre of the world . . . it is only the shamans and heroes who actually scale the Cosmic Mountain, just as it is primarily the shaman who, climbing the ritual tree, is actually climbing the World Tree and thus reaches the summit of the universe, in the highest sky. For the symbolism of the World Tree is complementary to that of the Central Mountain. Sometimes the two symbols coincide; usually they complete each other.[83]

As in "The Tale of a King, a Prince, and a Horse," traversing the mountain is to breach the final barrier to transformation:

> Off went the horse, galloping at a terrible speed. They had left behind them a long stretch when the boy noticed that the horse's hooves cut hard against the road. "Bend your head, dear master, and lean over me." When the boy did so, the horse, continued, "What do you see?"
> "I see immense brightness. But tell me, what sort of road is that under your hooves?"
> "We are passing through the glittering Glass Mountain of Fairyland. You see, those who want to carry off a fairy girl for a wife must cut their way through the Glass Mountain. But there is no other horse except me who could do it. You know now why I have asked you for the diamond shoes. Without them we would not be able to cross the Glass Mountain. But I dare say, by tomorrow morning all fairyland will rise against me. Just take a look back and see what havoc my diamond shoes have wrought on their beautiful mountain. But better not worry now . . . let us go ahead."[84]

In our story, the Bard travels in the inmost realm of the Underworld, Falias, and ultimately comes to the Castle of the Whiteladies, a towering stronghold carved from a single, perfect mountain. This mountain is the largest of the giants that form the range, a natural barrier of formidable proportions. Though reaching the last reserves of strength, the Bard realises the necessity of climbing the mountain. Moreover, the desire to climb the mountain is great — greater even than the dread surrounding the prospect.

The Bard dreads the final barrier in the Underworld because of the shamanic lore concerning the ultimate threshold. North, Earth, Winter, Old Age and Night are all metaphors for mortality. "'At the back of the North Wind' — a phrase used by Pindar to locate the land of the Hyperboreans — is still a popular Gaelic synonym for the Land of Death."[85]

Death is the final face the Goddess presents us. It is this aspect which is "shining white," like Guinevere. She is cool as marble and utterly inescapable. The many homilies and similes applied to Her include this reference by Robert Graves:

> Spenser's White Goddess is the Arthurian "Lady of the Lake," also called "the White Serpent," "Nimue," and "Vivien," whom Professor Rhys in his *Arthurian Legend* identifies with Rhiannon. She is mistress of Merlin (Merddin) and treacherously entombs him in his magic cave when, as Llew Llaw Gyffes to Blodeuwedd, or Samson to Delilah, or Curoi to Blathnat, he has revealed some of his secrets to her. However, in the earliest Welsh account, the *Dialogue of Gweddydd and Merddin*, she tells him to arise from his prison and "open the Books of Inspiration without fear." In this dialogue she calls him "twin brother," which reveals her as Olwen, and she is also styled *Gwenddydd wen adlam Cerdeu* — "White Lady of the Day, refuge of poems," which proves her to be

the Muse, Cardea-Cerridwen, who inspires *cerddeu*, "poems," in Greek, *cerdeia*.[86]

Knowing this, being a keeper of sacred knowledge and lore, a "repository of songs," the Bard accepts the challenge of the final barrier to the core of Self, and crosses the abyss beyond which lies entry to the World Mountain. Inside the castle, the Bard finds wealth and luxury. This is the realm of those deities who rule over the riches of the Earth. Hephaistos, the miner, smelter, and crafter of precious metals and husband to Aphrodite, is one such. Pluto, Lord of Riches, voluptuous Cerridwen, the elegant and luxurious Faery Sidhe, the magical Blacksmith of folklore, and the gem-laden Seven Dwarfs are all versions of this basic archetype. They are the keepers of the keys to the only thing of real value, from whence follows all the rest, that being the possession of one's essential, core Self.

Cerridwen's most ancient progenitors were akin to the "Stiff White Ladies," protectors of the soul in the Underworld, as well as guides to, and actual incubators of, rebirth. Cerridwen devoured Gwydion after he accidentally stole the year and a day's worth of wisdom She had been brewing in Her cauldron for Her son's enlightenment. After nine months, She gave birth to Gwydion, who was reborn as Taliesin of the Radiant Brow.

The White Sow Goddess is common to countless ancient cultures. She is the model for the "Whore of Babylon" who rides a pig into the Apocalypse in the pages of the Revelations of John in the *New Testament*. She is the Alabaster Goddess, Ishtar/Ashtoreth/Astarte, once called Lillitu or Lilith, adjured as the "Abomination" throughout the books of the *Old Testament*. She is the sow who devoured the rotting flesh of Llew Llaw Gyffes as he languished in a treetop in the form of an eagle, awaiting transformation into human form by his father, Gwydion. Her influence was once primary throughout the ancient world. Her myth has come down to us in a form distorted by patriarchy's prohibitions against self-knowledge, but still potent and evocative. Jean Houston tells a story from Cerridwen's lore: "Cerridwen is a flying pig, and as she flies, she gives birth to piglets. A Mystery School springs up wherever one of Cerridwen's piglets lands."

Pigs, like many creatures sacred to esoteric schools, were carrion eaters. Like the owl, dog, jackal, wolf, lion, and vulture, a pig is seen to transform death and decay into nourishment. These particular totemic animals compost waste into valuable nutrients. This is something like the way an oyster turns an irritant into a pearl, or how an artist turns suffering and pain into creative material or inspiration, or how a magician, shaman, seer, Witch or Bard turns experience into wisdom. It is because of these correspondences that the White Sow Goddess is associated with the idea of value, wealth and gain. "The root (word) 'alph' expresses both whiteness and produce: . . . alphe is 'gain' and alphiton is pearl barley and Alphito is the White Grain-Goddess of Pig-Demeter, alias Cerdo (which also means 'gain') . . . (Who has a) connexion with Cerridwen the Welsh Pig-Demeter, alias the Old White One . . ."[87]

Tibetan Buddhism sees the pig deity, or "Diamond Sow," as a guardian and bestower of discrimination. "The pig is, in its mystic aspect, the symbol of the Dakini Vajravarahi, the 'Diamond Sow' of Discrimination Wisdom, who in fact rules over all pearls of wisdom."[88] The Eleusinian Mysteries centred around the functions of germination and incubation, with Demeter's priestesses mixing the remains of sacrificed pigs into the seed grain, to be fertilised and enriched for the following planting season. These mysteries had their correspondences in Celtic myth. The hero, Llew, is resurrected "in the dead of Winter, in the season of the Old Sow, the time of the annual Athenian pig-sacrifice to the Barley-Goddess."[89]

Pigs were seen as signifying enormous wealth in Celtic lands. In the British Isles, countless old stories centre around pigs. It was in pursuit of pigs, symbolic of treasure, that many heroes harried the Underworld, including Arthur. "Phorcus, or Orcus, became a synonym for the Underworld; it is the same word as *porcus*, a pig, the beast sacred to the Death-Goddess, and perhaps as *Parcae* [or *Porchides*], a title of the Three Fates, usually called the Moirae, 'the distributors.' *Orc* is 'pig' in Irish, hence the *Orcades*, or *Orkneys*, abodes of the Death-Goddess."[90]

> Running through the Mabinogion, famed for its ferocity, greed and cunning (translate, "survival acumen"), is the boar or pig. Although pork was the staple diet of the Celts, this did not make the totem boar any less mysterious. It came from the Underworld, the gift of Arawn himself. A Twrch Trwyth, it ravaged countrysides, swept its devastating path across Wales, Ireland and Cornwall, before vanishing into the sea. It was also a chthonic beast and, when it appeared in the shape of a sow, was a messenger of the Dark Earth Mother herself, the feeder-on-carrion: Llew suffered her attention until released from his totemic shape by Gwydion.[91]

Graves sees the name of Cerridwen, the "Dark Earth Mother," to be derived from *cerdd* and *wen* — *wen* meaning "white," and *cerdd* in Irish and Welsh meaning "gain," and also "the inspired arts, especially poetry . . . Cerridwen is clearly the White Sow, the Barley Goddess, the White Lady of Death and Inspiration; is in fact Albina, or Alphito, the Barley Goddess who gave her name to Britain . . ."[92]

Pigs are also associated with many Celtic heroes. Magical swine are in the possession of the Underworld guardians, kings, queens, and divine powers. They are the objects of the hero's, hera's, or Bard's quest for ultimate regeneration. The Underworld lord, Manannan mac Lir, nourished the gods "from his pigs, which, like the boar Saehrimnir, in the Norse Valhalla, renewed themselves as soon as they had been eaten. Of these, no doubt, he made his "Feast of Age," the banquet at which those who ate never grew old.

Thus the people of the goddess Danu preserved their immortal youth . . ."[93]

Like the great Goddesses Cerridwen, Danu, Anna, Demeter and others, heroes and Bards sometimes shape-shift into pig form in the course of their magical feats. The solar hero, Cian, transformed himself into a pig (he struck himself with a Druidical wand) and wandered among the herd of a tribe of the Tuatha dé Danaan in order to hide himself from his enemies in the Bardic tale, "The Fate of the Children of Tuirenn." When these enemies, the sons of another tribe, found him out by turning themselves into hounds and driving him out of the herd, they killed him. His own divine son, Lugh, then demanded a blood-fine from Cian's killers, which involved an heroic quest to procure magical objects from distant and exotic lands.

These included the magical pig's skin of Tuis, King of Greece, which, "has two virtues: its touch perfectly cures all wounded or sick persons if only there is any life still left in them; and every stream of water through which it passes is turned into wine for nine days . . . And the seven pigs of Easal, King of the Golden Pillars; though they may be killed every night, they are found alive again the next day, and every person that eats part of them can never be afflicted with any disease."[94]

Pigs were the primary treasure of the Celtic paradise, which was located in the Underworld, within the hollow hills, or sidhe. "These sidhe were barrows, or hillocks, each being the door to an underground realm of inexhaustible splendour and delights . . . There were apple trees there always in fruit, and one pig alive and another already roasted, and the supply of ale never failed."[95]

The solar hero, Gwydion, guessed the name of the Underworld lord, Bran the Blessed, and thereby won entry to his realm, the Elysium of the gods.

> The last and greatest of Gwydion's raids upon Hades was undertaken to procure — pork! Gwydion had heard that there had come to Dyfed (in Wales) some strange beasts, such as had never been seen before. They were called "pigs" or "swine" and Arawn (another name for Bran), King of Annwn (The Underworld), had sent them as a gift to Pryderi son of Pwyll. They were small animals, and their flesh was said to be better than the flesh of oxen.
> . . . Gwydion set off, with eleven others, to Pryderi's palace. They disguised themselves as Bards, so as to be received by Pryderi, and Gwydion, who was "the best teller of tales in the world," entertained the Prince of Dyfed and his court more than they had ever been entertained by any storyteller before. Then he asked Pryderi to grant him a boon — the animals which had come from Annwn.[96]

Pryderi refused, for he had promised the Underworld king not to part easily with the magical pigs. Eventually, by battle and guile, Gwydion won the pigs from Pryderi. Pryderi is said to have pursued Gwydion and battled for possession of the pigs. There are five towns, throughout the several counties of Wales where this legendary struggle took place, named to commemo-rate it: *Castell y Moch* ("Swine's Castle"), *Mochnant* ("Swine's Brook"), and three named *Mochdrev* ("Swine's Towns"). A later version of this story casts Arthur in the role of the solar hero and semi-divine warrior who attempts to capture the swine of a similar Underworld prince, called March son of Meirchion. Arthur's foray into the Underworld is depicted in the epic Welsh poem, attributed to Taliesin, called "The Spoiling of Annwn," in which Arthur seeks the magical Hallows, or sacred objects of the Underworld.

Even Merlin, The Enchanter, is said to have taken final refuge in the Underworld paradise within the Hollow Hills. His "Crystal Cave" is located everywhere and nowhere, in "a place that is not a place, a time that is not a time," but which magically underscores all places and all time. One mythical location of Merlin's paradisiacal cave is Bardsey Island, off the western tip of Caernarvonshire, in Wales. "Into it he went with nine attendant Bards, tak-ing with him the 'Thirteen Treasures of Britain' (The Hallows), thenceforth lost to men."[97]

These sacred Hallows, the pigs, and all other Underworld treasures sym-bolise not only the vital aspects of the personal Self, but of the collective soul. The hera, hero, Bard, artist or shaman not only redeems and regenerates her or his own creative integrity, but that of their community and the world. Caitlin Matthews explains this age-old spiritual tradition beautifully in *Mabon and the Mysteries of Britain*:

> . . . a young and vital saviour is, of her or his own free will, made prisoner of an older cycle of spiritual bondage; by breaking the pattern — usually by means of a simple affirmation or belief or by a redemptive offering — she or he estab-lishes a new pattern of responsibility . . . This process of redemption is unfor-tunately often misunderstood by those who have only experienced its applica-tion in a narrow religious context. To revalue the process of redemption — which only means to "buy back" or ransom from (a kind of) prison that which has been improperly aligned or diverted from its prime purpose — we need to observe the recurrent patterns of cyclic renewal in many traditions. The re-deemer or ransomer, who can be male or female, stands in the place of Mabon, whose task is to share the common lot of the prisoner, the unredeemed, for the sole purpose of ending all imprisonment; in order to realign creation and its creatures with their primal directive.[98]

The truth is that, magically and spiritually, artists heal not only them-selves, but culture — and, through it, society and the souls of others. The Path of the Bard is a shamanic service role, and anyone who penetrates to the deep-est realms of Self, the Underworld of the creative forces (or gods) knows this with certainty. It demands, and is in fact the transformative threshold of, absolute integrity. It is life-giving and life-renewing. Quite simply, the world needs the magical arts. Creativity is a path of responsibility. The treasures of personal and collective soul-nature, symbolised by the Hallows, are redeemed by great effort and dedication on the part of the seeker.

Within our native British tradition, the model of service is the Pendragon ("Head of the Dragon") and his court (who) must guard the treasures and traditions of the land — often represented by the Hallows, which are the regalia bestowing Innerworld power. These are not freely given nor thoughtlessly bestowed. Since these Hallows reside in the possession of the ancestral guardians, the Pendragon must venture into the Underworld in order to fetch them. And here, the Pendragon makes a commitment to the Otherworld also: for whoever ventures there to fetch the Hallows, becomes the candidate for Innerworld Guardianship.[99]

Speaking of the initiatory roles of two major, Underworld archetypes, in the tale of "The Two Magicians," (Cerridwen and the Blacksmith figure) Matthews says, "Both have climbed down the Tree of Tradition, pursuing the totems ever deeper until they find their true selves and oneness with the Ancestors. The totems are symbolic of the initiatory changes which are wrought within the subject."[100]

The totems of Falias include the owl and the pig. In the magical, transformative symbology of the Celtic Otherworld, pigs are also Dragons. Sometimes pigs turn into Dragons. In other stories, pigs and Dragons alternate as symbols for the same kinds of consciousness, and of the land itself. In one Welsh myth, a terrible unrest (in the form of a "scream") unsettles Britain every May Eve (Beltaine), causing madness, miscarriages and impotence. The princely brothers, "Llud and Llefelys," conspire to end this "plague," one of three which are harrying the land.

They found that the scream was the result of a mighty, airborne battle between two Dragons, one white and one red. They dug a pit at the exact centre of the Island of Britain (said to be Oxford) and placed a vat of mead within it. After the Dragons had fought, they sank down into the vat of mead "in the form of piglets," drank it all up, and fell asleep. The brothers locked them in a stone chest, then buried them "in the most secure part of the kingdom," that being Mount Snowdon in Wales.

The fact that the dragons become pigs may seem curious at first, but, as we noted in "Mabon," they are chthonic creatures, that is, associated with the Underworld whence they are supposed to derive. . . . During his madness Merlin (who was, himself, said to have been fathered by a Dragon) addresses his remarks to a pig in the forest of Celyddon . . . In this obscure poem, "Yr Oianau" ("The Greetings"), the pig seems to represent the dormant spirit of Britain. It would seem that there is a distinct sequence in which the beasts that are emblematic of Britain become dragons when the land is active and pigs when the land is passive.[101]

When the Bard follows the Ermine, it is similar to Alice in Wonderland following the White Rabbit. Alice, too, encounters a deep, dark tunnel to "fall" into. This image signifies the final surrender of the Self to its deepest, most ancient nature. The truly magical, immense potential of the Self can be seen in the creature which breaks the Bard's fall: the snake. The snake, like the pig and the Dragon, is a chthonic figure. It symbolises the wisdom of the Earth, and of the body. "This is the symbol of the awakened Kundalini, the serpent energy latent within each psyche, centred in the base region of the subtle body . . . and its tendency to move upward, breaking through all barriers."[102]

In many eastern European folk tales, the "Garaboncias" (shaman or magician), is portrayed "riding" a dragon or snake, just as the "Taltos daughter" (female shaman or Witch) is depicted riding a flying pig or broom. In stories like "The Dragon Rider," and "The Man Who Lodged With Serpents," the magician is seen to ride the snakes or dragons through the air. "The Man Who Lodged With Serpents" falls into a deep pit, where a garaboncias is keeping his serpents. He raises the two huge serpents in the pit for seven years, after which time they are "strong" enough to be bridled and ridden through the air by the magician. During this time, they are fed on water and salt crystals only.[103]

"The Dragon Rider" is himself a boy when he starts raising his dragons from hatchlings. After seven years, he comes back to the mountain where the dragons have been maturing on the forested slopes. The young man catches the dragons and mounts them, "and then both animals took a leap into the air and like a shot they were off."[104] In both stories, the ride of the hero/magician engenders a mighty storm. "Never had there been such a storm in Bakonybel as on the day the garaboncias was carried off by the two dragons," and when, "off went the garaboncias and his two snakes . . . all along their way they were followed by a terrific storm with hail . . ."

Achieving orgasm in Tantric sexual practice, or attaining ecstatic, heightened awareness during trance in Hindu and Buddhist spiritual disciplines, is referred to as "raising the wind and the rain." The storm is a metaphor for the ecstatic (spiritual or erotic) release which accompanies the "raising of the Kundalini." Kundalini is the ancient Vedic term given to the conscious energy which spirals up and down the spine. The serpentine motion of this dynamic of the nervous system is the reason for its metaphoric snake image, and also its undeniable conscious nature. Its imaging as two snakes evoke the twin serpents on the caduceus or Staff of Hermes, symbol for the spinal column, the axis mundi and also for the Tree of Life.

The Kundalini is a quality of continual motion, on the one hand, but it is also the process responsible for the functions we identify as consciousness. In other words, the Serpent is the combined activities of the brain and neural system, as formatted along the spine, with its seven major plexi of nervous system, which feed every structure, function, organ, tissue, cell and sensory activity of the body, the result being that complex awareness we call intelligence, or consciousness. Consciousness does not merely occur in the brain, but all over the body, through the astonishing network of the nervous system and its bio-electrical activity, which, when seen as arrayed upon the axis of the spine, looks like a tree.

When perceived in terms of the weight or density of these stratified layers of consciousness, this activity might also look like a rainbow-hued ziggurat (similar to those constructed by priestly orders in ancient Babylon), a seven level-pagoda (the stylised "soul-tree" from Asian shamanism), a conical structure, or mountain (symbol of the godhead, or place of power, in many cultures around the world). The heavier-hued regions are those arrayed lower on the spinal axis, the reds and oranges, golds and emerald greens are more readily perceived within the prismatic array than the more delicate and diffuse aquamarine, or violet.

Colours are frequencies, vibratory rates, or "cadences" of light. So it is with the chakras. They resonate to a graduated scale of vibratory rates, or frequencies. If perceived as colours, they would range from deep red to violet, as in the seven-tone refraction of light (through a prism) and if heard as sound, they would range from the note C to B, as in a seven-note scale.

The Feathered Rainbow Serpent of Mayan myth is an image of this dynamic of magical, creative consciousness. A stepped pyramid at Chichen-itza ("The Mouth of the River of the Itza People") in Mexico has the outline of the Feathered Serpent, Kukulcan, carved upon one of its sides. Every year, on the Spring Equinox, the pyramid's stratified edge casts its shadow onto this outline, filling it out and creating the image of the snake. The Feathered Serpent is seen to fly down to earth, carrying its fertilising waters and regenerating crops and livestock. The Dragon fulfils the same beneficent role of rainmaker in Chinese mythology, where its flight is seen to bring the seasonal monsoons, so necessary for the fertility of the parched earth.

The base of this perceived structure of the World or Self Mountain (which is actually a formalised self-concept or magical, idealised construct) houses the serpent energy. It is depicted by Asian Tantric (magical and healing) disciplines in its passive aspect as being coiled at the base of the spine, waiting to be awakened. In its active aspect, it is depicted as being "arisen," or "raised." The ascended Kundalini serpent is crowned and feathered, or winged, symbolising the capacity of the active, "risen" human consciousness to travel in astral, abstract realms of awareness, aware of its own true nature and "royal" divinity.

When a fetus is forming in the womb, the first bone to form is the one at the base of the spine, the coccyx. Within it is the "serpent brain," the neural hub or primal nervous system of the forming zygote. As the fetus rapidly grows, it builds the structure of the spine, and the nervous activity within it. From this source, the entire human system grows, but the first "brain" is the primitive system of neural matter aligned along the spine and terminating at the base of the skull. This is the conscious apparatus we inherited from our earliest ancestors on this planet. It has features in common with Earth's primal life-forms, the reptiles and amphibians, the dinosaurs and primitive winged creatures, the "dragons" and "serpents" of old. As humans, we still "think" with our "serpent brain" during most processes. It is the foundation for autonomic functions of the body, and the repository of millennia of stored survival instinct, our genetic legacy from ancestral species, and aeons of learned, encoded, instinctual behaviour we could as well call special (or "species") wisdom.

Households in the ancient world, around the Mediterranean and elsewhere, maintained the custom of keeping a live snake as a sort of family mascot, in the foundations of the house. This snake was fed and cared for, and was actually revered as an ancestor. Its health, age and size was an indicator of the wellbeing of the family or clan, and the family domicile. Whole lineages of snakes were maintained for years, their survival linked to the survival of the clan, family or tribe in a mystical bond. This was a formalisation of the early awareness of our ancestral and mythical associations with the serpent totem, both as a symbol for our earliest manifestations as a species and as individual fetuses. Well into this century, charcoal-burners in Britain kept a snake in a box in their hut when working in the woods at their trade.

The serpent also serves as a glyph for the quality of motion which is the nature of our primal consciousness, the spiralling dynamic in the spine. This mystical association has been made since the earliest times; prehistoric rock paintings and pictographs show this mythical association between the serpent and the tree (or spine), with the Woman or Goddess in the Paradisiacal Garden, and its link with consciousness as the agent of wisdom, or knowledge.

In contemporary folk and fairy tales, the "little snake" is still affectionately portrayed as being the agent of awareness which perceives, ferrets out, or discovers the truth, aiding the hero or hera in the eternal quest for knowledge. One such fairy tale, "The Nine Ravens," perfectly sets the snake as "the faithful servant" of the king, who, on loan to the hero, enables the transformation of a darkened realm, a "wilderness of mountains," back into its native, healthy, "rich" and gentle beauty.

The hero, Dick, enters a door in an oak tree, and finds within a passageway. This he follows until he reaches another, golden door. This swings open, and he enters a golden room where an old man sits on a golden stool, feeding a little snake. This, of course, is the former king of the land, but now he and his lands are under an enchantment which has imprisoned his nine children in the forms of ravens, and made of his kingdom a wild, hostile and impenetrable place. The king gives Dick the little snake as a guide into this wilderness of the spirit, to gain redemption of the king's land and children, and restore them to their proper forms.

The snake shows Dick how to fly through the enchanted territory, over a river of flames, to the endarkened citadel where the nine ravens are held hostage. Dick does this by waving a raven feather over his head three times. "At the first wave his feet left the ground, at the second wave he was lifted high into the air, at the third wave he was flying fast, faster, away over the valleys, plains and mountains with the little snake coiled around his neck."[105]

In a fairy tale from the Grimm Brother's collection, called "The White Snake," there "lived a king who was famous throughout the entire country for his wisdom. Nothing remained hidden from him, and it seemed as if he could obtain news of the most secret things through the air. However, he had one strange custom. Every day at noon, after the table was cleared of food and nobody else was present, a trusted servant had to bring him one more dish. This dish was always covered, and the servant himself did not know what was in it, nor did anyone else, for the king did not take the cover from the dish and eat until he was all alone."[106]

One day the servant was overcome by curiosity. "He lifted the cover and found a white snake lying inside. Once he laid eyes on it, he had an irresistible desire to taste it. So he cut off a little piece and put it in his mouth. No sooner did his tongue touch it than he heard a strange whispering of exquisite voices outside his window. He went over to it to listen and noticed some sparrows talking to one another, telling what they had seen in the fields and forest. Tasting the snake had given him the power to understand the language of animals."

This new-found, magical ability saves the servant's hide more than once, and ultimately leads him on a quest for travel and knowledge. He ends up competing for the hand of a beautiful princess. If he wins her hand in marriage by completing three magical tasks, he will (of course) gain the kingdom and crown of that land. He is aided in completing the nearly impossible tasks, or shamanic ordeals, by the animals he has helped on his travels, and whose speech he can now understand.

The final task given him by the princess requires the greatest of magical powers, for it is the most difficult test ever posed the heroic seeker in the worldly garden. Jason, Gilgamesh, Merlin, Herakles (Hercules), Adam, Paris, and countless other figures from story and myth have faced this ultimate threshold to wholeness, creative, magical power and integration. "Even if he has accomplished the first two tasks," said the princess, "he shall not become my husband until he has brought me an apple from the Tree of Life."

The hero feels defeated in the face of this final task, but sets out "with the intention of going as far as his legs would carry him, even though he had no hope of finding it." After he has travelled through three kingdoms, he reaches a forest and, like Newton, sits down under a tree to rest and think, whereupon a golden apple falls into his hand. At once, "three ravens flew down to him, landed on his knees, and said, 'We're the three young ravens whom you saved from starvation. When we grew up, we heard you were looking for the golden apple. So we flew across the sea to the end of the world, where the Tree of Life is standing, and we've fetched the apple'."

The young hero brings the apple to the princess, who finally yields to his suit, and marries him. "They divided the apple of life and ate it together, and her heart filled with love for him. In time they reached a ripe old age in peace and happiness." Integration and harmony is achieved by means of the secret magical knowledge (the shamanic ability to understand the speech of animals), brought about by eating of the white snake in the king's chamber.

When the Bard in our story perceives the true identity of the Serpent (the conscious, foundational wisdom of the world), the chamber reveals itself to be wrought of the lowest frequency, the base note or home key of the conscious colour scale. It is red, the deep red of garnets. The subterranean chamber itself is seen to be wrought of a "single, massive ruby."

The Serpent becomes three, then nine shining white women, which is to say, nine "Gwynhevars," or sovereigns — the council of queens which rules the land, its traditions and forms. Reform may only happen by their special wisdoms, which have to do with such matters. Each of the Whiteladies proffers the pentacle of her unique angle on the theme of manifestation. The pentacle is the symbol of the element of Earth, for it perfectly expresses the Earthrealm's ability to manifest elemental energy (air, fire, water and earth) into form. The pentacle represents the four directions plus the centre: "ether," or spirit. From the alchemy of thought, will, desire, form and spirit are all things wrought — the "Endless Knot" of cause and effect in motion.

The pentacle has long been the symbol of human perfection. The five fingers, five senses, the four elements plus spirit, and many other images of wholeness or completeness are entailed within the glyph of the pentacle. It is one of the oldest symbols ever scratched into a rock or cave wall.[107] Gawain wore a pentacle as his device, on shield and armour, because he was the perfect knight.

> *First he was found faultless in his five wits,*
> *Then the fellow failed not in his five fingers,*
> *All his faith on earth was in the five wounds,*
> *Of Christ on the cross, as the creed doth tell,*
> *Where 'er this Man in melee was placed*
> *His thoughts were upon them above other things;*
> *So that all his force he found in the five joys*
> *That the Fair Queen of Heaven had felt in her child.*
> *For this cause had the Knight in comely fashion*
> *On the inside of his shield her image depicted,*
> *That when he viewed it his valour never failed.*

On his shining shield shaped was that knot,
All with red gold upon red gules
Called the pure pentangle among the people of lore.

The pentacle presented to the Bard turns into an encompassing cube. The cube is the foundational shape from which all other shapes are hewn. The molecular geometry of the five perfect solids are whittled from a basic cube. Spheres, octagons, and polyhedrons of all subsequent complexity are extracted from a primary cube by lapidarists, who first cut their mineral into a cube, then remove material along given angles. Blocks of clay for sculpting come from the art supply in cubes. This shape contains all others. The cube is the starting point and matrix for form in many media.

Shape, and the perception of shape, is the magical, heightened sense of the realm of Falias. The root chakra rules the primal sense of smell, which is the first sense to develop, and which is accomplished by the detection of molecular shapes by their impression upon olfactory nerves.

A cube provides the floor, four walls, and ceiling of possibility. This is the shape of one's limitations, which are concretised, habitual ideas about oneself. Within these limitations, one can create great works. One can contract or expand the parameters of personal limitations and those imposed upon us by the world by the secret and powerful wisdom of self-knowledge. One can carve, sculpt, mould and stretch them, to accommodate growth and evolution. The cube is the rough matrix which houses all the varied ideas you may have about yourself. It is a construct, and it can be built, demolished, renovated, or rebuilt. But, first, you have to know it is there, at the very foundation (and *as* the very foundation) of your being.

As soon as the Bard realizes this, the Whiteladies begin to rapidly transform and change, becoming a kaleidoscope of possibilities. The World card of the Tarot conveys this understanding. Anything is possible, within the limitations of one's ideas concerning possibility, for everything is, at base, an idea — or shape of thought. But these shapes are very real, and accrue reality and (ultimately) matter, around themselves. They must be respected as consummately real, as well as their ensuing realities. Then, when they are accepted and honored, they can be danced with, painted with, expressed, articulated, choreographed, orchestrated and conducted in new ways and evolving patterns. The snowflakes dancing upon the air, which are the final forms of the nine Whiteladies, evoke the infinite range of possibilities for these crystalised forms.

Chapter VI

The Realm
of
Finias

A small cup
filled to the edge
Edging its way to
my shadowed heart
A heart forged
with armour to hide in
Hiding the songs
of my own true bard
Bard songs travelling
light as wings
Winged daughters
of the truthful blade
Blades of wild grass
piercing the wood
Wood protecting stone
and challenging waves
Waves of tears
sheltering the small
A small cup
filled to the edge

THE CASTLE OF THE NINE SYLPHS

As soon as I had begun to climb the silver stair I felt the atmosphere begin to change. With every step the air became distinctly different. I began to notice a relief of the weight of gravity upon my body. The lethargy and contracting cold that had settled upon me as soon as I entered Falias, the Earth realm, was lifting. The higher up in the Tree I climbed the more I felt a sensation like a softening, shifting, melting. The air itself seemed to become more fluid. My movement flowed more easily and I began to have the sensation of swimming in a medium finer than that of Earth and more like that of Water.

After a long climb in the thick, red atmosphere, winding up and around, around and up, I emerged into the next realm of the Tree. It was the grotto of the Castle Murias in Avalon. There was the clear lake, its surface glassy and calm, fed by the underground spring. I knew that the same spring flowed down into the earth to feed the garnet pool, which in turn fed the taproot of the Tree of Life. The relationship of the Tree and the realms of Abred was becoming clear to me.

The Nine Nereids were there waiting. Morgan Le Fay stepped forward and presented me with a small but perfect vessel. The stem was wrought of silver and the bowl carved from a single carnelian. The rim was also of silver and studded with pearls. I gazed at it in wonder for I knew it was my own cup.

"It is yours by right," said The Fay. "You have gone to the deepest realm of the Underworld and returned. Now all of the treasures of the Tree can be yours if you want them, even those of Ceugant, the Celestial Sphere. But first you must journey to the Castle of the Sylphs in Gorias, higher in the Tree. Follow the silver stair."

With that she was gone, and her sisters with her. They turned into a moist mist which spread itself upon the water like a veil. But I felt their touch like a soft caress as I began, once again, to climb the stair.

Up and up, around and around, I climbed through the gentle glow of the carnelian hall. The atmosphere of Murias was moist and soothing and felt distinctly different from the hard, cold air of Falias. For what seemed like ages I climbed in circles in the swirling orange mist of the Nereids' chamber. Then the atmosphere began to change, and I emerged into the next realm of the Tree.

I knew I had ascended through the ceiling of Murias into Gorias because the light changed and became a fiery gold. I recognised the Hall of the Creatures of the Flame, with its golden emblems, winged disk, breastplates and helmets high upon the walls. Here was the singing manticore, and the Griffin. Here too was the Eternal Flame in its golden dish and the Nine Muses beside it.

Melpomene stepped forth and gave me a golden wand. A brilliant topaz glowed at its tip. "This is yours," she said. "You inherited it when you delved to the root of the Tree. It is yours to use as you will."

She started to glow herself, and soon she and her sisters had returned to their true nature, that of flame, flowing back into the Eternal Flame of Memory. I turned again to the silver stair. Around and around, up and up I climbed. On and on in the blazing fiery light. Flames danced in the air around me as I ascended. Then the atmosphere subtly changed, becoming lighter - finer. I realised I had reached the element of air, the realm of Finias. The light was shifting from gold to greenish gold, and I felt the sensations of a subtle alchemy occurring in my body. Before long the light had shifted along the spectrum to clearest, Emerald green. I knew I had entered Gorias, the heart of the tree.

Though I had not recognised it as such, I had been here in the realm of air before. This realm coincided with the Glass Castle in the Garden of Gwynedd. It was the place from which I had begun my journey of the Tree. This was the Emerald Hall from which I had entered the first of the four realms of Abred, the Underworld. I realised that Gwynedd, the Shining Realm, was the way to all other realms of the three worlds of the Tree.

I stepped from the stair onto the Emerald floor of the hall and looked up at the columns of pink-veined marble and vaults of alabaster. The seven Ambassadors stood in their alcoves, each holding the emblem of her realm, as before. But there was one thing quite different about the hall, something that had not been here upon the first occasion of my presence in the Glass Castle. For there in the centre of the Emerald floor was a great stone and in it was thrust a shining sword. And round about the stone and sword was a circle of winged women.

I gaped at them, thinking they must be angels. But they laughed and the nature of their laughter convinced me they were not. They laughed in high, chirping, fluting sounds, and chattered in a strange language, like birds. When they quieted down, one of them stepped forward. She said:

"We are the Nine Sylphs of Gorias. I am Allalu, and these are my sisters, the Winged Ones. We are entities of Air and of the heart. Welcome to our realm in the heart of the Tree. The Glass Castle in the Garden of Gwynedd is a place you have been before, many times, but not realised it. The sword in the stone is yours but you must feel entitled to draw it out."

As I looked at the stone, with the sword thrust in it like a nail, all the hardship and suffering of the journey rose before me. All the struggle and effort of my entire life thus far welled inside me like a flood, and the sadness of it made me weep. All the tears I had never shed, and renewals of the ones I had, poured from my eyes. It felt as if a lump that had lain in my heart rose to my throat, then poured from me in the form of teardrops. I was sobbing so hard I gulped for breath and the air hurt me as I gasped it in. All the while this was going on the Nine Sylphs did nothing. They just waited, quietly and respectfully, as if it was ordained that I should weep uncontrollably, like a child.

When the storm of grief finally abated, Allalu gave me a handkerchief and said, "How do you feel?"

I noticed that I felt a sense of lightness shining through my tears, like the sun after a downpour on a spring day and said as much. At this she smiled and it was as if the sun had come out.

"Then you may remove the sword from the stone that was your heart," she said. To my delighted surprise, I found I was able to do so. The sword slid from the rock as from butter and came into my hand as if made for it. It was forged of a fine metal alloy and the hilt held a perfect, faceted emerald.

"The sword belongs to you, and is for you to wield. It confers the gifts of clarity and reason, focus and equanimity, balance, justice and fair words. It brings you resourcefulness, swiftness and mercy, as do we. These are our gifts to you, and your entitlement by right, from Finias, the last of the realms of Abred."

Then, with a flutter of wings and chirping laughter, Allalu and her sisters were gone. This was the strangest of my passages yet, for all I had done was cry to win my prize. I placed the sword within the scabbard that now magically lay by the stone, and belted it about my waist. I was armed with the knowledge of my own grief. My mind had never before possessed such clarity and resonance. My thoughts had never been so unclouded. I knew my own heart.

The stone was dissolving, becoming naught but a scent, like roses. As it faded and disappeared from view completely the aroma increased, becoming the most delectable sensation. I could almost taste the refreshing perfume — like that of a rose garden in summer. My heart opened to it. Then it, too, began to fade and in its place I saw a small, exquisite, golden harp — lying on the floor where the stone had been. It was humming softly, singing and thrumming with a gentle rhythm and quiet, piercingly sweet tones. I picked it up, filled with wonder, for it looked like an angel's wing strung with golden wires.

As I held it, it began to sing the louder. It started to vibrate in tune with my beating heart, then turned into a singing shape, made of pure, greenish-golden light. It flowed into my hands and arms, filling my chest with its warm vibration, and flowing into all the bones and muscles, tissues, organs, and systems of my body. I could feel the vibration extend even to my toes and fingertips — my scalp and hair. It filled and encased me, as if I was formed of and surrounded by my own, ever-changing song. The harp had become me — my bones: its frame, my senses and responses: its strings — and I had become the harp.

I turned and saw an Emissary, the one who held the sphere of Light and Sound, come forth from her alcove. "Come with me," she said in a voice of surpassing loveliness. "It is time for your ascent to the stars."

As the Bard climbs the silver stair, the atmosphere changes, becoming finer and lighter than that in the Serpent's chamber in the Castle of the Whiteladies. Gravity is claiming less of an influence upon the Bard's body. It is becoming lighter and the sensations of movement more fluid. Falias, the Earth realm at the root of the Tree of Life, is the realm of densest energy. Here, the vibration is the most compressed, contracted and involved, manifesting as palpable forms. The silver stair is a conduit to the other three realms of Abred and, as with all evolutionary journeys, is a spiral.

> The spiral tendency within each one of us is the longing for and growth towards wholeness. Every whole is cyclic, and has a beginning, a middle, and an end. It starts from a point, expands and differentiates, contracts and disappears into the point once more. Such a pattern is that of our lifetime, and may well be that of our universe. Only the time-scale has changed.[108]

The spiral is the way in which we are conscious of ourselves. The dichotomies of Self and Other, or of subject and object (up and down, inside and outside, Yin and Yang), are approached through spiral awareness. Reasoning in the dialectical mode produces a spiral movement where *thesis* and *antithesis* function as the two poles, between which results *synthesis*, a resolution which begins the process again by becoming the thesis of the next logical equation. The spiral describes our consciousness itself, its function and form. The ancient Egyptian hieroglyph for "Self" portrayed this spiral, like a repeating figure eight or lemniscate, eternally describing seven circles.

The cycles of becoming, the rounds of existence, spiral on and reveal their source by the creation of a vantage point; from its own opposite pole the source may view and hence become conscious of itself. The separation of heaven and earth gave the light of consciousness by which all is seen and known . . . This cyclic becoming appears in mythology as the protecting serpent or dragon which coils around the World Tree or Mountain — the central axis, the Axis Mundi . . . The theme recurs in a more or less explicit form in most traditions; the world materializes and man [sic] spiritualizes along the same spiral. It is the breathing of the cosmos. With the exhalation the spirit contracts, creates, and involves or winds into matter . . . With the inhalation, matter evolves or unwinds into spirit. Man is the heart and microcosmic controller of this pulse . . .[109]

All life processes are cyclical. When this dynamic shape is added to the notion of evolution, or progression, the cycle becomes a spiralling motion. Movement through the fourth dimension of Time means that our experience of life, though cyclical, is also linear, producing an evolutionary, spiralling passage through space/time. All vital and organic functions echo this pattern.

If life is a path "through" time, and therefore a continuum, we may also imagine it as a line; and further, since it returns and yet flows on, it is a spiral. Only if it were possible to come back to the same point in time could it be a circle. Any circular movement carried into the fourth dimension (of space-time) becomes a spiral; which is why apparently cyclic processes in time never repeat themselves. Even the earth's orbit round the sun is a spiral in time, and every year is different from the last.[110]

On this part of the journey, the ascent through the elemental regions of the Tree of Life, the Bard now knows the way. This is a return trip, taking the Bard through territories now familiar. The journey in the Underworld is now a conscious process of remembering and reclaiming aspects of Self and specific powers previously unguessed at.

Looked at on a single spiral, the path to consciousness has to be seen as a return along the same path; on the spherical vortex, the return is a continuation. At the point of maximum contraction, the expansion begins . . . As each individual spirals down the Tree of Life, he [sic] involves into matter . . . he thus brings heaven down to earth at the moment of birth, at which point the process is reversed, and through life he spirals back up the Tree, evolving or aspiring into spirit. He takes earth back to heaven, remembering in consciousness his original path. Indeed, all recognition, all knowledge of life, is a conscious remembering of the pre-conscious knowledge of the involving path.[111]

Because of this process of remembering, the treasures and powers of Abred's conscious realms are delivered up as the Hallows. These symbolise the knowledge and powers of the four elemental realms. The Hallows actually were in the possession of the Bard all along, as the essential nature of being in the Earth plane. The wisdom signified by the Hallows is encoded within the spiralling path of the Serpent, or conscious energy, through the four realms of Abred (the Underworld, Inworld, or physical experience of life in the body) upon the axis of the Tree of Life (the spine). "The course of the Kundalini's path, which may be straight up the central axis or spiralling, according to Gopi Krishna, 'zigzags through the spinal cord, exactly like the sinuous movement of a white serpent in rapid flight,' her rising energy awakens each of the seven chakras."[112]

As Thomas the Bard, the protagonist in Jodie Forrest's novel *The Rhymer and the Ravens*, perceives as he gazes upon Yggdrasill, the Tree of Life: "Something he could only describe as *movement* was occurring there, movement that he did not see but sensed. Layers of motility all around and above the tree and deep in the earth beneath it. Vast ponderous spiralling motions, complex and intertwined, revolved around more than one center. And the centers themselves were in motion . . ."[113]

When these centres (or realms) of consciousness of the body are intimately known, recognised, or remembered, their specific natures can be identified. They can be selected out, and experienced as vibrational qualities. This articulated perception of energetic signatures, and a familiarity with their corresponding realms of power and influence, is the treasure-trove of esoteric wisdom sought by Bards in the Underworld. It is this magic knowledge which is referenced by the Witch's collection of the four elemental talismans of the four directions, and their corresponding areas of wisdom, within the magic circle of the Self. The pentacle, cup, wand, and blade are the four magical "tools" depicted on the altars of traditional Tarot "Magician" cards. They represent specific, finely-tuned, articulated types of Gnosis, re-membering, integration, or experiential wisdom.

> These lotuses, centres of energy at the root of the spine, the generative centre, the solar plexus, the heart, throat, third eye and crown of the head, roughly correspond in their positions with the various glands and plexuses controlling the different systems within the physical body. As kundalini rises and pierces the successive chakras — each of which is itself a mandala spiralling around the central axis — the chakras unfold and transmute her energy into progressively finer vibrations. This is the reverse of the original process, whereby the vibration and sound of the oscillating three principles, or gunas, brought these levels into being as the gross elements.[114]

As we realised in the realm of Falias, in the deep, underground grotto of the Whiteladies, undergoing this conscious, spiral journey doesn't just benefit and empower the personal Self. This is an heroic journey, a shamanic feat, which restores the wasteland outside as well as within. "The hero who descends to the Underworld becomes the guardian of the Otherworldly Hallows."[115] The Self, the family or clan, the community, one's society or culture, and the world at large stand to benefit. The planetary soul is reclaimed by increments.

Journey of the Bard

We are the incremental saviours and we accomplish our heroic feat by becoming our true selves as much as possible, and by expressing that truth. This process can be called fidelity, authenticity, or art. It doesn't much matter what it is called. The point is that this is what will save the world, restore the wasteland, and enable us to act with integrity on behalf of the planet, each other and ourselves.

Caitlin Matthews recounts the story of the solar hero, Arthur, who "goes in his ship, Prydwen, to reive the inner empowering symbols known as the Hallows. We see him in his mythical guise, fulfilling an ancient, redemptive action which will rebalance the land of Britain."[116] Early communities understood that mythic, magical feats of this sort were not only personal, but collective soul rescue. "He journeys to Annwn in order to win the Hallows, which will heal the land and empower him."[117]

The redemptive role of the hero or hera who ventures in quest of the inner world treasures is a royal sense of purpose. It is a sense of responsibility, to the Self, so as to be a fit vehicle for the energies activated within the psyche, the body and the outer world, to the community, and to the land — to the earth itself. "Sovereignty" here means a state of self-rule, acting by one's sovereign will in harmony with the greater good. The "good of all" is understood to also represent the best interests of the Self. For the Self and the other, the individual and the collective, the inner and the outer, the body and the land are understood, in Finias, to be but multiple expressions of the one unity.

> Invariably, Sovereignty gives to drink of her cup to the rightful kingly candidate or champion. In this, as we will later see, she is the prototype of the Grail Maiden. More importantly she is the guardian of the Hallows, the Otherworldly empowering elements that underlie the kingly regalia of the king-making ceremony. The Hallows — often formalized into the spear, the sword, the cup and the cauldron, though appearing in many variations — may not be handled by any save the rightful king or most worthy champion.[118]

The Bard's spiralling ascent leads back to the beginning, the point of entry into this journey into Abred. The Bard began the descent into the Underworld realms from the very hall the spiral stair ultimately leads to. This same realm of Finias, corresponding to the element of air, juxtaposes the next sphere of the Tree of Life, the Overworld, or garden of Gwynned. Finias and Gwynned share the same space/time, though they inhabit just slightly different dimensions. Gwynned is the experience of Self in the present moment, from which all other realms and states of being are entered. And Finias, coinciding with the heart centre of the physical body, is the urge to connect, to become unified with that experience.

Finias is where we experience our unity and connection with others and with our environment. It is the impulse to reach out, to merge and flow with our world. The heart centre rules the sense of touch. The skin is the physical organ by which we experience tactile feeling. It is also the largest, most extended, flexible and expanded organ of the body. The skin provides many life functions for the body, nourishing cells and systems and transforming toxins. The skin breathes; it is a respiratory organ, responsive to air, which covers the entire body. It is the surface upon which we feel both our separation from and our connection to our environment. Our skin is how we feel the air which surrounds us. It is the sheath which contains us. It is the border and the bridge, between what is "me" and what is not "me." Through the sense of touch, we connect with others, establishing a link, communicating and receiving volumes of subliminal, sensory information. While the physical sense governed by this realm is that of touch, the heightened or extra-sensory perceptions are those of empathy and compassion.

The same organ by which we experience our separation, our "otherness," is the one by which we feel our unity most strongly, when we touch. Intimacy is established by touching. The ultimate joining of sexual conjugation involves the bonds formed by giving and receiving tactile pleasure. The realm of the heart is the place in consciousness where the sacred marriage, the Conjunctio, or Hieros Gamos, is realised. It is ruled by that element we all share. Air is the medium, surrounding the planet, by which we are all joined, skin to skin. We all breathe the same air.

Alchemy is the transformative magic of the heart centre. The joining of separate beings, and separate natures, is the perfect essence of alchemy. Alchemy achieves synthesis or metamorphosis by combining two dynamic elements. They then act as catalysts for each other, galvanising the creation of a new, third element, the "Divine Child" of the original two, "parent" elements. This is the mystery mythologised as the "Virgin Birth," and it occurs even at the most basic, material level. As Deepak Chopra states, in *The Way of the Wizard*:

> In the lore of alchemy, the four elements — earth, air, water, and fire — mysteriously combined to arrive at a magical end product called life. It is undeniable that you are made of earth, air, and water that have been reshuffled from some earlier form, such as food. The fire that sparks these lifeless materials into life can't be distilled, however, because it isn't a visible fire, or even metabolic heat. It is the fire of transformation, pure and simple. Therefore, you are the transformation, the transformer, and the transformed. You are your own alchemist, constantly transmuting dull, lifeless molecules into the living embodiment of yourself. This is the most creative and most magical act you will ever undertake.[119]

The Merlin character in *The Way of the Wizard* tells us: "Alchemy is transformation; Through alchemy you begin the quest for perfection; You are the world; When you transform yourself, the world you live in will also be transformed; The goals of the quest — heroism, hope, grace, and love — are the inheritance of the timeless."

The child of the Virgin Birth is a renewed, resurrected Self. It is this renewed consciousness which is referred to in terms such as the "Divine Child," the "Magickal Childe," or "Child of the New Aeon" of ceremonial magical lore. This is the aspect of Self who acts from the heart, with empathy and compassion, attained through the impulse to merge with another and to understand their reality, their sufferings and their joy. Joseph Campbell discussed this phenomenon with Bill Moyers in *The Power of Myth*:

> You know the idea of the ascent of the spirit through the different centres of archetypal stages of experience. One begins with the elementary animal experiences of hunger and greed, and then of sexual zeal, and on to physical mastery of one kind or another. These are all empowering stages of experience. But then, when the centre of the heart is touched, and a sense of compassion awakened with another person or creature, and you realize that you and the other are in some sense creatures of the one life in being, a whole new stage of life in the spirit opens out. This opening of the heart to the world is what is symbolized mythologically as the virgin birth. It signifies the birth of a spiritual life in what was formerly an elementary human animal living for the merely physical aims of health, progeny, power, and a little fun.[120]

Many a hero-Bard, champion or messianic figure is born of mysterious origins. The paternity of these shamanic characters is left in doubt, suggesting that their mothers may have conceived them by a spirit or daemon, or by some angelic suggestion, like Hebrew Mary, Miriam or Elizabeth. Merlin, Moses, Christ, Lohengrin, Lancelot, Galahad and countless other divine, shamanic heroes are born as the results of magic intervention, or as "Virgin Births."

> That's what the virgin birth represents. Heroes and demigods are born that way as beings motivated by compassion and not mastery, sexuality, or self-preservation. This is the sense of the second birth, when you begin to live out of the heart centre. The lower three centres are not to be refuted but transcended, when they become subject to and servant to the heart.[121]

Arthur was a hero and a demigod, whose birth was mysterious, and who was whisked away into magical fosterage by Merlin. His harrowing of the Underworld was gruelling, an ordeal which brought him understanding of suffering, or compassion. There is also a sense of his sacrifice, the winnowing which accompanies any decisive transformation. The old Self is left behind. Part of oneself dies. All that is not authentic and essential falls by the wayside, defences and illusions are shattered and composted. Only the integral core remains, the truth as it is experienced in the seven conscious centres. There is often a feeling of loss attending this kind of growth. "According to ancient tradition . . . Arthur sailed to gain the empowering Hallows of Sovereignty, reiving them from the Underworld of Annwn: a feat which, says the poet Taliesin, caused him to wear a 'mournful mein,' since out of three shipfuls of men only seven returned from that place."[122]

The lure into the beautiful Otherworld, the Hollow Hills, abodes of illustrious, magical ancestors, the fairy hills of dream and fantasy, is seductive. Legend has always endowed the lure of the spiritualising journey into the Underworld with an inviting glamour. The journey into the magical world "below" was undertaken with excitement and only a little trepidation by the Bard in our story. But the climax of the quest, and the exact nature of the ultimate treasure retrieved from the harrowing of the Underworld, was a painful reckoning, a confrontation of all the pain which has scarred and hardened the Bard's heart throughout life.

> Later Celtic and early medieval tradition invested the Otherworld with castles or caers from which the Otherworldy archetypes operated. Even earthly castles take on supernatural roles in Branwen, Daughter of Llyr, and The Dream of Macsen Wledig, where real places come under Otherworldy rules. Even Glouster, Caer loyw, has its place in legend as the site of Mabon's imprisonment, and a similar shining fortress appears in Owein, where, in place of Peredur's nine witch tutors, an array of beautiful maidens and youths wait on the hero. These Otherworldly castles are treasure houses also, like the Fort of the Golden Bowl, whose powerful magic lures Rhiannon and Pryderi into enchanted servitude, or like the Castle of Wonders, where Peredur sees the undying splendours of the Hallows exhibited. But the treasures are often housed within the dark caers of Annwn, to which both Pwyll and Arthur descend. Pwyll's experience of Annwn is of a magnificent palace of entertainment and joy, while Arthur's face is said to be scarred with anxiety after the experience of the raid upon Annwn for the cauldron and other empowering Hallows.[123]

To fully metamorphose into one's own pure potential, it is necessary to let go of all that is not a part of one's authentic Self. Any projections which one wears like ill-fitting, uncomfortable clothing, any self-perceptions which are actually distortions, will undergo a natural death at this point, necessitating a mourning process. One must release anger, sadness, and grief. One must feel them all over again. The cathartic release which permits this looks like acute sadness or rage, but is in fact cleansing. In order to release such feelings, one must know them, name and identify them. This is the magical, intellectual function symbolised by the sword in shamanic lore.

> The work of the Blade is varied. One of the functions of the Blade is to cut obsolete or regressive tendencies from the Self, and to pare and trim outdated circumstances from one's life. The Blade works with the medium of Time in interesting ways, due to its quality of opening portals and inaugurating new possibilities and realities . . .

The activity of the Blade . . . is that of pin-point accuracy and an exact identification of meaning. It is also significant of efficient, direct action with no wasted motion. The Blade . . . would represent a part of the mind, in tune with the senses . . . that would hone in on an accurate "naming" of the thing or dynamic under scrutiny. As such, it would represent the power to have control or mastery in a situation by bringing the ability to analyse and define the locus, or hub, or its dynamic.[124]

This naming, identifying and paring away of regressive "baggage" is the shrivening, or "harrowing," described in Taliesin's tragic epic, *Preiddeu Annwn* ("The Spoiling of Annwn"): "Three shipburdens of Prydwen entered the Spiral City. Except seven, none returned from Caer Sidi." A host of illusory projections, "three shipburdens" of them, may have entered the spiral process of self-confrontation in Annwn, the Underworld. But only the actual Self, the seven centres of consciousness which are the self's true, core nature, returned from the process, which is to say, emerged as the survivor of the "harrowing" in the Underworld. This essentialising process, though painful, represents a spiritual victory. It marks the attainment of an entirely new, divine condition — that of personal sovereignty.

As the Merlin voice says, in *The Way of The Wizard*: "Wizards do not grieve over loss, because the only thing that can be lost is the unreal; Lose everything, and the real will still remain; In the rubble of devastation and disaster are buried hidden treasures; When you look in the ashes, look well."[125]

This new condition, rising from the ashes of loss or sacrifice like a Phoenix bird, is the result of the successful completion of one return-trip within one of the three worlds of the Tree of Life. The Bard has descended into Abred, the Underworld, and returned — bearing the royal treasure which represents the state of sovereignty, or "regalia." Having spiralled down, "involving" into matter and understanding matter at the cellular level, the Self has been awarded the insignias of victory by the Self. The Bard then "evolves" to the conscious, intellectual air realm, which endows the ability to articulate and name the qualities of experience entailed within the journey.

The final insignia, awarded by the process, in the hall of the heart, is the blade — symbolising this ability. It is a function of analytical intelligence commemorated by the regalia of this realm, and the objectivity which comes as a result of self-knowledge in each of the four dimensions of earthly existence — physically, emotionally, spiritually and mentally. As I have written elsewhere:

The "Hallows" are the magical tools of the Craft of the Wise, or sacred Power Objects of Celtic Lore. . . . The Thirteen Hallows [of Britain] reduce to four, primary sacred motifs: the Cup (or vessel); the Stave (or wand); the Sword (or blade); and the Disc (or pentacle). These, in turn, signify the four earthly elements of alchemical transformation: earth, air, fire and water. Witches turn to the four directions to invoke their characteristic, elemental energies, then to the centre to address the archetypal, androgynous Self. . . . These five points of focus are symbolised within the pentacle, the points being the four directions/elements, plus spirit, within the circumference of the World/Self.

East is the direction of air, eliciting the qualities of mentality, analysis, definition, and clarity or exactitude. . . . The magical working tools that Witches use to engage these elemental energies are: the Athame (or Witch's dagger or blade) in the East to evoke the element of air and the qualities of Thought, mental definition and prowess . . .[126]

In the Tarot, the King of Swords court card indicates the ability to be emotionally clear. This, in turn, bestows good judgement and practical discernment, otherwise known as "business sense." The reasons for these attributions of the King of Swords are clear. When you know your own heart, you are less likely to be fooled on emotional grounds. You are less likely to be coerced or manipulated because you can track your own reactions, desires and vulnerabilities. A major part of self-knowledge is the ability to name your demons, as well as to identify and articulate your truths.

This is how the intellectual, defining quality of the sword serves our emotional wellbeing. The sword both pierces and protects the heart, by bestowing compassion. The self-penetration which occurs when one has knowledge of one's heart is like that consummation depicted in Bernini's sculpture, "The Ecstasy of St. Theresa." The "Sorrowing Mother" archetype is an icon for this bridge to the compassionate state.

She represents the great figure of an ancient mythology and religion who had human qualities as well as divine, the goddess Isis, Ourania, Queen of Heaven, crowned in the highest and enthroned in the hearts of men [sic]. She who was also known as the Lady of Wild Things, Our Lady of Nature, the Lady of the Moon and Night Sky. She who sorrowed and searched for dismembered Osiris, who knew bitter grief and searing disappointments.

We can see in her the same figure that has been built up for us in Mary the Mother of Jesus. Both of them have been known as the Mother of God, the Star of the Sea, the Gate of Heaven. And as Isis had the grief of searching for the body of her consort Osiris, the Divine King, who had been betrayed and killed and mutilated, so is Mary the Mater Dolorosa, the Sorrowful Mother, whose heart was pierced with the Swords of Anguish, who stood at the foot of the cross and received into her arms the dead and mutilated body of her son.[127]

There is cathartic pain, but the release which ensues is an ecstatic state of liberation. It ushers in a state of grace — of harmonious, personal balance. The marriage of heart and mind, thought to feeling, right lobe to left, inner male with inner female, right hand to left — the poles of being, in other words — produces the completion which is, itself, an awakening. The quest for unity experienced at the heart initiates the inner marriage, the highly cognitive,

Journey of the Bard

lucid, expanded state of awareness which occurs when all is acknowledged, owned, accommodated and accounted for. Or, as Jill Purce puts it in *The Mystic Spiral*:

> Lama Govinda shows the development of consciousness as a double spiral. Moving outwards from the centre, from an original unconscious unity like that of the child, its development gets progressively differentiated towards the periphery, which represents the usual surface-consciousness and maximum of differentiation. This is the turning point and the start of the inward spiral towards the centre, towards the conscious unity of the enlightened.
>
> The vajra, or "diamond sceptre," in the Buddhist tradition, is the symbol of the highest spiritual power. It shows the original point, Bindu, containing its potential spiral unfolding. Although never moving from its central position, the point unfolds and becomes the central axis — the polarity and union of opposites — surrounded by the lotus petals of the four directions. The spiral at the centre is both the original subjective knowledge and that gained by the balancing of opposites (of subject and object). The diamond sceptre thus shows the primordial unity of consciousness, its outward path to the periphery and its return to the centre.[128]

The Bard sees a large stone in the centre of the rose and alabaster hall (a symbol of the chamber of the heart). This "stone of sovereignty" is a Celtic version of a motif which signifies the centre in countless, world mythologies; "it is the Rock of Living Waters, the Ka'aba of the Heart, the Philosopher's Stone, the Stone of Sure Foundation, the pearl or jewel"[129] at the heart of the lotus. In our image, it is surrounded by nine Sylphs, or supernatural winged women. According to Barbara Walker, "Sylph" is "a female spirit of the element of air: an invisible angel, whose voice might be heard in the breeze. In medieval times, 'sylph' became a synonym for 'witch'."[130]

The earliest concepts of angels were far closer to this image of sylphs than the current, aesthetic, Judeo-Christian concepts allow. "The earliest angels were heavenly nymphs, like Hindu asparas, who dispensed sensual bliss to the blessed ones. Vikings called them Valkyries. Greeks called them Horae. Persians called them Houris, or Peris (fairies). A guardian angel was a personal Shakti who watched over a man and took him into her ecstatic embrace at the moment of death. . . . Like the queen of the Holy Grail palace in bardic romance, the angel was a 'Dispenser of Joy'."[131]

Our current ideas around angels are conflated with images from the earliest civilisations. "Angels were often confused with seraphs and cherubs. The former were six-winged fiery flying serpents, the lightning-spirits of Chaldean myth. The latter were Semitic kerubh, from Sheban mu-karib, 'priests of the moon;' sometimes they could take the form of birds. Angels accompanying the Hindu Great Goddess were able to fly on the wings of garuda birds."[132]

It is significant that ideas around angelic beings, the descendants of ancient, pagan elementals, or "Sylphs," have changed greatly from their original, magical/spiritual sources. It is important to reclaim a kind of amorality for the guardians of the heart. They must not be invested with notions of "good" or "bad." Their true value is as emissaries of truth — that is to say, personal, subjective truth. No judgement can be brought to bear on feelings. They have their own context and logic — or illogic. They exist in their own right and on their own terms. They are "wild," and untamed — in other words, primary, elemental energies — and are simply to be owned and acknowledged.

Only by such measures are feelings, or emotional truths, to be transformed and released, not by any attempt to "tame," judge, or control them. This is why, originally, Sylphs, or "angels," served no particular ideology or code. "There were no really well-defined distinctions between angels, demons, familiars, fairies, elves, saints, genii, ancestral ghosts, or pagan gods. Among supernatural beings one might always find many hazy areas of overlapping identities, even 'good' or 'evil' qualities being blurred."[133] Their loyalty was to the truth of the heart; they served only the healing, harmonising or alchemising of the Self.

"Alchemy" is a word derived from an Arabic term, *Al Khameia*, meaning "the matter of Egypt." *Khemenu*, "Land of the Moon," is an ancient, Middle Eastern name for Egypt. Arabs attributed the development of the mystical philosophy and practices of alchemy to Egyptians. Alchemy was really just another approach to magical synthesis, a sort of substantive Tantra. In European medieval alchemy, energies and substances were construed as catalysts for each other, producing third substances or energies as the results of their combining. These quasi-miraculous secondary creations were given allegorical names referring to personal alchemy, such as "the Divine Child," the "Virgin Birth," the "Divine Androgyne," the "Crowned Hermaphrodite," or the "Glorious Child."[134]

> As a system of mysticism, alchemy was permeated by sexual symbols. So-called "copulations" and "marriages" figured in alchemical procedures. Sexual drawings enlivened the texts. The Alchemical Rebus was the usual bisexual image of male and female powers in union, "a Hermaphrodite, born of two mountains, Mercury and Venus." [i.e. Hermes and Aphrodite] Sun and moon were shown as naked male and female figures . . .[135]

These sexual metaphors addressed the healing and creative unification of opposites or polarities in the *conjunctio*, or "Sacred Marriage." Its issue was the *filium philosophorum*, or "Glorious Child," the magical offspring of the original substances, or *prima materia*. The new, transformed and resurrected consciousness born of the unification, or "wedding," of heart to mind (intellect to feelings, articulation to emotions, or right brain cognition to left) is, likewise, the Glorious Child — the renewed Self who rises, Phoenix-like, from the ashes of self-confrontation.

"Mary the Jewess" was said to be the first great alchemist. She discovered distillation of alcohol in the time of the Caliphate, and invented the double boiler, still called bain-Marie, (Mary's bath) in France. During the Renaissance some female alchemists were burned as witches. Julius, Duke of Brunswick, roasted one of them alive in an iron chair in 1575, because she could not tell him how to make gold out of base metal.[136]

The assaults of early Church fathers upon alchemists, and their arts construed as heretical, were doubly misguided as alchemy actually centred around the very core of Christian mysticism — the Virgin Birth. Fundamentalist teachings within the Church, and the insistence upon making these allegories into literal truths, were (and are) in contravention of thousands of years of established, sophisticated mystical beliefs and practices surrounding the "matter of Egypt." (The word "sophisticated" itself is from the Greek *Sophia*, meaning "Wisdom," the patron Goddess of Gnosticism and its art/science, alchemy.)

The "Philosopher's Stone" was another name for the *prima materia* of mystical transformation and rebirth. It was sometimes called the "Sophistical Stone." The crucible within which change took place — the chamber of the heart — was often symbolised as a heart-shaped vessel, following a pattern established millennia ago in Egypt. This vessel, or "vase," signified the womb of Isis in the pictographs (or hieroglyphics) of the ancient kingdoms, but medieval alchemists sought the same principle in the *vas hermeticum*, or "Womb of Hermes." This equated to the *vas spirituale*, or Virgin Mary of Christian Mysticism. Another term for this crucible, as well as those metaphors for the spiritual vessel or the chamber of the heart, is the "Mystical Rose."

The Mystical Rose is at the heart of the Rosicrucian mysteries, blossoming at the intersection, or heart, of the axes of the mystical Cross — really just another image for the Tree of Life as a path of sacrifice. The Rose is the experience of the miracle of life, the "Virgin Birth," occurring at the level of the heart within the body consciousness. It is the experience of the Sacred Garden, "Gwynnedd," within the secret enclosure of the heart, or "Finias." This is the *cunjunctio* — where the spiritual axis (or "spine of consciousness") intersects and merges with the material plane (or total, physical experience of the world experienced at the level of the heart and outstretched, embracing arms). The spiral approach to this consciousness is symbolised by the seven perambulations around "the centre, the square stone of the Ka'aba ... the 'Temple of the Heart' and the world axis ... Since the pilgrim spirals around the Ka'aba as the heart of the Universe, it is also his own heart; and so the vortex being created is his own receptivity ..."[137] Or, as Ibn 'Arabi describes in his *Meccan Revelations*, "I am the seventh degree in my capacity to embrace the mysteries of becoming ..."[138]

The heart chakra, or Finias, is the last of the four earth realms of Abred, the "inworld" or Underworld. These realms are also the "four directions," which in combination with the spiritual centre becomes the pentagram of self-orientation. "The centre is equally the centre of any place, or the centre of any person or being. In Greek philosophy, in the *Upanishads*, in the Cabbala and in Sufism, the centre within the human being is considered to be the heart, designated respectively the seat of Intelligence, of Brahma, of Solomon and the Universal Logos."[139] The arrival at the heart, where the conscious dynamic marries the physical plane signifies the conscious totality of our experience as planetary beings. This is the true significance of both the symbol of the cross, and of the idea of "sacrifice" upon the cross (of consciousness and matter), and has been since the dawn of abstract symbolisation.[140]

"Sacrifice" means "to make holy." A worldly life is construed, in some philosophies or from certain points of view, as a process of suffering, meaning simply to endure and to experience feelings, physical and emotional. This process is conceived as the road to compassion. "Compassion" simply means "with passion." "The Passion" is a mystical Christian term for the "sacrifice," or "making holy," of the "Divine Child," or resurrected Self, upon the mystical Cross, or Tree of Life. The sacred state or "holiness" gained is the compassionate state. And the first and foremost recipient of any such compassion gained must always, first and foremost, be the Self — for only by such "sacrifice" can compassion be extended to the "other," be it another human being, humanity-at-large, or the world itself. Suffering is useless unless the pain endured is treated with the utmost compassion by the sufferer; for only then is the cathartic state of any real value, as the crucible for a renewed and expanded state of awareness and health — or wholeness.

The Mystical Rose was called the "Flower of the Alchemists." It had five petals, and was sometimes called the womb of the Glorious Child. It also symbolised the Virgin Mary.[141] The Catholic "Rosary," dedicated to Mary, was adapted from the Arab prayer beads, *wardija*, or "Rose Garden," which in turn was adapted from the Hindu *japamala*, or "rose-chaplet," the necklace of Kali Ma.[142] The first bead of the Rosary, from which the other beads were said to "spring up," was a vase-shaped bead, symbolising the "Holy Vase," or Mystical Rose — the spiritual womb of the resurrected Self. The *Rosarium Philosophorum* (Rosary of the Philosophers) said the soul of the world is made of male and female, the *Anima est Sol et Luna*.

> Alchemists usually rejected the church's teaching that matter was "evil" or "fallen." As Gnostic animists they thought the "saviour" destined to emerge from the alchemical matrix (mother womb) was both an anthropomorphic Glorious Child or filius macrocosmi, and a "miraculous stone" or Philosopher's Stone, possessing corpus, anima, spiritus, the "redeemer" of the inanimate universe.[143]

The unfeeling or anaesthetised heart has no vitalis, or "life," but is inanimate and cold. It reflects a state of compassionlessness, in other words, "without passion." As such, it is the *prima materia*, or *matrix* for transformation.

Quickened, fertilised, or pierced by the blade of awareness, the "Sword of Anguish," it softens, comes to life and becomes organic like a womb or a rose — or a garden. The stone becomes a living theatre for conception and renewal — the "Passion" — like the secret, enclosed or "virginal" garden — in which grows the "Sacred Rose Tree" or Tree of Life.

When the Bard in our story pulls the sword from the stone, the stone dissolves and is transformed into the fresh and beautiful scent of roses. The sword is the final emblem of sovereign regalia, signifying a successful conclusion to the Underworld quest. The Underworld of the Self has been harrowed and its treasures redeemed in full. The Bard is anointed with the scent of the Rose, awarded the insignia of Self-knowledge, and shown to be fit to rule the kingdom of the Self.

Arthur was recognised as the rightful king of England when he drew the sword, Excalibur, from a stone or (in some versions of the tale) an anvil. These images were later adaptations of the stories of Arthur's magical descent into Anwynn to retrieve the Hallows, which included the Sword of Enlightenment. The stone and anvil are, themselves, symbols of the Underworld. The anvil is the insignia of the Underworld shaman, Mars, Hephaistos, or Vulcan, showing up as the ubiquitous, magical Blacksmith in countless fairytales. A stone often serves as the symbol for an Underworld imprisonment in the old tales. There is the "enchanted prison" under the Stone of Echymeint in very early Arthurian tales, the stone under which Lunet is trapped in "The Lady of the Fountain," and the rock or tower which encloses Merlin within the Crystal Cave of his imprisonment by Nimue. The stone serves as an image for the entire Underworld sequence and is analogous with the redeemer's sojourn there. In the words of Caitlin Matthews, "For the purposes of practical research each captivity (within or beneath a stone) may be considered as part of an initiatory cycle of 'imprisonments' within the Otherworld where Hell is Harrowed, and where Arthur joins the Succession of the Pendragons, becoming in turn the guardian or porter on the threshold of the worlds."[144]

The legendary Stone of Fal ("stone under a king") was said to cry out when the rightful king of Tara was placed upon it. The Stone of Scone is another such stone of sovereignty. It rests beneath the British coronation throne in Westminster Abbey. The "cry" is that of someone who acknowledges his or her pain and therefore has power with it. Self-knowing, they are self-authorised; they are the authors of themselves and their acts. They are connected with themselves and their feelings — fit to rule themselves or to lead others.

Swords of heroes and sacred kings typically came out of a stone, a tree or water, having been forged in fairyland or under the earth by magical beings. On the hero's death, the sword returns to its origin. Some famous magical or holy swords include Arthur's Excalibur, Lancelot's Arondight, Saint George's

Ascalon, Siegfried's Balmung, Dietrich's Naglering, Roland's Durendal, Oliver's Glorious, Charlemagne's Flamberge, Sigurd's Gram, Beowulf's Hrunting, Ogier's Sauvagine, Fergus's Caladolg, Paracelsus's Azoth, Ali's Zuflagar. Often, the breaking or loss of the sword signalled the loss of royal authority or of heroic mana, and the hero's consequent death.[145]

In ancient Celtic myths like Culhwch and Olwen, the sword is identified with the Sword of Light, "Caledfwlch," or Excalibur. The fairytale, "Apple Staff and Silver Crown," recounts how the hero experiences the painful knowledge of his own anger and grief through his connection with his sword of recognition:

Garth stood in silence, full of shame, and a long sadness began in him, like a grey lump of ashes where hot anger had been. He still held the hilt of the shattered blade in his hand. Its light had gone out too, and the jewels on the scabbard were blackened, and the metal dull and streaked, as if the weapon had been seared by fire. And the hand in which he still held his blunted weapon was burned too, so that in a moment he dropped the broken sword hilt and clutched his pain-wrapped hand to his breast with a cry. He fell to his knees crouching over the burned hand and began to weep like the child he had been not many years before. Garth wept on until all his tears were spent.[146]

In our story, the removal of the sword from the stone signifies the death of our hero's last remaining ties to all that has limited or impeded movement, vitality and growth. It is the end of numbness and buried grief. This heralds the death of an old Self, the one who remained disconnected out of fear of disowned, emotional pain. When the Bard finds and holds the golden harp, a new Self is born — one who is vulnerable and feels everything strongly, for whom life has grandeur and meaning, in whom emotions course with fidelity and power, and for whom responsiveness is no longer synonymous with pain.

Part III

Celestial Ascent:
The Three Realms Of Ceugant

Chapter VII

Ascent
to the Stars

All
my bones
resound
with music

Music of waking
in the body
Body of night
and my own blood
ascending

Ascending to silences
and the polished
stars in clusters
Clusters of notes
for the heart to remember

Remembering and releasing all
All my bones resound
with music

THE SILVER STAIR

I noticed that I felt lighter than I had ever felt before, as if a great burden had been lifted from me. The hall was in the process of change. Once again, my environment seemed to reflect the transformations occurring within me. The air was clarifying, becoming crystalline as in Falias, the realm of the Whiteladies. But this time the air held a vibrant warmth, a peculiar live quality which lent a subtle, vibrating edge to things, as if everything around me was alive and emanating its own light.

I watched for a while as the hall continued to change — to demonstrate the fact that all things are continually in the process of dynamic change. I was just starting to notice the startling patterns thronging the air, like radiations of shape around each object, the destined, evolved shapes all things carry within them like blueprints made of light. Then I noticed the stair. It was back in its place in the centre of the hall, linking the realms above and below. I knew it was time to pursue the journey the sylph had spoken of and climb the stair to the starry realm above.

I followed her to the winding silver stair and began to climb. On and on I climbed, around and around. Up and up I went until, strangely, elusively, as with my descent to the Underworld, I began to hear the most beautiful, stately music. It was like the harmonies of many voices or the chords of a great, celestial pipe organ. Impossible to describe, the sound was slowly building the higher I climbed. It increased in volume and intensity, the delicious harmonics weaving in and out, as octave after octave of sound joined the chorus. After a while I began to feel as if the music was reverberating inside my body. I could feel it in my bones and teeth, moving through my body like a song, pulsing in my hands and feet. I could almost taste it on my tongue, the delicate flavours like colours of sound tantalisingly defying description. They kept blending and changing, building and ebbing, rising and descending the scales of some etheric harp. The Emissary of Light and Sound drew me up and up the silver stair. The higher I climbed the more the divine sound increased in complexity, beauty and power.

It was at this stage that I began to feel I was flying. The rhythm in the sound began to invoke in me a trance of swirling movement. I felt borne aloft by powerful wings, as if I rode a surging, flying horse or winged serpent. At times I felt I was soaring on the scaly, blue/green back of a great dragon, flying higher and higher in ever-climbing circles. A sound like thunderous hooves or the reverberations of a powerful drum spurred me on in my flying trance.

Then, all at once, the stair ended in a platform that seemed, for all intents and purposes, to be a diving board. I crept gingerly to the edge and looked over. Before me (and below, above, and all about me) sprawled the starry reaches of space. Blue/black night, thick with flashing, winking stars, surrounded my small platform at the top of the slender silver stair. The implications were obvious. I was being invited to jump, to dive to the depths of star-strewn space.

The Emissary began to telescope away from me at an alarming speed, becoming smaller and brighter and more distant every second. I felt a pang of fear at her rapid departure, similar to that which I had felt at being abandoned by the Maiden of the Flame in the Hall of the Fire Creatures.

"Fear not," said the Emissary as she turned into one of the seven stars of a distant, blue cluster, "and do not despair of seeing me again, for you shall find me many times. You have successfully entered the first of the three realms of Ceugant, the Celestial Sphere. Here you will gain the etheric power of the Word and find enlightenment concerning the cardinal creation of the world. You will hear the nature of expression of which the universe consists, in all its variety. Look beyond. What do you see?"

I looked beyond, but all I saw was an overwhelming, starry void.

After the initiation of the heart, when the burdens carried at the emotional level have been transformed into realisation, the immediate sensation is one of extreme lightness. All that had once seemed inescapable, inevitable or fated, is now perceived to have been a construct of belief.

The primary realisation resulting from the release of emotional pain is that an assumption about the Self, one's position, value, or place in the world, has been mistaken for objective reality. What amounts to an idea — a self-concept — had been held in the emotional body as a posture, a stance adopted toward all of life, the world and everyone in it. Whatever distortions of self-image, wrought over the span of a lifetime and its experiences, had been worn like a heavy and constricting garment, affecting the way in which the self approached each and every opportunity or event. Moreover, this mental structure or self-concept had infused the very infrastructure of the body and soul. Its shape had underscored the alignment of muscles, bones, viscera, tissues, tendons, and all the organs, forms and functions of the physical body, becoming its language and expression. A self-concept is clearly communicated to the world through our physical expression, though we may not realise it.

The "enlightening" of this idea concerning the Self — the review and perspective gained upon the true self-nature — is comparable to the effect of a sudden lifting of the spirit. The sheer realisation that nothing is set in stone, nothing is eternally "true" or irreversible, whether with regard to identity or perception, is liberating. This consciousness is like being lifted up out of what had seemed "fated" — airlifted out of inevitability in a hot-air balloon. Vantages widen, the horizon expands, and an eagle's eye perspective is gained on the matter of earthly existence. Everything looks subtly different, workable — responsive to transformation and change. The environment begins to "reflect the transformations occurring within . . ." and a sense of clarity is gained. While the shapes and patterns of all things may now be perceived as the blueprints of growth and evolution, they are also perceived as relative — connected to and in communion with each other. The evolving patterns of all things are contingent upon all other patterns, all other "realities," mental or ideational structures.

This threshold of awareness verges on another world of thoughts, feelings and sensations. Though having the sensations of leading to an "altered state," exalted in traditional lore as the "shaman's flight," it is in reality, just another dimension of the body-consciousness. The Celestial Realm is simply another level on the Tree of Life, the consciousness of the spine — the innate physiology of Self.

We have all experienced these flights of the spirit, when things come into a new and unfettered perspective, and we feel let out of the cage of our own limited beliefs — even if only for a moment. It is this experience, when formalised into doctrine or ceremony, which is known to shamans everywhere as the soul's flight. This is the flying trance or celestial ascent courted within ritual by magical practitioners, and within meditation by mystics. All human culture has records of it, in story, myth, folklore and song. This is because it is a common human property, not reserved for particular individuals or traditions. It is the result of self-nature becoming aware of itself at the heart level of the body-consciousness and, momentarily unburdened, effortlessly rising into the more abstract regions of consciousness. These correspond, on the body, to the throat and head.

Patterns for flying trance-type initiation, as well as Celestial Ascent, Underworld Descent, and mystical death/rebirth (dismemberment/rememberment) initiatory trances, exist within shamanic culture worldwide. In *Shamanism: Archaic Techniques of Ecstasy*, Eliade describes Australian initiations as highlighting ". . . the ecstatic experience of an ascent to the sky, including instruction given by celestial beings. Sometimes initiation includes both the candidate's dismemberment and his ascent to the sky . . . Elsewhere, initiation takes place during a mystical descent to the Underworld. All these types of initiation are also found among the Siberian and Central Asian shamans. Such a parallelism between two groups of mystical techniques belonging to archaic peoples so far removed in space is not without bearing on the place to be accorded to shamanism in the general history of religions."[147]

The Buryat people of northern Central Asia recognise the "... initiatory death and resurrection that consecrates a shaman."[148] But it is "... the candidate's triumphant journey to the sky ..." which constitutes the "initiation proper." Every Teleut shaman has a celestial spouse who lives in the seventh heaven. The Teleut shaman ritually avows, "We shall go up the 'tapti' (the spiral groove cut in the shaman tree) and give praise to the full moon." Among the Dyak of Borneo, "A third ceremony, which completes the shaman's initiation, includes an ecstatic journey to the sky on a ritual ladder."[149] Altaian shamans enjoy "the protection of a 'spirit of the head,' ... during ecstatic journeys ... [or of a] ... grey horse"[150] to ascend to the sky.

> The dakinis, fairy sorceresses who play an important role in some tantric schools, are called in Mongolian, "they who go to the sky." Magical flight and ascending to the sky by means of a ladder or rope are also frequent motifs in Tibet, where they are not necessarily borrowed from India, the more so since they are documented in the Bon-po (shamanic) traditions or in traditions deriving from them. In addition ... the same motifs play a considerable role in Chinese magical beliefs and folklore, and they are also found almost everywhere in the archaic world.[151]

Certainly, our own Western shamanism allows for the mystical flight of magical persons. As Eliade states:

> A universal belief, amply documented in Europe, gives wizards and witches the ability to fly through the air ... the same magical powers are credited to yogins, fakirs, and alchemists. We should make it clear, however, that here such powers often take on a purely spiritual character; "flight" expresses only intelligence, understanding of secret things or metaphysical truths. "Among all things that fly the mind (manas) is swiftest," says the Rg Veda. And the *Pancavimsa Brahmana* adds: "Those who know have wings."[152]

And:

> The long-haired (kesin) "ecstatic" (muni) of the Rg-Veda declares in so many words: "Exhilarated by the sanctity of the Muni we have mounted upon the wind; behold, mortals, (in them) our forms! ... The steed of the wind, the friend of Vayu, the Muni is instigated by the deity ..."[153]

Rainbows as bridges to celestial realms are a particularly common theme. In Norse mythology, the magical bridge *bifrost* is a rainbow. For Australian shamans entering the "Dream Time" of mythical dimensions, "The ascent is made by way of the rainbow, mythically imagined as a snake, on whose back the master climbs as on a rope."[154] Similarly:

> It is always by way of the rainbow that mythical heroes reach the sky. Thus, for example, in Polynesia the Maori hero Tawhaki and his family, and the Hawaiian hero Aukelenuiaiku, regularly visit the upper regions by climbing the rainbow or by means of a kite, to deliver the souls of the dead to meet their spirit-spouses.[155]

The combination of light and sound were also, in and of themselves, considered to constitute vehicles for celestial ascent by Eurasian tribal peoples.

> The ribbons employed in Buryat initiations are called "rainbows"; in general, they symbolise the shaman's journey to the sky. Shamanic drums are decorated with drawings of the rainbow represented as a bridge to the sky. Indeed, in the Turkic languages the word for rainbow also means bridge. Among the Yurak-Samoyed the shamanic drum is called "bow"; the shaman's magic projects him (her) to the sky like an arrow. Furthermore, there are reasons to believe that the Turks and the Uigur regarded the drum as a "celestial bridge" (rainbow) over which the shaman made his (her) ascent. This idea forms part of the complex symbolism of the drum and the bridge, each of which represents a different formula for the same ecstatic experience; celestial ascent. It is through the musical magic of the drum that the shaman can reach the highest heaven.[156]

Not only refracted light ("rainbows" or as generated by prisms) and sound, but objects which symbolise the octaves of light and sound, engender the mystical "flying trance." Native shamans of North America, as well as Australia, South America, and elsewhere, consider the prismatic or refractive properties of quartz crystals to facilitate celestial ascent. "A young chief of the Ehatisaht Nootka tribe (Vancouver Island) one day came upon some rock crystals that were moving and striking against each other. He threw his coat over some of them and took four. The Kwakiutl shamans receive their power through quartz crystals. We have seen that rock crystals — in close relation to the Rainbow Serpent — bestow the power to rise to the sky. Elsewhere the same stones bestow the power to fly — as, for example, in an America myth recorded by Boas, in which a young man climbing a shining mountain, becomes covered with rock crystals and immediately begins to fly."[157]

Far from being an "altered state" of awareness seldom achieved, it is the one most habitually occupied in our culture. The "Age of Reason" and its aftermath has located European civilisation in the intellectual realm of abstract (left-brain) reasoning, a world of ideas, words and numbers. This place in consciousness is rich in theory, but shy on practical implications. This is how a freeway can get planned, designed, and halfway built before enough people truly notice it was wastefully pushed through a populated neighbourhood, a problematic water-table, or an ecologically valuable wildlife sanctuary. Things have a way of existing too materially on paper, before the actual space/time physicality of the object or event is accounted for. As a result, we have a top-heavy, theory-driven society — like the roof of a house without benefit of a base or foundations. We are, in a way, a culture of disembodied heads.

The irony of this priorising of cognitive functions associated with the head is that Celtic culture once so prized the head, of all the limbs or members of the body-consciousness, that they collected them. Legendary heads abound in Celtic myth — prophesying or uttering inspired poetry — on plates, on battlements, or on poles. Images of heads were emblazoned upon standards, armour, and shields. They were prized as chariot ornaments, battle trophies or venerated oracles. Celts were head hunters, reaping the heads of venerated heroes and enemies alike.[158] Countless stories revolve around heads rising out of wells and speaking, or decapitated heads giving sage council — sometimes for years on end, as when the head of Bran the Blessed entertained the knights (for eighty years) in the elyrion of Gwales (though it seemed but a day), and "kept them good company."[159] The Norse had a similar view: the head of Mimir, the wisest Aesir, was preserved as a talking oracle by Odin.

We haven't really changed; those of us with Indo-European roots and Celtic ties still venerate the head over other limbs and members of the body consciousness. But we've found more sophisticated ways to justify it. An adoption of Greek philosophy and thought, implemented and appended by church clerics and state philosophers like St. Augustine and St. Thomas Aquinas, facilitated the world view of the head chakras. Even the abstract application of the Holy Trinity as the model for the dialectic by Aquinas (after Augustine, after Aristotle) was a function of the victory of abstract reasoning over the more foundational awarenesses of the heart or belly.[160] For we do "think" in these "lower" places as well.

In fact, "thought" occurs throughout the body, through the activity of the nervous system in communication with bodily systems, tissues, structures and organs. This activity or "thought" is synthesised by the brain, becoming the conceptual tool of abstract symbolisation. It is supposed to serve us, not run us. That level of activity, or "thought," is an instrument — not necessarily a reflection of objective "reality." Abstract thought is an imagistic template by which to view, quantify, qualify, and interpret reality, not the real thing. Cultures of the past, or so-called "primitive" cultures of today, believe that thought occurs within other centres of the body. Early Greeks attributed much thought to the heart and stomach. North American Native philosophy would advise thinking with one's heart.

When we are in touch with the regions of consciousness "below the earth," (those realms located in or below the level of the air element in the body, or heart) we automatically understand this. We then have a dexterity, flexibility or facility with this concept, gained by the initiatory journey known in shamanic lore as the descent to the Underworld. This facility is the "wisdom" which endows the Self with the power to alter "reality," a power recognised as "magic." Putting the roof of reason on the foundations of sensation creates a house — the temple of Self. Connecting the head to the rest of the body gives access to intuition and instinct, ancestral memory and profound, instant "knowing."

Street-survival manuals for kids prompt them to heed the instantaneous sensations in the belly or diaphragm in order to recognise a dangerous situation. This is wisdom we, as a species, cannot afford to lose. The degrees to which we already have lost touch with bodily wisdom are reflected by our societies. Western society has built, manufactured, created and promoted things no-one in their right body-mind would consider giving material form in a million years. Some inventions of war suggest a complete inability on the part of their makers to imagine what the effects of such a weapon would feel like. Like the Classical Greek notion of "progress," some ideas look great on paper, but cannot withstand unchecked application.

When we have a better perspective of the synaptic occurrences in the brain our culture identifies as thought, we are able to choose "wiser" applications of theoretical models. Ideas come into proportion and balance with intuition and feeling. We are less inclined to disregard the material reality of a situation, person, place or thing. We can better gauge the greater implications of ideas. Long hindsight grants equal foresight; deep roots support even more wide-reaching branches and vital growth. Sound foundations are necessary to support height, breadth and extension of any structure — human or other. The greater the memory, the more far-reaching the projections of vision. The resplendent crown of a tree directly reflects the spread of its root base within the nurturing earth.

When the Bard's spirit begins to fly — to ascend to what is theoretically possible as an astral projection of thought — limitations fall away. The fact of the matter is, that anything and everything is real at the abstract level. The mind, when liberated, need know no bounds. If the ideas, shapes and models invented by the mind are in touch with the lower body's consciousness, this deeper wisdom is in a position to inform as to whether or not these inventions are desirable as applied realities.

Ideas are very real templates for reality, and energy will obligingly come to fill ideational shapes and give them form, depending only upon the thinker's (conscious or unconscious) go-ahead. If the creators of energy-holding mental shapes and structures (or "thoughts") doesn't understand the inevitability of thoughts becoming reality, they are out of control of this powerful mechanism. Furthermore, if they are not being guided by their deeper knowledge of what is good for them and their world, the results can be disastrous, as we see clearly in the examples of highways being routed through wildlife sanctuaries, or in the proliferation of nuclear weapons and innovations in biological warfare.

Modern physics reveals that energy and matter are intimately related.

Their relationship is described by the equation $E = mc^2$ (with E representing energy, m representing mass, and c being the speed of light, a constant). In effect, matter and energy are simply two states of existence. Another way to say this is that matter can be seen as energy bound by shapes.

In a similar manner, one can say that ideas will manifest as fact. Reality is manufactured from our thoughts, which we often mistake for reality in any case, unconsciously giving the go-ahead for manifestation, regardless of whether we really want this change. Better our thoughts be informed by holistic, bodily wisdom, for then they become a compounded knowledge of conscious thought — or, thought which is conscious of itself. With true consciousness, possible only with support from foundational awareness, the understanding of "magic" manifestation is built-in. The decision to manifest thoughts, to give them the "go-ahead," then comes under our conscious control. We can *decide* which of our thoughts will shape our realities and manifest as form.

In the Chaldean Oracles, and in other models of neo-Platonic philosophy, there is the figure of Hekate, who acts (in this capacity) as a kind of valve for, or transmitter of, thought — a sort of go-between for Universal Mind and humankind. Her role is that of the function of choice — selecting ideas from the infinite pool of possibilities available (known as "Idea," "Ain," "Ceugant," "Cosmic Consciousness," and other appellations in different systems of thought), and translating them into usable forms.

The Bard again sees the spiral stair reappear in the centre of the hall. The spiral stair is actually the Bard's own spiritual axis, the axis mundi of being — the structure of self-knowledge. We are connected to our life by this slender, elastic spiral form. The silver stair is encoded in the body as the DNA. All we are, have been and will be, plus random, personal possibilities, are linked upon it. The silver stair is that same inner mechanism or structure of enlightenment represented by the initiatory ladder of Eurasian shamanism. But it is not only here that the ladder or stair symbolises the dynamic of self-knowledge. According to Eliade, the Egyptian *Book of the Dead*

> . . . preserved the expression *asken pet* (*asken* = step) to show that the ladder furnished them by Ra to mount into the sky is a real ladder. . . . "I set up a ladder to heaven among the gods," says the Book of the Dead. The gods "made a ladder for N., that he may ascend to heaven upon it." In a number of tombs from the archaic and mediaeval dynasties, amulets representing a ladder (maqet) have been found. Similar figurines were included in burials on the Rhine frontier.[161]

These funerary ladders equate to the burial poles which marked the graves of peoples native to Vancouver Island and other parts of the west coast of North America. Frazier documented the "little ladders of dough" the Russians of Voronezh baked in honour of their dead, "and sometimes represent seven heavens on them by seven bars." A seven-runged ladder is documented in the Mithraic mysteries, and ascent to Hera was achieved on a ladder by the legendary prophet-king, Kosingas.[162]

In Islamic tradition Mohammed sees a ladder rising from the temple in Jerusalem (preeminently the "Centre") to heaven, with angels to the right and left . . . Jacob dreams of a ladder whose top reaches heaven, "with the angels of God ascending and descending on it." The mystical ladder is abundantly documented in Christian tradition; the martyrdom of St. Perpetua and the legend of St. Olaf are but two examples. St. John Climacus uses the symbolism of the ladder to express the various phases of spiritual ascent . . . The symbolism of the "stair," of "ladders" and of ascensions was constantly employed by Christian mysticism. In the heaven of Saturn Dante sees a golden ladder rising dizzyingly to the last Celestial sphere and trodden by the souls of the blessed.[163]

Orphic initiation included an ascent by ceremonially climbing a ladder or stair, and the symbolism of ascension by means of stairs was known in Greece. "The ladder with seven rungs was also preserved in alchemical tradition. A codex represents alchemical initiation by a seven-runged ladder up which climb blindfolded men; on the seventh rung stands a man with the blindfold removed from his eyes, facing a closed door. The myth of ascent to the sky by a ladder is also known in Africa, Oceania, and North America. But stairs are only one of the numerous symbolic expressions for ascent; the sky can be reached by fire or smoke, by climbing a tree or a mountain, or ascending by way of a rope or vine, the rainbow, or even a sunbeam . . ."[164]

Climbing the stair restores a motif typical of the spiralling motion of movement upon the silver stair — that of music. The oscillation of energy is, in three-dimensional reality, a spiralling movement through space. Energy "waves" are perceived as flat when looked at on end, or from the side. Only in linear, two-dimensional representation are energetic spirals perceived as waveforms. Starhawk describes the movement of energy, active in all things, in this manner: "The waves are the waves of orgasm, light waves, ocean waves, pulsating electrons, waves of sound. The waves from spheres as swirling gases form stars. It is a basic insight of Witchcraft that energy, whether physical, psychic, or emotional, moves in waves, in cycles that are themselves spirals. (An easy way to visualise this is to borrow a child's 'Slinky' toy — a coiling spiral of very thin metal. When stretched and viewed from the side, the spirals appear very clearly as wave forms.)"[165]

Energy moving in any direction produces a vibration which can be perceived as sound. The oscillations produce tonal frequencies, or "notes," at specific intervals. Frequencies of light waves are sensed by our optic nerves as colours, frequencies of sound waves are sensed by auditory nerves as notes. In both cases, these energetic frequencies are perceived upon an approximate, seven-tone scale. Though there are infinite shadings of every colour or note, human physiologies the world over seem to agree on something between six to nine pure tones of both perceived light and sound. Exceptions include the Irish Pentatonic scale and archaic Greek and Chinese musical scales. The Tantric chakric system has six energetic centres, while the Vedic system has seven. Mongolian shamans perceive nine chakras. Some East Indian Ragas are structured upon a nine-note scale. Traditions disagree about the exact number of colours in the refraction of light — much as they disagree, within a small margin, concerning the number of chakras along the spine, "realms" within the World Tree, or number of "pure" musical tones, for that matter. But the similarities are greater than the discrepancies, for the underlying truth is that we, like all of the manifest universe, cohere to the same, basic harmonic scale, set of frequencies, or "Logos."

Matter occurs at specific intervals or frequency patterns, manifesting cohesive form where energy "waves" (which, in three-dimensions, are actually spirals) intersect. Substance is an energetic compound, concretising, gelling and cohering at the intersections of energy patterns (or "shapes"), relative to contingencies of their movement through space/time. Energy performs within certain parameters. Everything is energy, at some frequency of vibration — including us, our individual and combined consciousness. New physics and archaic magic demonstrate that we are more intrinsically linked to our universe than ordinarily supposed. At a certain level of vibration (energy, consciousness, or "understanding"), we *are* our universe. And we are also the sound from which, to certain sensory perceptions, it is made.

Sound, like light, is a perceived emanation of the vibrating universe. Deaf people can "hear" by touching a vibrating object — the floorboards beneath a piano or the soundboard of a harp or guitar. The first sound we hear, and possibly the last, is the heartbeat. While still in the womb, our uterine mother's heart beat duplicates the cosmic heartbeat — the "thrum-thrum" — oscillating rhythm which underscores all matter and being.

As energy vacillates between the poles of positively and negatively-charged particles, its alternating current can be heard as compound sound, vibrating back and forth, ebbing and flowing, waxing and waning, advancing and receding, in an eternal turn and return of sound, or rhythm. Many religious systems (Sufi, Tantric, Hindu, Buddhist, etc.) identify this sound, the "heartbeat of the universe," as a rhythmic drone — "O," or "Ohm." To Yogis the sound is a mantra, "Su Ham," or "Ham Sah," the sound of the ebb and flow of breathing, which says, "I Am," "I am That," or "I Am That I Am." It is the sound duplicated by a trance-inducing drumbeat, or the sound of the sea against the shore. It is the rhythmic drone of insects or the sound of our own pulse in our ears.

One of the most amazing sights I've ever seen was a cluster of spiders "dancing" rhythmically on my ceiling. They were gathered in a corner of the ceiling, standing on each others' backs with their many legs, forming a sphere or dome of spider-bodies. Rhythmically, in unison, they collapsed and extended their legs, so that their combined, spherical structure appeared to "breathe," collapsing and expanding, swelling and shrinking, like some kind of cosmic, three-dimensional, spider-circle-dance. I remember wondering what they were hearing that I wasn't.

Within the thrumming of vibrating energy which is the created world can be heard counter-rhythms, tonic scales, and harmonies. All of the possibilities and relationships of sound can be perceived within the basic, heartbeat rhythm of life. For they are all there, complete and constantly playing, waiting to be perceived. Mediaeval cathedral builders sought to give form to this dynamic relationship of space and sound by creating vaulting domes, to be filled with choral sound. Tibetan monks chant in cycles of breath, creating a droning rhythm. They create complete tonal arrays or frequencies, producing sound in chordal patterns from the breath vibrating within the vaults of the body and head, each monk sounding like a pipe organ in concert with other pipe organs. The members of the Steven Hykes choir of New York City likewise produce sympathetic sound frequencies and secondary harmonics. Etheric chimes and whistles, occurring somewhere in the air above their heads, are the results of sound vibrations building and compounding upon each other, or colliding in midair. All of these musical/spiritual practices seek to reduplicate the primal, cosmic sound, the infinite breathing of the Universe ("uni-verse," or "one song"). In the words of the renowned twelfth century abbess, philosopher, and composer, Hildegard of Bingen, "every element has a sound, an original sound from the order of God: all those sounds unite like the harmony from harps and zithers."[166]

Octaves of sound can descend or ascend beyond the audible range — or, at least, beyond the range of our "normal" senses, just as light "waves" can range beyond the visible spectrum. Our extrasensory sight and hearing, clairaudience ("clear hearing") and clairvoyance ("clear sight") can perceive the full spectrum of both light and sound, however, which is (of course) circular, or more properly, a spiral. Following light or sound as far as your expanded awareness will take you will always bring you back to your home note — with a difference. You will have travelled "forward" in time, arriving back at the same note, but in a different place — both with the cosmos and yourself, because the sound itself is creative, and changes whatever it touches, or "vibrates."

Sound vibrations change form. Sonic baths are used to clean jewellery and dentures, dislodging calcified debris, even cement. Sound is credited with bringing down the walls of Jericho. In Biblical lore, the Hebrew tribes are said to have circled the ancient, walled city seven times, then "shouted with a loud voice" in unison, causing the walls to crumble into dust. Teams of chanting priests may have been employed to vibrate huge stones into place in sacred structures of Egypt and MezzoAmerica, the sonic vibrations of their chanting causing the molecules to dance into seamless proximity. Vibrators are used in the dental industry to flow plaster mix into the tiny crevices of dental impressions. Sound waves cause molecules suspended in fluid to align into circular patterns like mandalas. In Frank Herbert's science fiction epic, *Dune*, the mystical desert warriors used wrist devices to set up vibrational frequencies into which they would shout a war-cry at a certain pitch, disintegrating their foes. Sound, like any life energy, can be both creative and destructive. It can build universes, and break down rigidified form.

The building power and complexity of sound in our story causes the Bard to experience the sensation of flight. The flying trance experienced by shamans and mystics of many cultures is equated to soul travel upon a magical steed, a winged horse or dragon. The Bard is mesmerised by a rhythmic sound "like thunderous hooves or the reverberations of a powerful drum . . ." Shamans' drums are used to induce this kind of trance among tribal people of Europe, Asia, and the Americas. As Eliade has noted, "The iconography of the drums is dominated by the symbolism of the ecstatic journey, that is, by journeys that imply a breakthrough in plane and hence a 'Centre of the World.' The drumming at the beginning of the seance, intended to summon the spirits and 'shut them up' in the shaman's drum, constitutes the preliminaries for the ecstatic journey. This is why the drum is called the 'shaman's horse.' (Yakut, Buryat). The Altaic drum bears a representation of a horse; when the shaman drums, he is believed to go to the sky on his horse. Among the Buryat, too, the drum made with a horse's hide represents that animal . . . the Soyot shaman's drum is regarded as a horse and is called *khamu-at*, literally, 'shaman-horse'."[167]

> Ecstasy induced by the drum or by dancing astride a horse-headed stick (a kind of hobby-horse) is assimilated to a fantastic gallop through the skies. As we shall see, among certain non-Aryan peoples of India the magician still uses a wooden horse or a horse-headed stick in performing his ecstatic dance.[168]

The one time a flying trance nearly got away from me, or felt out of control, was when I was performing a purposeful chakra meditation on a train. I was focusing my awareness in each of the centres in turn, having started at the root, when I suddenly had the sensation of spiralling upwards very fast. I experienced myself flying up through the roof of the train and bobbing about above the upper atmosphere. I felt like a cork with too much flotation, bobbing about on the surface of some vast ocean — though my proper location was somewhere on the ocean floor.

I was a little alarmed; I didn't seem to be able to get myself back down into my body, which (I knew) was seated in a train, hurtling along on some tracks midway through Idaho. I remembered the connecting silver thread, the same elastic structure as the spiral stair — though in my case it had turned into something like the string holding a helium balloon. Strangely enough, I had to imagine myself hauling myself back down, hand over hand, through the atmosphere and into my body, before I could gain a sense of rejoining my-

Journey of the Bard

self. This was the only time in my life when the flying sensation was so irresistible or compelling, and I attribute this to the simple fact of the train's rhythmic sound and momentum.

Momentum, movement and speed are associated with shamanic flight. According to Eliade: "Miraculous speed is one of the characteristics of the *taltos*, the Hungarian shaman. A *taltos* 'put a reed between his legs and was there before a man on horseback. All these beliefs, images and symbols in relation to the 'flight,' the 'riding' or the 'speed' of shamans are figurative expressions for ecstasy, that is, for mystical journeys undertaken by superhuman means and in regions inaccessible to mankind."[169]

The fact of the matter, however — contrary to what Eliade has to say about it — is that the means of ecstatic flight or mystical journeying is undertaken by purely human means. Ecstatic flight is a natural means of journeying to regions not only accessible to "mankind," but native to humankind. These regions are represented within us as the chakras, which form our own "rainbow bridge," prismatic refraction of light, or seven-note scale. We are the rainbow bridge, the spiral ladder, or ecstatic flight. These experiences are our true, conscious nature. In some circumstances (like those of my journey on the train), they are difficult to avoid. These regions are readily available for exploration, whether experienced as the World Tree, the Cosmic Mountain, or the Chakric worlds within the spine — the "Seven Heavens." Iris is the Greek Goddess who signifies this aspect of Self. Her forms are both the rainbow and the many-hued flower that carries Her name.

> Ecstasy brings about harmony, the "music of the spheres." Music is a symbolic expression of the vibration that is a quality of all beings. Physicists inform us that the atoms and molecules of all things, from an unstable gas to the Rock of Gibraltar, are in constant motion. Underlying that motion is an order, harmony that is inherent in being. Matter sings, by its very nature.[170]

The Bard is led "up and up, around and around" to a platform suspended in space, where the spiral staircase abruptly ends. The Emissary of Light and Sound transforms and departs, becoming a tiny point of light among the vast sea of stars. The Bard feels a pang of fear, because the implied response to this situation is to leap, with absolute, radical trust, into the overwhelmingly vast abyss of cosmic space.

This threshold is the same as that symbolised by the "invisible" sphere on the Cabalistic Tree of Life — the one suspended in the "Abyss" between Tipareth and Kether, the Heart and Crown. This sphere is immaterial, elusive — appearing and disappearing in the sea of space like the Isle of Avalon in the Lady's lake — shrouded, like Isis, by a veil of mystery. It is made of nothing but faith. It requires faith to perceive it is there in the first place, and to keep it in place, like a stepping stone across the void. It is called *Da 'Ath* in Hebraic mysticism, the "mysterious" and "unseen" realm, called the "bridge across the abyss."

The challenge posed the Bard by this unsuspected brink represents the moment when the magical traveller is asked to step into her or his own future. All that has gone before is here transmuted into a basis for unquestioning faith in the Self. This is the zero card of the Major Arkana in the Tarot — the Fool's leap into empty space from the precipice of the "known" into the "unknown." This is the moment when, mustering courage and turning the wisdom of experience into something entirely new, one jumps first and asks questions later. Or, one jumps first, and figures out how to land on the other side of the decisive moment. The "something entirely new" is belief in the Self's ability to know how to land. What is called for here is trust, abandon and surrender — as well as the deep, inner confidence that one will survive risk.

Things you never thought possible for yourself become possible at this threshold, because you become open to them. You know, now, that what formerly limited you were beliefs about limitations, nothing more. What had seemed like large or overwhelming forces containing or constricting your potential were in actuality structures formed from your own beliefs and suppositions about yourself. In possession of greater clarity concerning your true, unlimited nature — informed by discernment and discrimination as to what is desirable and truly in your best interests — the self-confidence necessary to open yourself (to make yourself vulnerable) to new possibilities is available to you.

You are entering the realm of Ceugant, the yet-to-be-formed. This is the place where the future is projected — imaged, named, voiced, shaped, and modelled. This is where the templates and patterns for reality are formed as various kinds of "thought," becoming vessels for energy, which rushes to fill them, to make them realities. This is where the release of personal limitations affecting the nature of your thoughts begins to radically alter your life for the better. In Ceugant, your own future can begin to guide you — your own best destiny can begin to draw you to itself, like a beacon in Time.

While the descent to the Underworld put you in touch with whatever it was you needed to remember, the ascent to Ceugant poses a different challenge altogether — that you become your own possibility. The most eclipsed or shadowed parts of your experience or heritage, genetic legacy or childhood traumas, lived-on in the memories of the mind, body and emotions. The ascent to the abstract, astral realm of possibility represents another kind of abyss, one for which there is no map — only absolute certainty of your arrival at the throne of Mystery.

We are born into a generation that requires us to look into two abysses. The one is the abyss of ourselves. It is deeper than we had supposed . . . The other abyss we must look into is the abyss of infinite being, in which all the gods are swallowed up. This is a good, a necessary, a humbling experience, as it was to the forest sages of India in the century of the Upanishads. The people who refuse to look into these two abysses are not safe for our time. Unbelievers, those who cling to some 'ism' are dangerous in this nuclear age. The need is for those true believers who doubt much and cannot accept any easy good or an easy God. They see themselves in perspective. They are not a humanity turned in upon itself, but aware of kinship with other creatures and able to respond to the transhuman magnificence of things.[171]

Chapter VIII

The Realm
of the
Cardinal Astral Powers

Flight of a star
falling to earth
Earthborn
my soul grows
in rings like a tree
A tree rising
into the universe of suns
Suns blazing forth
with music of light
Light falling
through the wings of birds
Birds encircling
and becoming four
Four voices
in the elemental song
Songs gathered
and released in flight
Flight of a star
falling to earth

The Four Birds of Enchantment

As I stood suspended on the plat-
form, it was not that I felt fear precisely. It was more a kind of nervous
anticipation I was feeling, a kind of bubbling excitement. This is not to say
there was no fear concerning what I was about to do. But it was the eager
productive fear attendant upon all significant thresholds, something like
stage-fright.

I hovered for a moment on the brink, gazing over the limitless expanse.
The music still played. Indeed, it had become an immanent presence. It
now seemed to be the very fabric of the universe, space itself. The cosmos
and all its splendour, the infinitesimal particles, the great, slow-wheeling
galaxies, the planetary spheres, the points of light, the blazing suns, majestic and infinite in number were wrought of this sound. A whirling, rushing
sensation took me into its momentum. I felt as if I entered the flow of the
music, the tide of its movement, or that it entered me. All of a sudden,
without even thinking about it, I found myself leaping, arms wide, diving,
soaring, lunging into space, trying to embrace it all.

This was, of course, impossible, at least from the perspective with which
I was operating. But my attempt gave me such impetus that I found myself
cruising through space at blinding speed, past all manner of celestial phenomena. At somewhere close to the speed of light, I buzzed myriad galaxies, all wheeling sedately in their own graceful parabolae. Brilliant starry
clusters burned fiercely into my eyes. Some of these would turn out, upon
inspection, to be illuminated clouds of space dust. What looked like smoke
rings from a distance proved to be all that was left of giant star systems up
close. Comets, asteroids, planetoids, binary stars engaged in courtly rota-
tions, and the radiance of millions of glittering planets caught in the orbits
of countless blazing suns swept by. The rays of their illumination bent
through the entire spectrum of light in the wake of their passage, or rather
my passage, as it was I who was flying through space like a shooting star.

At last the momentum of my journey slowed, and I began to rotate
slowly, softly, like a gyro in perfect balance. I began to take stock of my
surroundings. They had altered, in response to my speed, to a different
configuration of reality. Gradually, as I watched, the structures of the great
tree began to re-materialise around me. The stair reappeared, winding its

way above and below, through the astronomically immense trunk. My platform returned, providing a seat upon which I could perch, like a bird, and survey this new realm.

Superimposed upon the vistas of the cosmos were the impossibly huge, grandly familiar outlines of the Tree. I seemed to be perched in the lower branches of its immense crown. All about me transparent leaves were sprouting, the stars winking through them like stage lights. And in the branches appeared thousands and thousands of birds, all conversing in a strangely familiar, lilting language. It sounded, in its fullness, like the rustling of the leaves.

No ordinary birds, some of them had heads of human appearance. Others had bird's heads and the bodies of women. Some looked like ordinary enough birds, except for their supernatural size. At last I noticed that four of these latter type of bird were significantly arrayed around me. They formed a neat circle with me in the middle. They sat silent, regarding me. I wondered if they ever spoke in the strange language of the other birds.

At that precise moment, one did indeed speak. This was a bird with the appearance of an immense falcon. Its eye was fixed on me with a frightening intensity. In a voice like molten glass it said, "You are in a region few discover until death, outside of dreams. Yet you, while still within a mortal life upon the earth, have made your way to this realm of the Tree.

"You must have therefore braved the Underworld, abode of death and becoming, enabling you to consciously travel here. This is where souls wait between lives, choosing their pathways and byways, resting and deliberating and flexing their wings, which are made of will. All that can be said or sung can be done. All that can be heard can be embraced and understood. All that can be felt as vibrations of sound can be created — for the created worlds are made of this alone, the inspired utterance of Fire.

"We are the Four Birds of Enchantment. We represent the four elements of invocation. We impel sound into cardinal movement for the magic of creative expression, the magic of becoming, from which all things are made. We are the guardians of the enchantments of form, the Word made flesh."

No sooner had the great falcon finished speaking in its voice of fire and glass when another of the winged giants spoke up. The one that had the appearance of a great vulture lowered its head, which swung around, swivelling on the long, naked neck, regarding me from small, piercing eyes.

"My sister misleads you, though not intentionally," said the vulture in a silky, musical voice. "It is simply her point of view, of course, for the Universe is not wrought of spoken Fire but of the songs of Water. It is the expression of oceanic depths and tides, the fluid movement of sound that gives rise to the medium of space and its infinite forms, just as the sea is the mother of life of Earth.

"Listen! Hear the sound like the sea, the slow, rhythmic surf of white noise, the crashing of energy waves on distant shores. That is the utterance of which the world is made, the background whisper mistaken for static.

"That aside, it is true we are the guardians of the enchantment of spirit into matter."

At this, the third bird interjected, the one who resembled a large crane. "What's all this?" she said. "It is obviously air that when shaped and defined into a vibrating sound gives birth to all things. The breath is the rhythm of the Universe itself, its inhalations and exhalations the ebb and flow of primal force, the dance of energy between the poles of positive and negative charge in an eternal, balanced flow. This is the Aeolian harp upon which the divine breath composes the song that is the world.

"Can you not hear the sound like the wind in the leaves of the Tree of Life, moaning in the lonely reaches of space, whistling in the vaults of time, breathing secret words of power, telling you truths and messages? It is the cries of triumph and loss, the whispers of becoming, the rushing here and there, the constant flux and movement of air that creates all things, like an orchestra made up entirely of wind instruments.

"Besides that one error, the Vulture is correct in what she says. We are indeed the guardians of the actualising of sound."

I turned to face the fourth bird, whom I knew would address me next. "Don't listen to my sisters," said the Raven. "Naturally it is the element of Earth, whose sacred crystalline geometry, when uttered, gives rise to form. This is the shape and organisation of any utterance, any composition, any sound. Before it can manifest, it must reflect a logic, it must be organised. Isn't that apparent?

"Listen to the Music of the Spheres. Hear the perfect mathematical precision, the measured melodies, the geometric harmonies, the exponential resonances. Can you not hear the structures of the sound, the building blocks of form, the basic solids as sound shapes? Can you not hear the rhythmic structure of one grand orchestration? If it were not so well structured of form itself it could never give rise to such an ordered dynamic as this Universe!

"That aside, my sisters speak truth when they say we are the guardians of the manifestations of enchantment."

After the Raven had delivered this statement, the four birds regarded me silently. All the while, the cosmic music was continuing in the background and the thousands of soul birds were keeping up their lively, lilting chatter. Then, gradually, the many separate sounds began to reorganise in my perception slightly differently. I became able to detect the bass rhythms and melodies as distinct from the airier sounds, like brushes on cymbals, that interspersed them. I could clearly make out the soaring, inspirational strains like a thousand violins, and the percussive sounds and counter-rhythms, like the bass rhythms and accents of countless, syncopated drummers.

Heartfelt sounds like flutes and clarinets wove through it all, creating exquisitely plaintive harmonies, reflecting the breath of the one great mystery that breathes us into being. The oceanic nature of the combined sound was impossible to deny. I realised the sounds of all four elements were required to make the cohesion of matter. It was their orchestration that provided the universal glue, the bonding agent that married spirit to matter and spun it into form.

As soon as I beheld this realisation the sound echoed my coherence by cohering into a single, unified note. The note was rounded like an oval or an egg. It was self-perpetuating like a closed circuit of energy. It was a sound like "Oh."

When the universe struck this reverberating chord, the giant birds began to dissolve. They transformed rapidly through the spectrum of light, refracting out of my range of perception, finally turning into pure sound. They flowed away into the general flux of sound I had come to recognise as the Universe. I mused on the meaning of the word, "universe," and realised it meant "unified verse."

I noticed the constellations of Aries, Cancer, Libra, and Capricorn begin to glow with increased brightness, thrumming with energy, and I belatedly recognised the nature and identity of the feathered guardians of cardinal movement and sound. The Four Birds of Enchantment are the four cardinal signs of the zodiac. I looked above, searching the higher branches for their cargo of stars, for stars now signified more to me than they ever had previously.

Though each and every realm of the Tree of Knowledge signifies a threshold, this one is particularly scary. For many years, the number one phobia (unreasonable fear) in the U. S. A., among men, was the fear of public speaking. Among women, it was the fear of being burned alive (which makes you wonder about exactly how much the western world's collective unconsciousness remembers about the Burning Times, the period of time when the Inquisition was most violent).

Whichever way you slice it, for both genders the act of speaking out, of expressing one's personal truth aloud, is terrifying. For one thing, culturally, we're trained not to do it. (And this, more than anything else, was the true message behind the Burning Times, and other such policies of terrorism and persecution.) While terrorising examples have historically been made of those who would express an unorthodox or unsanctioned point of view, so too have examples been made of anyone who might speak out to protect victims of torture, execution, or milder forms of oppression (which is where the fear of public speaking comes in). People attempting to live their lives by their own lights have been assaulted in the interests of preserving the interests of oppressive structures. Not only they have been persecuted, but also any and all advocates, those who would stand by victims of oppression and protest their murders or mistreatment.

There are some other practical reasons to be afraid of speaking out, many of them too subtle to be accounted for by collective stigmas or mass-memories of apocalyptic abuse. There are pressures against self-expression not nearly as overtly traumatising as institutionalised persecution or organised genocide, but very effective in their own right. Though obvious examples exist, such as the persecution of Witches in the Middle Ages, the Jewish Holocaust, and the current genocidal attrition of Kurdish villages in northern Iraq, many more insidious discouragements are aimed against the unique expressions of the "inner voice."

For the most part, people in western culture are discouraged to even find or locate their personal voice. Though individualism, independence of mind, and personal initiative are given lip-service as virtues in our society they are, in actuality, penalised. That is, they are penalised right up to the moment it becomes apparent that the creative (inner or personal) voice is not going to shut up. Then, when all attempts to repress such a transfiguring force have been exhausted, the audience — society's structures and forms — gives up and, in some cases, capitulates. It is even possible, once it is apparent you will not be stopped, that you will be recognised and rewarded for your unique creative expression. But this can only occur when all resistance to your own truth, within you and without, is overcome — usually by sheer, plodding persistence. Perhaps this is how the world tests new ideas (and their harbingers) for consumer safety — although that notion doesn't account for Adolf Hitler or Saddam Hussein. In their cases, their own methodical practices of covert and public acts of terror effectively suppressed the inner voices that must have been silently screaming "No!" We must assume that personal conscience had been objecting in a far greater proportion of the German and Iraqi populations than had ever had the chance to be heard, without fear of a murderous reprisal.

In Hitler's case, as in many others, his voice overwhelmed the "still, small voice" at the heart of every listener, and resonated, instead, with their fear.

Then too, the widespread "hearing" of a particular, personal message or agenda apparently depends upon whether or not the message is an idea whose time has come. It appears to work this way even if it is a bad idea whose time has come — to be clearly seen and questioned perhaps. To many, Saddam Hussein would appear to be a bad idea whose time has, nevertheless, come. He seems to do such a good job of demonstrating just what is so terribly wrong with certain, atavistic thinking processes. But, though his acts and policies constitute atrocities, it doesn't seem time for the world to purge him — for we can learn much by watching him. For, it is true, if he exists out there — rampaging in our world — then he, and his kind, must also exist within each of us. There is a certain point at which we all have to look into that inner abyss, and just say: "No more. This abuse ends here and now, with me. I will perpetuate it no further." Only then can we give ourselves the courage and confidence to leap, as a participating, formative player, into the second abyss — the abyss of the not-yet-formed: the future.

We have to trust ourselves absolutely in order to manage this leap of faith. It is all about faith; faith is its fabric and substance. We must have it — but not located outside of ourselves in some "ism" or tribal ideology. That's how the Hitlers and Husseins of the world get into trouble. We have to give ourselves the trust required to speak and act from our hearts, which requires that we have an unshakeable trust in our own motives. This means we must examine our motives, often and without suspicion or dislike — examine our hearts, searchingly but never dishonourably. We must treat ourselves with tenderness and respect — with affection. Taking into account the many levels of motivation we may experience in any given moment, we can maintain awareness of ourselves. We can be self-aware at every level of manifestation, accessed through our understanding of the many realms of Self encompassed within the Tree of Knowledge. Self realisation is here translated into the kind of knowledge that is required at the portal of Mystery, the yet-to-be. "Know thyself" was engraved at the entrance to the Oracle at Delphi. To "know thyself" is to be able to trust yourself. Only then can you know and accept your own motives, and therefore have the power to choose which to implement.

This is the moment when, holding all that you are (have been and will be) in your hands, you step out onto the stage and begin to juggle. Mustering all the song you've ever heard within you, you open you mouth and sing. Having learned the Book of Self by heart, you emerge from the wings and improvise. Extemporising like crazy, you make your pitch, rooted in the vital compost of all-that-went-before. The cardinal creation of the future requires that you be willing and able to project.

Because more of yourself is present than ever before, your perceptions undergo a radical shift at this point. This threshold, like all the others, is an initiation, though resembling more the initiatory rebirth experience in the Castle of the Nereids in Murias. The throat chakra threshold is the realm of

Journey of the Bard

the Cardinal Astral Powers, meaning: the cardinal signs of the zodiac. The cardinal signs have the qualities of movement, expression and action. They are "generators" of activity — ambitious and aggressively creative.[172] The will to accomplish is a "cardinal" power. These qualities, symbolised in astrology by the signs of Aries, Capricorn, Cancer, and Libra, precipitate creative action by expressing it, giving voice to it — by uttering the magically creative "Word." These are what Joseph Blake called the "Four Mighty Ones . . . in every Man [sic]; a Perfect Unity . . . the Four Zoas," and "The Four Faces of Humanity, fronting the Four Cardinal Points of Heaven, going forward, forward irresistible from Eternity to Eternity."[173] "In the Beginning, was the Word" is a biblical representation of this concept, though the power of the spoken word is recognised by primitive societies the world over as the initiator of creative genesis.

This is why the realm of the Cardinal powers has the quality of a rebirth, like the rebirth from the cauldron of the belly in the Castle of the Nereids in Murias, and why heads and wells are wedded in Celtic Mythology. Current examples of these unified motifs exist in the boon-granting "Three Heads of the Well" of English fairytale, or the legendary "Well of Heads" monument on the edge of Loch Oich outside Invergarry in Scotland, which "may represent resumption of the pagan Celtic practice of head and water worship."[174] But the initiatory birthing of Self that occurs at the throat is that of creative cardinal self-expression and it betokens a radical exogenesis. We are reborn through faith — in ourselves.

The element which corresponds to the throat chakra is Ether, which, like Water, is a medium for dreams, visions, intuitive knowing, and nurture. In the Tarot, this concept is symbolised by the Star card of the Major Arkana. At the belly, the Water element is a creative font, nourishing the creative functions of all other centres and functions of the body-mind, with emotional energy and consciousness. The throat centre is also a font, but in this case, of astral consciousness, which is visionary experience informed by greater, more expanded, apparently "random" possibilities. These are possibilities which issue forth from more than our personal experience, which we access through a greater, expanded capacity for communication at the etheric, vibrational level. One of the meanings of the Star card of the Tarot is that of the ability to channel astral nurture (or "manna") to others through creative expression. We identify this outpouring as "inspired," a word which actually means "breathed in." Artistic expression, in some respects, is simply the capacity to take energetic messages in, and to let them back out — to communicate them in some form, or to "express" them.

The throat chakra — the realm of the Cardinal Astral Powers — governs artistic expression. This is where the writers find their "voice," the singers their own sound, the painters their own imagistic style. This is where the artist, in any medium, channels a universal message through a personal mode of expression, and so manages to communicate to many — at a level we perceive as "great," or expanded. Artists working this way, funnelling greater understandings through highly individual modalities, seem to have something of value for everyone encoded within their messages. Art produced from this level of alchemy holds a message special to each individual — one which is both unique and universal. It does this by making an expanded ("cosmic" or "greater") concept into a personal statement which nevertheless conveys the original expanded concept with fidelity. When this happens — with a painting, novel, dance performance, or film — the creative work has succeeded as a work of art. Successful works of art have the effect of bringing people home to themselves, to their soul recognition. This is the aspect of Self which is cosmic, universal, eternal, immortal and undying, for it is a quality of consciousness. It is the part of us which is writing the script for all the phenomena we experience as our life (or lives).

The throat chakra governs the sense of hearing, which is a perception of vibrations upon the eardrum. It is here that the vibratory medium is experienced as sound. The shape-symbol associated with the throat chakra is the alchemical sigil for ether — an upright oval, signifying an element medium constantly stretching, pulling and evolving itself along the spinal axis — a medium continually translating itself into other forms, in other places. It is all-sound, encompassed in the word/mantra, "Oh." Ether doesn't remain in one place. It is always in motion — a mercurial awareness. Greek (bewinged) Hermes and Egyptian (Ibis-headed) Thoth are divine archetypes associated with this elemental consciousness. Both are couriers of souls, or psychopomps. The astral deities are typically associated with birds, and have bird forms. This is the meaning of the birds' wings at the crown of the Staff of Hermes, or "Caduceus." Venus is identified with Aphrodite, the *Stella Maris*, or "Star of the Sea," and was symbolised by the dove millennia before the Christian saint, Mary, has any such image or appellation. The Morning Star, or Venus as it appears on the horizon at dawn was identified with Adonis, Osiris, Attis, Tamuz and Damuzi. The Milky Way itself is associated with Lat ("milk"), Latona, Leda, Oestre, and Eurynome — all of whom had bird forms, usually swans or geese (the originals of Mother Goose). The stars were allegorised as their eggs.[175] "The Lover Who Came as a Star" is an eastern European folktale about winged Eros coming as a star and shape-shifting into a gander, to woo Psyche as (variously) a goose-girl or a milk-maid.[176]

In our story, the Bard flew among the stars with the speed of a beam of light. The Bard's perception of reality then transformed, returning the allegorical image of the Tree to its central position in the journey. The Bard's experience is of occupying the lower branches of the crown of the Tree, along with a lot of feathered, winged creatures, or "soul birds." The imaging of the soul as a bird exists in mythologies the world over, including Tibetan, Dongson, Siberian, Magyar (Hungary), Lapp, Sea Dyak, Indonesian, Dusun (Borneo),

Mentaweian (Sumatra), Yaruro, Tupinamba (South America), Tlingit, Haida, Apache (North America), Celtic (Irish), and many others.[177] The soul-bird is "kept safe in a nest hidden among the leaves of a tree . . ." in the imagery of the shamanism, folklore and fairy tales of Eurasia. "We may also note the motif of the giant bird that hatches shamans in the branches of the World Tree; it has wide application in North Asian mythologies, especially in shamanic mythology."[178] "With the propagation of Islam among the Turks of Central Asia, certain shamanic elements were assimilated by Moslem mystics . . . (according to legend) Ahmed Yesevi and some of his dervishes could turn into birds and so have power to fly . . . But the ability to turn into a bird is the common property of all kinds of shamanism, not only the Turko-Mongol but also the Arctic, American, Indian, and Oceanic."[179]

Central Asian shamans address the Markut, the Birds of Heaven, to signify that their trance has brought them in contact with the celestial realm.[180] Part of the ascent may take place on the back of a goose, and tobacco is offered to Karakus, the Black Bird who is the shamans' ally.[181] The Yakut and Dolgan tribes erect "trees," or stakes with birds atop them to symbolise the ascent. These have roughly the same significance as the funerary poles of North American Nootka, and the bird-topped house poles of tribal cultures around the globe. The Buryat, Manchu and Reindeer Tungus of Manchuria may erect trees in numbers of nine or compounds of nine, with a symbolic ladder for a celestial ascent. "Among the ritual objects present are numerous figurines of birds, examples of the well-known ascensional symbolism."[182] One is put in mind of the thousands of "figurines of birds" unearthed across Asia and Europe (especially the Cycladian Islands). Dating from the Goddess cultures of the Paleolithic and Neolithic eras, they have outspread wings and outstretched necks, like swans or geese in flight. Many of them are incised with marks or chevrons on the body to indicate breasts and vulvae, as well as lines on the head and neck to mark a resemblance to an erect penis.[183]

> The snake and Bird Goddess was a predominant image in the pantheon of Old Europe. As a combined snake and water bird with a long phallic neck she was inherited from the Magdalenian culture of the Upper Paleolithic. Though usually portrayed as a hybrid, this divinity could also be a separate Snake Goddess. She is the feminine principle . . . The presence of the Bird and Snake Goddess is felt everywhere — on earth, in the skies and beyond the clouds, where primordial waters lie. Her abode is beyond the upper waters, i.e., beyond meandrous labyrinths. She rules over the life-giving force of water, and her image is consequently associated with water-containers . . .
>
> The bisexualism of the water-bird divinity is apparent in the emphasis on the long neck of the bird symbolically linked with the phallus or the snake from Upper Paleolithic times and onwards through the millennia. This "bisexualism" may derive from the fusion of two aspects of divinity, that of the bird and that of the snake, and not from male and female principles. The

image of the phallic Bird Goddess dominates during the seventh and sixth millennia in the Aegean and the Balkans.[184]

William Irwin Thompson described one of the most ancient images known to human culture in this context — the bird-headed shaman-figure painted on the cave-wall at Lascaux:

> In the centre of the picture is a staff with a bird on the top, and this seems related to the fact that the man is shown with a bird's head. The staff with a bird on top, whether as totem pole or caduceus, is an ancient and universal symbol, and this painting from Lascaux may in fact be an expression of the source in Paleolithic religion from which all the later images derive . . . the bird symbolises the higher realms of consciousness, the being which is liberated from earth and can fly off to Heaven. In different cultures around the world this knowledge is rendered in the imagery particular to a place . . . In Mexico the image is a tree in the jungle; its roots are in darkness and its spinal trunk rises up in the dappled light, and there on the top of the tree . . . the brilliantly coloured Quetzal bird makes its nest. To teach a snake how to rise up the trunk to become a bird, or a plumed serpent — a Quetzalcoatl — is how Yoga was expressed in ancient Mexico . . .[185]

Some of the many fairy tales about metamorphic divinities who shape-shift into bird forms include (to name but a very few): "The Three Witch Maidens" (Transylvania); "The Nine Ravens" (Hungarian Gypsy); and "The Vulture Princess" (South America).[186] All of these folk tales feature magical women who transform into birds by donning a "feather dress." In each of the stories the hero gains their magical co-operation by stealing their feather dresses and refusing to return them until the fairy maidens agree to marry him (or lead him to the treasure, take him to her magical realm in the sky, etc.). These feather dresses have the same significance as those worn by shamans to fly to the sky, and are still thought of as having originated with a divine woman. In northern Europe, Freyja was considered the owner of magic feather garments that enabled magicians to fly through the air like birds. The Mayan and Aztec priesthoods had elaborate feather garments which probably had the same original function, to facilitate their soul-flights.

> The Emperor Yao's daughters, Nu Ying and O Huang, revealed to Shun the art of "flying like a bird." We observe in passing, that down to a certain date the source of magical power lay in women — a detail that, with some others, might be construed an indication of an ancient Chinese matriarchy.[187]

Other stories which involve shape-shifting or the gaining of wings include "Prince Swan," "The White Dove," "The Goose Girl at the Spring,"[188] "Wayland Smith," and "A Stork is not always a Stork."[189] In Celtic myth, the stork, crane, or ibis has a similar significance, that being as soul-courier, or psychopomp. In "A Stork is not always a Stork," the bird is actually a shape-shifting, Egyptian magician, who is mercurial and has the effect of infecting people with wanderlust. The Egyptian motif ties the stork/magician in with Hermes/Thoth, the ibis-headed divine son of the Goddess, Ma'at. Ma'at is the Justice/Libra archetype of the ancient Egyptian pantheon, and in our story, the crane signifies the cardinal, mental power of Libra to judge, measure and weigh. The crane also embodies the creative power of language. The invoking "Words of Power" were the magical property of Ma'at's archetype. These and other Libran qualities are evoked by the Justice card of the Tarot.

Ma'at had the task (in which Thoth assisted Her) of weighing the souls of the dead against an ibis feather. If the soul was light and unburdened, she or he could enter into the company of the greater divine powers, or "gods," in the Otherworld. Robert Graves stated in *The White Goddess*, "Mercury in Egypt was Thoth, the God whose symbol was a crane-like white ibis, who invented writing and who also reformed the calendar."[190] Mercury (and Manannan as well as Ogma) are said to have invented the alphabet after watching either the mating dance or migratory flight of cranes, when their long legs form letters and signs. Thoth is said to guard the Moon Gate of Heaven, just as the Three Cranes of Celtic myth are said to guard the gates to the Castle of Magic.

Cardinal Libra is always attempting to balance and adjudicate, to bring harmony and concord to the polarities of life. "In ancient Ireland the association of the crane with literary secrets is suggested by the augury given by its sudden appearance: a cessation of war; for one of the poet's main functions was to part combatants . . ."[191] As Libra, the crane guards the advent of winter in the Northern Hemisphere, in late fall. The Celtic, lunar month associated with Libra is Elder, or Ruis, resonant of the themes of death/rebirth and soul's journeying. The Rune for the month of Ruis is Raido, meaning "journey" or soul travel. The entire compiled wisdom and knowledge of the Druids is referred to, in some contexts, as the "Crane Bag" of Manannan mac Lir.[192] This Sea God is the original model for the "King Lear" of Shakespeare and fairy tales such as "The Swan Children of Lir." "The Bonny Swans" is a folk ballad about this legend, in which King Lir's children are transformed into swans due to jealousy. In earlier versions of the tale, Lir's relatives are turned into cranes.

Like Mercury's magical bag, Manannan's bag "carried the Treasures of the Sea (i.e., the alphabet secret of the Peoples of the Sea) in a bag made from the skin of a crane . . ."[193] Its treasures were visible when the moon was full, its contents poured out upon the full tide. At ebb-tide "they would vanish,"[194] indicating this was lunar, or female, wisdom and magic. The Crane Bag was said to actually be made "of the skin of a woman," which was also construed to be feathered, as this was a divine, shape-shifting, magical woman — the Great Mother in the form of a crane. According to Caitlin and John Matthews, "there is a strong Celtic tradition that cranes are people transmogrified into bird-shape . . . One of the wonders of Ireland was supposed to be a crane which lived on the island of Inis-Kea, County Mayo; it has been there since the beginning of the world and will live there until the day of judgment ... Generally, the crane was associated with the Calleach (Goddess), and was a secret, magical bird. Its skin went to make Manannan's Crane bag ... The contents of the crane's bag correspond to the Hallows of Annwyn and to the treasures guarded by Twrch Trwyth."[195]

In her cardinal-begetting, Libra aspect, the crane's Calleach aspect was like Justicia, Minerva, Juno, and Ma'at. She brought fertility, transformation, and prosperity as well as divine wisdom. Cranes were encouraged to nest upon the roofs of barns and houses as Her totem birds. Her magical element is that of Air.[196]

The raven was also a bird sacred to Druidry, and to Celtic lands generally. Raven is the totem of the Morrigan, the earlier form of Morgan le Fay (Morrigan the Fate). Owein (Yvain, in French Romance literature) was a God of Underworld redemption, and sometimes took the form of a crow or raven. He was said to have been accompanied everywhere by his army of ravens as He came to retrieve the souls of the dead from the battlefield and escort them to the Otherworld. The Celtic Goddess, Coronis, and the Norse soul-couriers, the Valkyries, similarly took raven or crow forms to retrieve the souls of those fallen in battle.

The raven is also the totem of the Welsh God, Bran the Blessed. The name, "Bran," means both "Raven" and "Alder," as Alder month (January) and the cardinal powers of Capricorn (Saturn/Cronos) belong to Him. The Gaelic name for Alder is Fearn, and its Rune is Fehu, invoking land, possessions, and enduring tribal protection. Structure, organising logic and form are enabled by raven. Raven is an oracular bird, like the "Wonderful Head" of Bran, which prophesied, sang and (buried beneath the "White Mount," where the Tower of London now stands) protected Britain from invasion from the east (translate: Romans, Saxons and Normans). King Arthur dug it up, making what is known as one of "The Three Unfortunate Disclosures," thought to have magically precipitated the many invasions from the European mainland that were to follow in succeeding centuries. The Tower of London houses a complement of ravens within its walls to this day as the totemic protectors of Britain and representatives of Bran. The main keep is called the White Tower. "It is said that if they leave the Tower, Britain is doomed. It is for this reason that their wings are always kept well-clipped."[197] Raven belongs to the sacred element of Earth.[198]

The falcon signifies the Celtic lunar Hawthorn month, or Huathe, commencing after the Spring Equinox with Aries. Aries is the first sign of the zodiac, and represents the agricultural and astrological New Year of the ancient Mid-East. Osiris was reborn as the falcon-headed Horus, the divine Child of the astrological pantheon. Hagalaz is the rune associated with this archetype, with the meaning of shriving or purification. It is a Mars-ruled cardinal sign, and connotes rigour, extremity, intensity, and drive. The falcon is a predatory bird, associated with fire, temper, speed and vision. The focus and scope of a hunting falcon is renowned, and they were favourite hunting creatures of Mediaeval nobility.

Falcon's magical qualities are those of a honed and focused Will, unerringly fixed upon its objective. Merlin shape-shifted into the small hunting falcon for which he was named, and met with Nimue and other magical women in Hawthorn groves. One of the sites of Merlin's magical internment by Ninienne or Nimue was within a Hawthorn tree. Hawthorn month, or *Huathe*, of the Celtic lunar calendar corresponds to the time-frame of Aries. Hawthorn is protective, and augers a Tantric meeting of male and female, and the alchemising of thought and feeling, heart and mind. Inspired action is the strong suite of Aries/*Huathe*/falcon. "The ordinary Welsh word for hawk is *Gwalch*, akin to the Latin *falco*, falcon, and the court bards always likened their royal patrons to it. The mystical names Gwalchmai ('hawk of May'); Gwalchaved ('hawk of summer') better known as Sir Galahad; and Gwalchgwyn ('hawk of summer') better known as Sir Gawain . . ."[199] are Celtic avian Godforms in this pattern. Falcon's element is divine fire.

The vulture is among the most ancient of sacred, cardinal powers. Osiris and Jehovah are associated with the vulture totem, as is Boreas the North Wind. As Nekhbet or Mut, She is one of the most ancient forms of the Goddess in Egypt. According to Barbara Walker, She represents "an ancient matriarchal stratum. The Egyptian word for mother was the sign of the vulture. A hieroglyph for grandmother was the vulture bearing symbols of royal authority . . . In the Book of the Dead, the Vulture Goddess guards the first gate of the underworld and represents Mut's taking back of the dead into her own maternal substance . . . Vulture carriers of the dead (psychopomps) were worshipped also by the Persians . . . Parsees still place the dead in Towers of Silence where they can be eaten by vultures, in order to bring about their rebirth."[200] Vultures were the power animals of priestesses charged with handling of the dead and preparation of the soul for journeying in the Otherworld and eventual rebirth.

Along with Isis and Mut, Nekhbet forms a divine, maternal trinity. Their hieroglyph was three cauldrons which signified the wombs of the three births of life's major initiations: birth; death/transformation; and rebirth. Vulture corresponds to the astrological sign of Cancer. Ancient Chaldean and Platonic philosophers called this constellation "The Gate of Men," for through it souls were said to descend from heaven into human bodies. It is also called "House of the Moon," and is thought to be ruled by the moon. In Coptic Egypt it was the "Power of Darkness," and associated with Anubis, guide to the ministrations of Thoth and Ma'at in the Underworld of death and rebirth.[201] *Tseih She Ke*, "Exhalation of Piled-up Corpses," was its unpleasant title in China.

Cancer is the sign of the "World Mother," and represents "the process of the growth of the soul through the sustaining efforts of the life-forces."[202] Cancer therefore embodies the principle of tenacity. The time-frame associated with Cancer roughly corresponds to the Celtic lunar month of Hazel, or Coll. Hazel month signifies essence, content and meaning. It is like the emotional centre of processes or events, and represents their life-value. Hazel/vulture/cardinal/water-sign Cancer cuts to the quick, seeking the core essence, or viable soul, to nurture — even if that nurture means consumption and reconstitution. The Rune associated with Coll is Kano.[203] Kano is the torch which, like that of Hecate or Anubis, lights the way through the Underworld toward initiation and rebirth. And it is also the vessel which carries the soul across the waters of transformation — like the boat of Charon across the river Styx, or the coracle which couriers souls across the lake to Avalon. The power conferred by the vulture is that of emotional transfiguration.

Chapter IX

The Realm
of the
Mutable Astral Powers

Blue wings spread
like a feathered sky
Sky stretching
into a bright veil
Veiling the beasts
revealed
in the working of words
Words slipping
through the branches
like rain
Rain washing the disguise
of sombre gods
Gods born of laughter
and forgetting
Forgetting the barriers
of time
Time released
in the spark of blue
Blue wings spread
like a feathered sky

THE FOUR FABULOUS BEASTS

Left on my perch, I looked around at the other denizens of the lower branches of the Tree. The Soul Birds were still in evidence, not having translated themselves into other forms of energy as had the Four Birds of Enchantment. They ruffled their feathers and kept up a lively chatter in their lilting, musical language. As I watched, one detached herself from the others and approached my perch. She flew through the giant branches and alighted next to me, which set my bough to swaying. She had the body of a bluebird, and the head of a woman. Her hair floated around her head in the sound-disturbed ether. It was blue-white, though her face was young. When she spoke, her voice was young as well.

"Well, Bard, you've travelled far. Will you continue on your journey in the stellar regions, or are you now content to return to the earthly realms of Abred, perhaps to the timeless garden of Gwynedd? Surely, you can have no need of further tests. What can the abstract regions hold for you, who are so tied to your vital life in the actualised world?"

"I don't know the answer to that," I replied, for it was true. I hadn't thought that far ahead. The journey had seemed to beckon to me, suddenly opening the first of many doors when I was led into the garden in the grove, where the crow had spoken to me by the well. After that I had simply followed the signs that came to me, in the form of messages and instructions, hints or hunches. I certainly hadn't seriously considered ending my journey, at least, not since the challenge of the moat at the Castle of the Muses in Finias. This possibility now presented itself. There was no real need to go further; I had acquitted myself nobly and well. Indeed, I had already gone where few have gone with any hope of returning to life in Gwynedd.

The atmosphere was thin up here in the crown of the tree. Already I was beginning to forget the earthly realm of pleasures simpler than those of cosmic sound, the music of the spheres, and the speed of light. I was starting to forget who I was in the earth dimension, and to remember only my eternal Self, the one I am between lives, on different planes, as an immortal conscious entity.

I suffered conflicting temptations as I considered this. I was drawn, on the one hand, to return to what was familiar, normal, comfortable, more visceral, and less exalted than the strictly mental joys that I suspected waited for me in the topmost branches of the tree. Whatever was happening was having the effect of cutting me away from the Self I recognised in my life below, in Gwynedd. Up here I was something else, something not exactly human, something not yet born, something more like a word, or even just the thought of a word.

I had the feeling that this was the last of the realms of the tree that communicated directly with the earth. I felt the realms in the upper branches were somehow too busy with specialised, celestial tasks, such as drawing nourishment from distant stars, as the leaves of the trees in the grove draw nourishment from the sun. What manner of being would I turn into higher up in the tree if I was scarcely able to recognise my mortal Self already?

On the other hand, I was curious about what lay beyond. A prickling of danger cautioned me to suspect that, like Falias at the root of the tree, the crown might not easily suffer the traveller to return to the earthly plane. This is what made me hesitate, for I loved the Earth. I loved the grove and the garden. I was attached to my life there, and fond of it. It would be a short enough time before I, like the Four Fabulous Birds, was translated into other, unrecognisable forms of consciousness. Perhaps I would perch in these branches, a soul waiting to return to a mortal life in a physical body on the Earth, like my feathered companions. Perhaps not. Nothing was certain for everything was flexible, compounded of choices continually made, qualified, and changed. Indeed, I now knew that all is motion, a journey formed of directions taken.

The only thing that appeared certain was that, from this vantage, the mortal life on earth was a brief, brilliant flicker of light, like the flame of a candle — a candle unlike any other. It was fragile and delicate, totally unique, and extinguished all too soon. It was this awareness of the preciousness of my one and only earthly life as that particular form of "me" that made me hesitate in making my answer to the soul bird. I had never considered my existence in quite this way before.

But, in the end, Bardic curiosity got the better of such modest, prudent thoughts. Come what may, the adventure would make for a marvellous tale, many an anecdote, and perhaps even a ballad or two. Moreover, it was well known that a traveller in the realms of the Tree of Life gains the ability to heal the ailments of those regions of the spirit and body thus travelled. There was no turning back. I must continue.

"I will climb yet higher," said I to the Soul Bird. "For I will know what further wonders await me on this journey."

As soon as I had said these words, my companion spread her blue wings, and grew greatly in stature. "Climb aboard," she said. "I will carry you further on your quest, for it is worthy of flight."

I accepted her offer and sat astride the blue feathers between her wings. She leapt from the platform into empty space and my heart lurched. The mighty wings began to beat the waves of sound that still wove around and through us. We climbed higher, riding the tides and swells of sound like air currents. Her blue-white hair floated out in the static wind, igniting etheric sparks in the wake of our passage through the fine medium of sound.

Gradually, powerfully, she flew us higher and higher, climbing in spirals to a realm where dynamic changes were occurring to the clusters of stars. Unstable astronomical phenomena were increasingly taking place around us as we flew higher and higher in the clouds of shifting colours and vibrations. The universe had altered its appearance to become less the organised, majestic mechanism of physical laws it had heretofore seemed. I now perceived it as something composed of smoke and mirrors. Images of small, private universes blossomed and faded before our eyes as the Universe dreamed itself into being. Whole systems of spatial relationships, giant working models of alternate, parallel realities were born, realised, and died as we watched.

Thought forms in the configurations of the major deities and lesser gods wafted though the cosmic reverie that I was coming to recognise was the true nature of reality. Comic, wry and mischievous were these forms, at times, producing creatures made entirely of mental energy that were preposterous, even perverse. These shared dimensions with, or blithely overlapped, more dignified projections, and some that were sublime — notions of elegant simplicity and grace. Grand and noble visions were jumbled with burlesque fantasies as the whole projection continued to metamorphose before my eyes.

Our ascending spiralling brought us gently through the shifting ephemera to a place imbued with deep blue light. Like a star sapphire was this blue, like lapis lazuli in richness, cobalt glass in clarity and depth. Fathomless blue encompassed us in this new place, the branches of the tree visible as if cut from blue topaz, jewel-like and sparkling.

My winged courier alighted on one such glittering branch. As she touched down the energetic pattern of the branch shivered, then blossomed into an entirely different configuration of reality. As I hopped down from the soul bird's back, she began to fade from view, growing tinier by the second, becoming at last a brilliant point of light before disappearing entirely. Left behind, like a ghost, was the sound of her voice.

"Don't forget me," it said. "I am Asterope." The voice dropped to a whisper only I could hear. "If ever you have need of me, say my name and I'll be with you. Farewell and may you prosper on your path."

Then she was gone. I looked around and found myself in a dimension where everything consisted of electric blue light. "Welcome!" said a voice.

"Yes, welcome indeed!" said another, and another echoed it.

"Nice you could drop by," yet another voice agreed, and still I could see naught but a shimmering curtain of blue light.

"Yes, that is us," said the first voice.

"What is who?" queried I.

"The drapery of blue light. We are in it and of it. Can you see us yet?"

As the mysterious voice asked this question, I saw shapes begin to form inside the curtain of blue light — fantastic shapes! Then the curtain swept aside dramatically, like theatre curtains or a veil of blue gauze, and revealed my correspondents. They stood as if on a stage, bizarre, grotesque, slightly monstrous, and wonderful.

They were weird creatures, part human, part beast. There was one similar to the soul birds in that she had the head, neck, wings and feet of a white swan, and the beautiful body of woman. Another was in the form of a female centaur, with the body of a jet black horse and the upper torso and head of a woman emerging from the withers. Still another was a mermaid, with a glistening blue fish tail. The fourth and last of the creatures had the wings, feathered legs and feet of an owl, and a human female upper body, face and arms.

"We are the Four Fabulous Beasts of the Tree," said the swan. "We guard the manifestations of thought. All is thought made manifest. We are metamorphic beings, mutable energies. As creatures made entirely of the vibrations of thought, we are fabulous, inventive, or profound. We can be quirky, as you may have noticed. What do you seek in our realm?"

For once I was speechless. I had not suspected the greater altitudes would have a sense of humour. Strangely, I feared that if I opened my mouth I might, irreverently, start to laugh. The Universe itself seemed on the brink of hysterical laughter from this perspective. Perhaps that is how it expressed itself here.

I risked breaking into loud guffaws and opened my mouth to speak. Aside from a small, insane giggle, no unseemly outburst betrayed me, and I managed to say, "I come to seek the furthest mysteries of the Tree, for no other reason than that they exist. In this fantastic, unlikely realm of possibilities, I come to gauge the limits of possibility itself."

"Well said, well said . . ." exclaimed the swan woman. "You couldn't have come to a better place. We are delighted to see you. We get few conscious travellers here. Most people wait until they're asleep or daydreaming, and end up having little or no idea where they've been. Only artists, inventors, children, geniuses and fools know of us here — and, of course,

Bards. You are welcome to the gifts we have to bestow. I am the Swan of Tuonela, though some know me as Lat, Latona or Eurynome, mother of the world egg, incubator of forms. I bestow infinite, balanced creation and healing."

Next spoke the owl woman. "I am Lilith, sometimes called Nemesis or Anat," said she. "I am swift, ruthless and merciful. I am the deliverer from pain, the executer of truth. I am the spinner and the loom, creatrix and creation, the beginning and the end. I am fate and necessity. I bring the knowledge of destined forms."

The centaur spoke up, saying, "I am the Witch of the Westmoreland, the Fairy Pooka. I dwell between the river-marshes and twilight. I haunt the borderlands between earth and sky, land and sea, day and night. I bestow the ability to travel in any medium, and to convey wisdom and healing between the worlds."

The Mermaid spoke then, saying, "I am the fairy Melusina, though some may call me Freyja-Nerthus, bestower of blessings. All who desire nurture and healing, prosperity, generosity and love may drink from my cup of dreams. I am the fountain of fantasy and vision."

My brimming laughter died on my lips. Though their manner was as light as, well . . . light, their words had a sobering effect. They were talking about the forces which determined the very nature of life on earth, those being thoughts and ideas. Attitudes, beliefs and feelings fuelled the thoughts which then spun themselves into the forms we recognise as our selves and our world.

But here, these fabulous beings were telling me such forms were as mutable as light and as flexible as a thought. I was caught in a quandary between finding this both extremely profound and rather funny. I giggled again, uncertainly. Then, as my brow wrinkled in deep concentration, I was illuminated. A revelation broke through my heavy preoccupation with the nature of reality and left an exceedingly clear after-image that was, indeed, hilarious. Though ineffably simpler and clearer than when put into words, the revelation was as follows:

All is consciousness. Moreover, all is consciousness as it is experienced, here and now. Consciousness configures and reconfigures itself constantly, assuming various changing patterns, wave-forms, and vibratory levels. I myself am consciousness expressing itself in a particular, form, pattern, or rate of vibration. Hence, consciousness is me, is my nature. Here, in the realm of consciousness, I share in its nature of omniscience, omnipresence, and omnipotence. Therefore, I can know all, create all, be all, as is my conscious nature.

I can know present, past and future for it is all, simply, consciousness.

The past and future are present in the here and now, for consciousness is not limited by time. Consciousness exists outside of time and embraces it. Time itself is a construction of consciousness, there simply because we believe it is there.

All three dimensions change as I change. As I change, so the consciousness which is the Universe changes. As the Universe changes, so do I; we are symbiotic.

In this present moment I can see the past and future radiate in lines of possibility from the set of conditions here and now. The reason I can know which lines of possibility are to be fulfilled in the future, or even in the past, is because I can decide such things, here and now. The past and future both radiate and blossom according to my informed choice, which I make upon looking at the set of relationships we call reality from this vantage.

The answer to my question and the knowledge I had come to seek is that *anything* and *everything* is possible — for all is consciousness, given shape and form from something as ephemeral as a thought. There is nothing, therefore, which is not possible. My sense of humour was returning in waves of laughter that rose from the depths of my being. I had finally got the Cosmic joke, and I was the punch line.

Though people in our culture spend the bulk of their time somewhere between the root centre of Falias (trying to survive) and the head centres (trying to figure it all out), few people occupy these regions of consciousness with the ability to make the most of them. In other words, few people are aware of the truly amazing possibilities native to these centres — rather, only their limitations. All too often, we are caught (or blocked) in physiological functions (methodologies, or perceptions), under duress, nose to the grindstone, busily trying to muscle through with an idea. This is perfectly understandable. Root chakra issues, like food, shelter and clothing, need to be dealt with before the creative aspects of any realm can be accessed.

Another common situation sees the facilitator of abstract ideas, the theorist or speculator, protected from practical necessity. He or she may therefore be boundlessly creative, but without the sensual discrimination informing the wisdom or desirability of applied ideas. It is when the realms of body-consciousness flow into communication, continually irrigating, nourishing and informing each other, that we are at our miraculous best. True clairvoyance, psychism and the ability to use such expanded perceptions in harmony with the greater collective evolution issue forth from a confluence of consciousness in the body. This is the energetic font called "The Fountain of Youth" in legend, as well as "The Path of the Rainbow Serpent," "Shushuma," "The Path of the Arrow," "The River of Milk and Honey," "Soma," and by many other terms, in countless cultures.

The brow centre, known as "The Third Eye" to the Vedics, is a realm of sensory awareness which is visionary in nature. Its energy is focused in a gland which also acts as a locus for the crown chakra: the pineal gland. This mysterious organ dwells in a chamber in the midbrain, and its function is to process light into a quality of awareness. The brain hormone we know as melatonin is produced from the perception of light and its processing as energetic fuel in the pituitary. Melatonin production affects the rapid-eye-movement period of sleep in which physiological ephemera and stimuli are processed though dreams. Visual, emotional and sensory experience are part of dreaming, as well as conscious realisations and thought processes.

Light is fed to the pineal gland through the optic nerve. People born blind, or people in whom the optic nerve has been severed, do not access this nourishment of light through their eyes, and so have trouble sleeping in "normal" sleep patterns. This is why melatonin is prescribed for blind children and adults, as well as pilots and flight attendants, midnight emergency-room medical personnel, and anyone else whose sleep is disrupted by irregular production of melatonin and other brain hormones. Melatonin has been credited not only with enabling people with these problems to sleep, but with endowing clarity of mind, physical and mental flexibility, intense and fruitful dreaming, increase of "intelligence," and youthful rejuvenation. As with all hormones, production of melatonin decreases with age and this probably has a lot to do with the calcifying, not only of physical flexibility, but of mental attitudes in old age. Poor health and depression in populations of the far north, where there is little light during winter months, could have everything to do with low melatonin production.

Hormone production can be stimulated in the body, without artificial supplements, simply by cultivating a conscious awareness of light — not only as the medium for vision but as warmth upon the skin — especially the skin at the crown of the head. Light is not only perceived and accessed through the optic nerve, but through the crown; the thin skin of the scalp on this sensitive area of the head permits light to enter the pineal's chamber in the cerebral cortex (in Yoga, "The Cave of Brahma") directly. Too much solar radiation on this area of the head can overwhelm the brain, causing "sun-stroke," and the toxic (and intoxicating), hallucinogenic effects of delirium and fever known as "sun poisoning." About ten percent of the population experience a negative reaction from taking melatonin supplements, in the form of overly vivid, active, nightmarish dreaming.

The crown of the head is always slightly warm; heat escapes the body from the throat chakra and the top of the head. These are nerve-rich, energetic vents in the system. There is an exchange of vibratory forces at these locations of the nervous system, which act like valves or flues. The crown of the head is not only a chimney of sorts, but an intake valve. Light, and subtler energies, are perceived by the pineal through eyes (all three) and crown. The function of the pineal gland, long questioned by conventional, medical science, can be defined through an understanding of Yoga or of alternative medicine. One of the physiological functions of the pineal gland is the manufacture of spiritual consciousness.

Thought is mutable. It is metamorphic and ephemeral, mobile and slippery like quicksilver. Mercury, the male/female, elusive shape-shifter is an archetype of mental dexterity and speed — the totem of courier services and communications media. He is also the mascot of healing arts, signifying the health-producing confluence of bodily systems in clear, flowing communication with each other — especially the nervous system. Thoughts, like dreams, are surreal, linking up unlikely bedfellows on a regular basis. At their best, thoughts do not quail at hybridising concepts, grafting notions onto other notions, or engendering patterns for new ideas. One may not necessarily want to implement every nutty marriage of forms, or idea, but we need to entertain their momentary manifestations in our imaginations. In other words, we need to image them — to visualise and *see* them, for only by such imaginative play can the creative, random possibility enter and revolutionise reality.

Albert Einstein credited the habit of "wool-gathering" with the genesis of his most brilliant, revolutionary ideas about the nature of physical reality. Isaac Newton is pictured daydreaming under a tree when the apple of knowledge bonked him on the head and bestowed him with an understanding of gravity. Marie Curie was not limited by the same notions of "the possible" which beset her male colleagues. Fabulous forms were allowed to play, to form and reform, in the imaginations of these and other creative thinkers. We know this with certainty because, in point of fact, this is the only way invention can occur. Conceptualisations must be permitted to meet, mate and marry. Ideological barriers, moral approbations, beliefs about "order," or other walls enclose and limit the free working of a mind, inhibiting this mercurial, metamorphic ability of the mind to change form. An open, imaginative mind "informs" transformation simply by envisioning such metamorphoses. The mutability of the mind is its greatest power.

When the Bard arrives at the hub of this centre of consciousness, a realm so blended of vision, light, imagery, imagination, and thought, the first, single, clear impression is of blue light. A perception of blue light is one of the first manifestations that practitioners of meditational forms experience. This is true no matter if it is Transcendental Meditation, creative visualisation, or trance journeying which is practised. The underlying reason for this common experience is simply that the practitioner of meditative arts has fully entered this realm of awareness, known variously as the Brow Chakra, the Third Eye, the Cave of Brahma, clairvoyance, or (in our story) the Realm of the Four Fabulous Beasts. This is the quality of consciousness symbolised by the mutable signs of the Zodiac. Their astral energies are embodied in the astrological archetypes of Sagittarius, Pisces, Virgo and Gemini.

Gemini corresponds to the Celtic lunar month of Holly, or "Tinne." The rune which correlates to Tinne is Tiewaz, auguring warrior-like protection, the "Path of the Arrow," lightning, and phallic-activating rays (arrows or spears) of light which quicken the earth. God-forms associated with Tinne are Lugh Lambada ("Light of the Long Arm," Celtic), Llew Llaw Gyffes ("He of the Quick Hand," Welsh), Lancelot (British), and Lohengrin (Frankish). They are associated with the Sword of Light and other magical weapons among the Hallows, such as the Lance or Spear of Light. All of these archetypes are phallic light gods, and serve the Land as sovereignty. They are champions of the Earth and they are Her lovers, as well as Her fosterlings. The later, Christianised versions of Lancelot never quite worked. These renditions failed miserably to convey his true nature. He was, of old, the fecundator of Goddesses and Queens — and father of magical offspring. He was the lover of barren Guinevere, as well as Elaine of Corbyn, an avatar of Elaine, the Lady of the Lake — his fairy foster mother and, herself, an aspect of the Goddess. With Elaine of Corbyn, Lancelot fathered Galahad, who would become the Grail Champion.

An earlier form of Lancelot was Llew Llaw Gyffes, the divine son of Arianrhod. He was married to Blodeuwedd, a magical woman and an avatar of sovereignty, who was made from the blossoms of nine flowers. Like Guinevere, she was fickle, unmanageable, and infertile — a metaphor for the land when it won't co-operate with the husbandry of farmers and kings.[204]

Female archetypes for Gemini/Holly are Lucina, Oestre (or Eostre, the Goose Who Laid the Golden Egg), Lat, Latona, Leda (Mother of the World Egg), and the Valkyries. All of these have an association with swans; Leda's case is the most instructive.

Leda is related to Eurynome, who birthed the Cosmic Egg, which had been fertilised by Ophion, the World Serpent. Leda is a much older Goddess-form than the version of Her we see in the myths of Classical Greece, in which She was a victim of rape by Zeus. She is older than Zeus, dating from the early Neolithic, when the Zeus role was fulfilled by the Divine Serpent. In early depictions, Zeus is portrayed as Zeus Meilichios, a massive serpent. In some versions of Leda's myth, She gave birth to the World Egg, from which came Castor and Pollux (the *Dioscuri* or Divine Twins of Light and Dark), who became immortalised as the constellation Gemini. In other versions, there are two sets of twins: first Helen and Pollux, then Castor and Clytemnestra.

In the oldest versions of Leda's myth, it is not Her rapist who takes the form of a swan, for the swan is Her totem and the form into which She shape-shifts, like the Valkyries. The amazon-like Valkyries donned cloaks made of swan feathers in order to shape-shift into swans and fly through the sky. The Valkyries flew over the battlefields and "sang magic charms to deprive the enemy of strength."[205] As in many a fairytale, if an enterprising hero or Bard could manage to steal her swan-feather cloak, she would be compelled to grant his every wish. Valkyrian Brunhilde, like King Lir, had seven children who were turned into swans. Vedic Brahma assumed swan form, and in *The Aquarian Book of British and Irish Mythology* we read:

> The swan has always had a mystical significance in Celtic mythology. Its skin and feathers were used to make the poet's tugen, a ceremonial cloak of office, thus aligning the poetic function with "the language of the birds," the secret formulas once more typical of the shaman . . .[206]

According to Barbara Walker, "Swan maidens and swan knights associated with the Old Religion were common in European folklore throughout the Christian era."[207] An order of knights connected with the Temple of the Grail and the defence of women claimed descent from a divine swan ancestor; the noble families of Gelders and Cleves bore a swan on their heraldry to honour "The Knight of the Swan, servant of women," their legendary patron. The legend of Lohengrin issues from this tradition. He was a champion of women in the fashion of Lancelot and Galahad. Lohengrin is associated with one of the rumoured sites of the Grail Castle, Montsalvatch, a hotbed of Goddess-revering heresy throughout the Middle Ages and a shrine of one of the Isis-like, Black Madonnas of Europe. Lohengrin is associated with the worship of Venus as Freyja, Nerthus, Leda or Oestre, the concept of romantic love, and the Swan Maidens. He is portrayed in myth as bearing the sigil of a swan on crest and shield and was called the Swan Knight.

The swan image is that same conceptualisation which dates from Paleolithic times: that of twin souls, male and female, light and dark, joined and wed in erotic union, the violin-shaped body being female — a "Venus" — and the head and neck the "male," phallic extension of an aroused (battling, protective, or amorous) swan in flight. Its magical properties are those of quickening and illumination. The Twins make an androgynous unity, and the crafting of figurines of this type was most prolific during the Age of Gemini (approximately 8,000 to 6,000 B.C.E.). The mutable, metamorphic properties of Gemini/Holly/swan are those which signify the integration or "marriage" of opposites: the polarities of male and female; light and dark; yin and yang; heaven and Earth.

Another of the Fabulous Beasts is the Owl Woman, who tells the Bard Her name is Lilith. She represents an archetype who has been known by many names, however. Earlier versions of Hebraic Lilith are to be found in the Goddess Lilitu of the Assyrians, Lili Anu of Mesopotamia, Belili of Babylonia, and Lillake of the Chaldeans.[208] Her qualities are to be found in Anat, Anath, Anathena, Athena, Neith, Metis, Medeia, Medusa, Maya, Fata Morgana, the

Moirai (Trinity of Fates), Irish Moira, Nemesis, the Neters, the Norns, Niniane and Nimue. She deifies the ideas of fate, necessity, finality, divine justice, and fairness. She represents the Virgin/Crone, found among the stars as the constellation, Virgo. As well as the Owl, she has the Spider as a totem, and is also known as Arachne, Ariadne, Arianrhod, Athena, and Asterope. She is the Spinner archetype, called Spider Woman by First Nations. Her lunar tree month is Ivy, or Gort, which epitomises in its growth patterns the spiral of life.

The magical significance of Ivy is the spiral of the Self, encoded in the DNA, as the understanding of destined patterns and evolved forms. The Rune relating to these concepts is Gebo, exemplifying the partnership of spirit and matter, the wedding of consciousness and form. Their consummation is the perfected expression of Virgo, endowing the ability to live graciously on the Earth. Virgo is an Earth sign, bestowing comfort and aesthetic perfection. As the Spinner, the Virgin/Crone is a weaver of destinies, and ruler of Her web, the gossamer fabric of space and time — seen in motion as the eight-spoked Wheel of the Year. Arachne's web is also seen in the heavens as the ever-turning celestial hub — known to British Celts as Arianhrod's Silver Wheel.

The next Fabulous Beast is a Centaur, evoking the constellation of Centaurus and the zodiacal sign of Sagittarius, as well as the element of mutable fire. Centaurus is a southern constellation, hard to see in the Northern Hemisphere; it contains the nearest bright star to Earth, Alpha Centauri.[209] In our tale, the Centaur is the Fairy Pooka, the *Nacht Mare*, or "nightmare."

A British version of this creature is the Witch of the Westmoreland, who bestowed sexual healing upon a fatally wounded knight. The knight was dying of his mortal wounds, so sent his hound to fetch the Fairy woman, who shape-shifted between horse, woman and centaur. The Witch of the Westmoreland had the power to bring those she loved back from the brink of death. The threshold between life and death was her territory, the borderland between land and sea — the marshes and bracken of tidal flats, river banks and alluvial plains. Twilight was the liminal period in time, neither day nor night, when she went abroad, running through the high grasses in her magical, transformative body.

The knight's hound faithfully followed her master's command, and drove the fairy beast toward the felled knight. The Witch of the Westmoreland took pity on the suffering man, transformed into a woman, and made love to him. He was healed of his wounds, by her grace, and lived to see another day. The Fairy creature returned to her twilit realm between the worlds, reappearing only in those moments out of time, between land and sea — the "place that is not a place, and a time that's not a time."[210]

Like the centaur in Greek myth, the fairy pooka, "Nightmare," or Witch of the Westmoreland has the ability to convey healing between the worlds. Centaurs were healers and teachers to gods and mortals in Greek myth; Dionysos was taught by centaurs. Chiron is the model for Sagittarius, and both convey an understanding of the "original wound," which occurs in the area of sexuality. Chiron is wounded in the thigh, a euphemism for the genital area, or "loins." The entire tableau is a metaphor for the wounding infliction of sexual shame upon his psyche. He heals himself, an avatar of "The Wounded Healer" archetype. In this respect, Chiron is an embodiment of the shamanic process, whereby the shaman acquires the ability to heal an ailment through first suffering its depredations, thus learning how to heal it in others — often by learning the dysfunction's "demonic" or magical name. Chiron/Sagittarius is an archetype of sexual healing.

Mohammed rode the magical steed, Alborak, who had the body of a mare and the head and neck of a woman. She enabled him to traverse the realms of heaven and hell. In other words, he made a celestial ascent and an underworld descent through the agencies of this centaur-like being, whose gift it was to travel between the worlds. The lunar tree month Celts associated with the time-frame of Sagittarius is Rowan, or Luis. The Runic symbol is Laguz, signifying the ability to establish a flow between various levels of consciousness, channelling understanding, wisdom and inspiration from one realm to another. The mastery of fire and the shamanic ability to heal was said to have been brought to humankind by Chiron, according to early Greek myth.

The final metamorph to speak is the mermaid. She tells the Bard her name is Melusina, "Bestower of Blessings." Her ancestral archetype is Mer Lucina, or "Light of the Sea." Because the same root words, Ma, Mene or Me, mean both "mother" and "moon," her name also means "Moon Mother Light."[211] Other names for her include Stella Maris (Star of the Sea), Mary, Mari Ishtar (Star of the Sea), and Mari Anna (Sea Mother). She is seen manifested as fish-tailed Aphrodite, Marina, and Freyja-Nerthus. Freyja-Nerthus sometimes took the form of a crowned mermaid, and sometimes a double-tailed siren in the birth-giving position — a sort of aquatic Sheela-Na-Gig (a Celtic Goddess depicted with legs wide apart, similar to portrayals of the Mother Goddess in the renderings of cultures all over the world). She is identified with Aphrodite and the planet Venus, visible at dawn as the Morning Star and at dusk as the Evening Star. According to Barbara Walker, "Aphrodite's principal rites at Paphos took place under the sign of Pisces, the Fish."[212]

Melusina was depicted in Mediaeval French heraldry flanked by two wolves, further identifying her with Aphrodite: Aphrodite's consort is Mars, whose animal form is a black wolf. The legend of the fairy, Melusina, is that she was a "Maiden of the Well" (near Lusignon, a modernisation of Gallo-Roman Lusinia, named for the fairy — who was originally a totem Goddess). She had come out of her pool near the wellspring of the "River Source" and was sitting on a rock, splashing the water into sparkling droplets with her powerful fish's tail (although in some versions she has a serpent's tail). She is combing her long hair and singing in her beautiful, Otherworldly voice, when the Duke Raymond staggers up to the water's edge. He has had a disastrous battle with his cousin, whom he has mistakenly killed. He is therefore sick at heart. Having acquired spiritual wounds far worse than the physical damage, he is about to die.

The fairy Melusina sees his plight and takes pity on him. She grows two legs, like a mortal woman, and leaves her pool to join him on the land. She grants him heart's ease by nourishing him with the holy water in her Cup of Blessings, a symbolic act of multiple layers, for this is a rich and ancient image. The vessel confers the magical meanings of erotic healing, being a symbol of the womb, and also of initiation and transformative baptism. Raymond is returned to health, his spirit restored, and he asks her to remain a mortal woman and become his wife. In this, the story reflects the related tales of the Selkie — an aquatic, Otherworldly woman (a seal) who consents to marry a mortal man, often bringing him material as well as spiritual riches in the process. There is always a catch in these stories, however. The Otherworldly bride comes to her human husband with one condition which, if broken, means that she must leave him and return to her Otherworldly condition. The Inuit Goddess, Sedna, and First Nations legends about the "Seal Bride" echo these themes.

Melusina's condition is that Raymond never interrupt her in her bath of the Sabbath Eve. The esoteric Sabbath, named for Sabboath — Hebraic Saturn — is Saturday, so Sabbath Eve is Friday — named for Freyja, the Germanic Aphrodite. In Her honour fish has been eaten on Fridays, across Europe, for centuries — though the original reason is forgotten. The reason Melusina forbids the Duke to observe her in her bath is because she transforms back into a mermaid (or Lamia) at these times. She luxuriates in her specially-made, oversized bathtub — singing, combing her hair, and whipping the bath water into a froth with her tail. In this highly magical state, she is not to be seen by human eyes.

Raymond, being human, becomes obsessed with curiosity. Though he has promised, willingly, never to spy on his magical wife while she is in her Friday night bath, he is goaded into suspicion and distrust by his jealous brothers. This resonates with Psyche's experience with her sisters, and their jealousy over Psyche's divine husband, Eros. Like Psyche, Raymond finally surrenders to the temptation to break faith with his magical spouse, and attempt to observe her true nature. He spies on her through the keyhole of her chamber and sees the water spirit resplendent in her bath. As soon as she is seen, however, she realises it, grows webbed wings like a dragon, and rises from her bath with a terrible cry. Like Lilith, she flees into the wind, where she shrieks and moans like a banshee (or, more properly, *Bean Sidhe*). She flies around the towers of the castle, howling her mournful cry, and returns to utter her blood-chilling keening whenever one of the descendants of herself and Raymond pass over into death.

Melusina resembles many metamorphs of air or water, including the Sirens, the Hesperides, nymphs, and nixies. According to Gareth Knight, "This primeval creativity became transformed into those capable of ravishingly beautiful song, so beautiful that sailors feared them, for to hear their song was to be entranced by them forever."[213] Related to the Medusa (whose Aegis protected Athena), these "gorgons" (derived from *gorgo*, meaning "terrible" or "spirited") have the mantic power to heal, enchant, or to usher the listener into death. They are, in fact, the guardians to the mouth of the Otherworld, from which temporal reality issues and within which it is, in turn, swallowed up. The open mouth of the Medusa is like the birth grimace, the face of potent utterance, able to curse or bless, birthing reality with Her pronouncements. The "anathema" (which originally meant "sacrificial offering" or "dedication," and which came to mean "curse" or "accursed") is related to "Anath." Athena is cognate with these terms and their meanings — which is why the Gorgo is upon Athena's shield. Her potent grimace or utterance is a protective device, like the fierce expressions of Hindu or Tantric allies and guardian deities.

In the ages that have passed since these archetypes, formerly tutelary spirits, began to be defamed, fear has arisen in relation to their position at the gates of the Otherworld. This is reflected in fairy tales like "The Nixie in the Pond" and "The Water Nixie," in which the nymph (from which we get the modern psychiatric term, "nymphomania") seduces and entraps a helpless male, keeping him hostage in her watery realm. "The Orphic name for the primal Goddess hovering over the dark watery abyss at creation was Nyx: that is, Mother Night. She was what the Bible would later call the Spirit (of God) moving on the face of the Deep, after having changed her. Her daughters may well have been the nixies, whose Germanic mother was named Nott: that is, Mother Night."[214]

> It is a valuable exercise therefore to re-evaluate all the ancient powers of primeval mythology, particularly those associated with the sea and night. For these are the forces of the primal creation, the Ain Soph or Limitless Sea over which Spirit breathed the first eddies of manifest form, transforming it into Ain Soph Aur — the Limitless Light of form expression . . . Of these are included sisterhoods (usually three-fold), such as the Fates, the Graiai and the Gorgons. Many of them have semi-serpent forms; sometimes figures as fish tails like mermaids or mermen, or otherwise like dragons.[215]

The constellation of Pisces describes the shape of the *Vesica Pisis*, or "Fish Vessel," a womb symbol otherwise known as the mandorla, or "almond." This symbol was often depicted between the legs of Sheela-Na-Gig, and the double fish tails of Freyja-Nerthus. Christ, also associated with Pisces, is depicted in Mediaeval iconography ascending into heaven, or descending to earth, through a mandorla. The limitations and constraints of earthly existence are illustrated by the mandorla shape in the World card of the Tarot.

Another fish-tailed Goddess is Delphyne (Hera in Her prophetic aspect[216]), who gave Her name to Her priestess at Delphi, and also to the word "dolphin." "Delphyne" not only signifies "dolphin," but also means "cave" and "womb." The original oracular shrine of Delphi was located within a womb-like cave near a natural well, a typical site of oracle shrines. The Dolphin was a highly magical animal to ancient Aegean and Mediterranean civilisations, perhaps because it was a sea creature who had a womb. Dolphins are associated with the archaic Greek Goddess Posedija, and are depicted in Archaic and Classical Greek iconography as pulling the sea chariot of Greek Poseidon.

The Celtic lunar tree month identified with this archetype is Ash, or Nuin (or Nion). The Ash tree is identified with many sacrificial godforms, including Odin, Poseidon, Attis and Christ. The Runic symbol is Nauthiz, signifying constraints and necessary limitations. The magical meaning of Ash is the confluence of the inner world with the outer. The concepts of sacrifice and redemption are associated with Ash, as well as with the mutable water sign of Pisces. The idea of voluntary stasis, suffering or helplessness as an initiatory ordeal is epitomised by Odin's incarceration upon the sacred Ash, Yggdrasill. The God hung upside-down on the Sacred Ash, a glyph of the Tree of Life, in the cross-legged position of symbolic sacrifice. He suffered thus for nine days and nights until the revelation of the Runes was granted Him by the Norns (who dwelt at the root of Yggdrasill) — nine, of course, being the number of the moon. The Runes, like the messages accessed at Delphi, were oracular and revelatory. The gift of Piscean Melusina is the enlightenment to be found in creative dreams and visionary experience.

Chapter X

The Realm
of the
Fixed Astral Powers

Shattered
into perfect light
Light dancing
through a living web
Webbing from the one
to the many
Many miracles
of divided wisdom
Wisdom flowing
in a blessed unity
Unified reflections
sharing my likeness
Like a sphere of
unmistakable promise
Promises meant
to be shattered
Shattered
into perfect light

The Four Heralds of the Tree

No sooner had my revelation sunk in and I had stopped laughing when I noticed that I, like my hosts in the blue realm, had metamorphosed. I had sprouted a pair of fabulous wings. I flexed the shining feathers experimentally. The wings lifted from my shoulder blades and within moments I was flying.

It seemed the most natural thing in the world that I should now be flying, borne aloft by great shimmering wings, in a realm beyond the normal spectrum of light. It was as if I was adrift in a cloud of brilliant particles, or as if I had been caught up by the aurora borealis. The shifting lights phased in and out of varying frequencies, changing colour and lifting me up, ever higher, like updrafts of pure energy.

The divine music I had once perceived the universe as being was unified with the divinely humorous shapes of thought I had later perceived it to be. Here these two aspects fused into a kind of sacred choreography. The light dipped, swooped, swirled and crested according to a deliciously complex marriage of shape and sound. It was like being within a three dimensional kaleidoscope. The infinitely sweet nature of its graceful motion provided a fourth dimension of sensation beyond the power of words to describe. The closest I can come to defining this quality is to say it was a state of the most profound and lyrical joy. It was ecstasy. It was sheer, untrammelled bliss.

Here, in this flying, swirling motion, I was one with the music and its movement, and it with me. I inhabited it fully, and it dwelled within me. Whereas in the blue realm I had simply known this truth and that had seemed enough, here I *was* that truth. I was now beyond knowing it and was occupied with being it. The secret I learned from experiencing this state is this: the impulse that keeps the entire, vast apparatus of becoming in motion is love. It is like the word Yes; by virtue of a simple, joyous affirmation, the incredible complexity of the created worlds exists.

We exist because we are. At some level, we say "yes" to the whole idea, and the reason we do so is due to this impulse born of love. It is the sacred marriage that issues from the urge that inevitably says, "Yes, I will," for it is the nature of consciousness to do so. Consciousness is energy is love. Molecular love is the attraction between poles, the magnetism of opposites, the universal libido. I saw why Eros is a hermaphroditic god, uniting all polarities in one being, and dancing, like Shiva, the cosmic dance that is the creation of all things.

I saw, as if across a lake of violet flame, a miraculous being approach. It was whirling and dancing in divine movements, with invoking gestures of eyes and hands, feet and legs. Constantly in motion like a spinning top, yet radiating peace and calm as if from a still, deep centre, it suddenly split into four wonderful figures. One was a phoenix, another a winged lion, the third was a winged bull, and the fourth was an angelic human being.

"We are the Heralds of the Tree of Life," said the beings in an exquisite chorus that thrilled me. "We are the pillars of the Universe, the fixed stars, the archetypical foundations that never change but remain the same. Certain principles are eternal and undying, though their combinations are infinite and various. On this you may depend for we, like the Whiteladies, are the ground of creation."

At these words, I noticed that the colour of the light shifted continually from deep violet into purple and burgundy, then back to violet. I realised this was the very same realm as the root of the tree, from a different perspective. They were two poles of the same process. The unity of everything was becoming increasingly clear.

"I confer the tolerance to embrace all truths equally," said the angelic being. "You may gaze on the many visages of truth simultaneously and without prejudice."

"I bring the flexibility to dive to the lowest depths and soar to the greatest heights, without breaking," said the Phoenix. "Time and again you will experience the fall into generation yet not forget the firmament of stars. Though you die you will rise again."

"I grant the power to see your relationship to all things that exist," said the winged lion. "Though sometimes you may feel insignificant, you will always know your part in the co-creation of the world, and that you have power with it."

"I give the strength to see the reflection of your inner being in outer forms," said the winged bull, "for you are a reflection of the Universe and it of you."

With these words the Four Heralds of the Tree fused back into the winged, androgynous being who had danced toward me over the lake of violet flames. The entity stopped whirling and dancing and became very still. The great, prismatic wings folded down and the creature looked into my eyes. He/she was taller than a human and exquisitely beautiful. It seemed this entity was wholly complete, a perfected being.

"I am you," it said, shocking me. "I am your own, eternal Self as you

Journey of the Bard

appear here, between the worlds of cause and effect. I am the image of your own immortal soul."

It seemed the creature came closer, then closer still. It moved yet closer then disappeared. I felt a fiery bliss infuse me, and I realised the entity and I had merged. I was identified with it. I had embraced and become it. I gazed into the surface of the lake of violet flames and saw my own reflection. It revealed the shimmering, iridescent wings, the two genders I hold within me, the agelessness, the great size and stature of my true nature. I looked into my own eyes reflected there and saw the eternities my consciousness spanned.

Then my soul's reflection was gone, and I gazed into a violet flame springing from the heart of a purple flower, like a water lily. Then that too was gone, and I beheld the contours of the Tree reform below and about me. I was on a topmost branch, swaying in the cosmic wind. The space around me was vibrant with violet light which, I could see, turned into threads above. The threads wound around and around in a spiral like a skein of wool, disappearing into a mysterious, opalescent sphere. Like an immense pearl, it floated there, above the crown of the tree. From it emerged fibres of pearly, prismatic light, woven together to form a net or veil. Like a giant, three-dimensional web, it was a luminous fabric flung across the heavens.

In this realm, the Bard meets a metamorph of the kind that has expressed the idea of completion from earliest times, in cultures all over the world. For example, in South America, the Auraucanians are known to have grafted their own ancient concepts of ultimate divinity onto the prayers taught them by missionaries, invoking "Father God, Old Woman who art in heaven . . ." Shamans of the Ngadju Dyak tribe of Borneo are androgynous, arising from the fact that these priestess-shamans "are regarded as the intermediaries between two cosmological planes — earth and sky — and also from the fact that they combine in their own person the feminine element . . . and the masculine element . . . We have here a ritual androgyny, a well-known archaic formula for the divine biunity and the *coincidentia oppositorum* . . . the hermaphroditism of the basir . . . is based on the sacred value of the 'intermediary,' on the need to abolish polarities."[217]

Starhawk describes this dynamic paradox in *The Spiral Dance*:

The Goddess falls in love with Herself, drawing forth her own emanation, which takes on a life of its own. Love of self for self is the creative force of the universe. Desire is the primal energy, and that energy is erotic; the attraction of lover to beloved, of planet to star, the lust of electron for proton. Love is the glue that holds the world together.[218]

In Tantric Buddhism, the same concept is imaged as Samantabhadra and Samantabhadri in sexual union. "In this male/female Tantric aspect they represent the "non-dual perfect Buddhahood of peaceful compassion."[219] Their image corresponds to Hindu representations of Shiva and Shakti in divine union, who represent "Divine Love in its most sacred and benign aspect, the resolution of all dualities."[220] The traditional location within the energetic body, or Chakric system, according to Tantric practice, is "above the Moon of the Head centre," and "indicates the evolutionary archetypal ancestor of the human Spirit, to which we must all ultimately return."[221]

In our culture, the kind of creature the Bard transforms into would probably be called an Angel, but quasi-divine, androgynous, winged beings exist in many mythologies — and the idea of "angels" far predates Judeo-Christian conceptualisations. The Winged Androgyne is a consummately magical figure, prominent in mediaeval esoteric texts, alchemical and Gnostic lore.

Even within Judeo-Christian conceptualisations, the proximity of eroticism and spiritual bliss was acknowledged in former times. "The Jerusalem Temple also connected male and female 'cherubic' spirits within the Holy of Holies, realistically as a priest and priestess who were 'mingled and united,' as Josephus said, and symbolically as two angelic beings guarding the ark. In the third century it was written that the two cherubim demonstrated "the love of male and female."[222]

This is the experience where the spiritual becomes the erotic, and where the erotic is consummately spiritual. The experience of exalted sensuality we call "bliss" occurs here, a result of actualised, inner, ecstatic union. A marriage of opposites occurs within the Self, and transforms reality in as much as our perception of it changes. "From the annals of magic arose the concept of the guardian angel, amalgamated with the personal daemon envisioned by the Greeks as a familiar spirit, or part of one's self."[223] All things are now perceived as relative, reflecting a cosmic unity, made-up of infinite variety and continual change. This is the cosmic dance of Shiva, of molecules in constant motion, and of the Winged Androgyne in our story.

This dancing, androgynous figure can be seen on a card of the major Arkana of the Tarot. In the last image, called the World, there is a naked dancer framed by a living wreath of interwoven branches. At the corners are depicted a lion, an ox, a phoenix or eagle, and a winged human. The figure is dancing in the centre of a mandorla, "reminiscent of the vulva, or lips of the vagina, through which at birth a new being, now complete, emerges into a new world of light and air."[224]

The dancer has the face, hair, and breasts of a woman but her slender hips and sturdy legs suggest that she is an androgynous being who combines and integrates within her body the masculine and feminine elements. The opposites whose development we have been tracing (*through the Major Arkana*) are here combined in one entity. Its neuter sex removes it from the world of the personal into the realm of the transcendental, yet its flesh colour marks it as human. The dancer moves in an area of awareness often described as "Thou art that" and "I am that I am." The flowing scarf suggests the presence of the ever moving spirit. The dancer holds two wands, one in each hand, representing the positive and negative poles of energy. As she moves, these two move in relation to each other in a compensatory way, symbolising the constant and dynamic interplay of all opposites.[225]

The Bard has arrived at a place where, though conscious of constant motion, there is also an awareness of connection with an inner equilibrium. Marie Von Franz describes this state: "The experience of the Self brings a feeling of standing on solid ground inside oneself, on a patch of inner eternity which even physical death cannot touch."[226] This is the sensation of feeling great calm, utter certainty and balance — like the still centre at the eye of a storm — even while one is joyfully participating in that vital, whirling storm. "Here conscious and unconscious are united and instinct and spirit flow together as one being whose awareness embraces and includes both . . . She is contained within that sacred space where reality touches eternity."[227]

Jung described the state of being entailed within this archetype:

Experiencing the self means you are always conscious of your own identity. Then you know you can never be anything other than yourself, that you can never lose yourself and never be alienated from yourself. This is because you know that the Self is indestructible, that it is always one and the same, and cannot be dissolved and exchanged for anything else. The self enables you to remain the same through all conditions of your life.[228]

According to Sallie Nichols, dance symbolises the act of creation. In her book, *Jung and the Tarot, an Archetypal Journey*, Nichols cites the Greek Orthodox principle of *Sophia* ("Wisdom") and Her perpetual dance, as well as Zen imagery surrounding the Cosmic Dance. She points out that physicists posit our world, our bodies and all corporeal bodies, as a dance of particles. "At the microscopic level, all dichotomies — inner and outer, mine and thine, subjective and objective — become meaningless. The dancer in our Tarot is the World."[229] Nichols quotes Yeats in order to drive this point home:

> *O chestnut tree, great-rooted blossomer,*
> *Are you the leaf, the blossom or the bole?*
> *O body swayed to music, O brightening glance*
> *How can we know the dancer from the dance?*[230]

The fact that the dancer is portrayed within the living, organic mandorla,

a leafy *Vesica Pisis*, "creates a sacred temenos within which the dancer is pro-
tectively contained . . . It sets the dancer apart from all that is meaningless
and unessential — from all that does not belong to her. Yet she has space to
move — her own space — within which she is free to express herself effortlessly. In Jungian terms, she might symbolise the self, centre of psychic wholeness . . . The dancer's wreath creates a safe asylum for the newly emerging
self, so that its unity can never be disrupted by invasion from the outside. It
also creates a boundary to contain her energies and protect them from dissi-
pating. This protection is pictured as a natural one, indicating that it occurs
spontaneously at this stage of psychological development. Symbolically this
means that the self is now fully realised as an incorruptible entity. Regression
is no longer possible. For this reason the alchemists call the final stage of
their process *fixation*."[231]

The Winged Androgyne splits into four winged figures: a human, a bull, a
lion and a phoenix. These represent the four fixed signs of the Zodiac —
Aquarius, Taurus, Leo, and Scorpio. As such, they represent the four directions, the four elements, and "the four-walled city." "Like the four points of a
compass, they mark out the new dimensions of this wider world. Although
securely placed, they are alive and the dancer is in constant motion in relation
to them."[232]

> The dancer does not have to worry about being consistent. She has no need
> to recall what she may have said or done yesterday so that she can square
> today's behaviour with yesterday's. As long as she keeps contact with the four
> in the corners, she moves spontaneously in the present, secure in the knowl-
> edge that her reactions of today are in harmony with those of yesterday be-
> cause both have come from her deepest centre. As the Tarot so beautifully
> shows, she is in constant motion in relation to her environment, and her envi-
> ronment (the four figures and the wreath of branches), too, being alive, can
> interact as part of an evolving pattern. Her reaction today will no more be the
> same as it was yesterday than the events which called it forth will be identical
> to those which confront her today.[233]

These creatures have long symbolised the four archetypal powers. Astrology and Astronomy were a combined, magical science in the ancient Near
East. The "Chaldeans," or priestly caste of ancient Babylonia, are credited
with developing the practice of stargazing into an art and a science. An immense body of poetic metaphor evolved from the observation of the heavens
over the centuries. Nearly all terrestrial divinities have their counterparts in
the night sky. Constellations, planetary bodies, and celestial orbs were named
for them, just as earthly phenomena were named for the stars. Many a temple
complex, temenos or shrine has been laid out so as to mirror astral patterns or
constellations. "As above, so below" was an integral part of the ancients' magico-
poetic perceptions of the cosmos. "Long before the advent of subatomic phys-

ics, mystics, poets, artists, and philosophers of many cultures connected intuitively with the *unus mundus* underlying the "ten thousand things" of our everyday experience. That each individual is this world in microcosm has been beautifully expressed in Cabalistic writing."[234]

Through relativistic thinking, peoples as distant in time as our Paleolithic ancestors saw poetic correspondences in all things. This is how they, without telescopes, microscopes or magnifying glasses understood the resonances of certain shapes and dynamics. They somehow understood their relationship to the spiral form, as evidenced by their many renderings of this seminal shape (in rock carvings, cave paintings and pictographs), showing a philosophical sophistication that has only recently been rediscovered, largely as a result of the discoveries of modern physics. It is now, once again, commonly understood that everything affects everything else in the Universe, to some degree, and at some interface of time-space.

There is now a scientific basis for an understanding of "magical" principles, as physicists like Fritjof Capra (*The Tao of Physics*), Michael Talbot (*Mysticism and the New Physics*), and Gary Zukav (*The Dancing Wu Li Masters*) have documented. Erwin Schrödinger, physicist and winner of the Nobel prize for research in his field, said this, concerning the nature of reality:

> . . . inconceivable as it seems to ordinary reason, you — and all other conscious beings as such — are all in all. Hence this life of yours which you are living is not merely a piece of the entire existence, but is in a certain sense the whole; only this whole is not so constituted that it can be surveyed in one single glance. This, as we know, is what the Brahmans express in that sacred, mystic formula which is yet really so simple and so clear: *Tat tvam asi*, this is you. Or, again, in such words as "I am in the east and in the west; I am below and above; I am this whole world."[235]

This is what the Druid Amergin and the Bard Taliesin meant when they intoned the conquering poetic magic of "naming" in the service of their tribes as shamans. Going first onto the land, as the Milesians invaded Ireland by sea, Amergin incanted, "I am the wind that blows upon the sea; I am the ocean wave; I am the murmur of the surges; I am seven battalions; I am a strong bull; I am an eagle on a rock; I am a ray of the sun; I am the most beautiful of herbs; I am a courageous wild boar; I am a salmon in the water; I am a lake upon a plain; I am a cunning artist . . ." In other words, he was *everything*. He was the very land his tribe was claiming, therefore it was already theirs, for he had magically identified it with himself.

The Welsh bard Taliessen sings in the same strain as the druid Amergin his unity with, and therefore his power with, all nature, animate and inanimate . . . "I have been a drop in the air; I have been a shining star; I have been a word in a book; I have been a book in the beginning; I have been a light in a lantern for a year and a half; I have journeyed as an eagle, I have been a boat in the sea . . . I have been a sword in the hand . . . I have been the string of a harp; I have been enchanted for a year in the foam of water. There is nothing in which I have not been." It is strange to find Gael and Briton combining to voice almost in the same words this doctrine of the mystical Celts, who, while still in a state of semi-barbarism, saw, with some of the greatest of ancient and modern philosophers, the One in the Many, and a single Essence in all the manifold forms of life.[236]

Sympathetic magic can no longer be dismissed as the heretical dabblings of superstitious primitives. A grain of sand hangs together due to the same basic principles as does a solar-system, or a galaxy for that matter. Within the human body can be found functions which correspond to those operating the universe. Within the "part" the "whole" is represented, just as the part is represented in the whole. Nothing remains unaffected by anything else. Everything is contingent upon everything else. The results of so-called "controlled" experiments are influenced by the observer and the images and expectations they bring to the event. The speed with which a moving body passes a stationary one will alter the fixed object's shape, volume and mass.

Yet within this continually evolving pattern in incessant dancing motion, there remain certain fixed points of reference — constant and eternal. These are the physical laws themselves, those fixed powers represented by the fixed signs of the zodiac. These form the frame of the loom of creation, upon which space and time weave the fabric of existence. The four fixed astral archetypes symbolise the pillars of the Universe, the corner stones of structural coherence. They assure us that the way the Cosmos works remains the same, even while everything changes. Once we realise this we can relax and simply be. As soon as we accept that we are a part of, and not separate from, this grand choreography, we are able to surrender to our true nature. We can each then be the quintessential "Self" we went to the trouble of being born to be.

> An ageless being, this dancer existed before man [sic] was, and she represents the essence of man, not a goal beckoning from without, but an emanation unfolding from within. In her, spirit is embodied in flesh — flesh spiritualised in such a way that the two interact as one. Her presence is made manifest, not through a death of ego, but through a humanisation of the archetypal Self. The dancer's two wands suggest self-fertilisation — a constant dialogue between all opposites, with ego and self interrelating in dynamic equilibrium.[237]

As the Self, so the collective structure, at least as far as the ancient's were concerned. The cities of early civilisations were often built to correspond to the human spiritual body, or mandala. And so the collective entity of the Neolithic city-state was built with four walls, like the boundaries of Self, an heraldic gate in each one. Often these gates were watched over by the immense figures of the guardians of the sanctity of the city/self, called *Kerubhim* by ancient Hebrews. These figures are the ancestors of (but quite different from) the later *Cherubim*. They were venerated by Babylonians as totemic animal deities combining eagle wings, lion feet, bull heads, and human heads, "animal symbols of the four seasons, cardinal directions, and elements." Barbara Walker speculates that these archetypes "probably descended from Sheban *mu-karribim*, 'close-kindred,' guardians of the shrine of the Moon-Goddess at Marib."[238]

The Four Heralds of the Tree correspond to these ancient guardians. Their current forms are extremely ancient, dating back more than 4000 years to the Sumerians' identification of the constellations of Leo, Scorpio, Aquarius, and Taurus with the four totemic beasts. They have been appropriated by Judeo-Christian ideology to inform the biblical images of "The Four Beasts of the Apocalypse," "The Four Prophets," and "The Four Evangelists," among other archetypes. But they also show up in the visionary works of heretical mystics, alchemists and poets throughout the Age of Christianity, fulfilling their original function of empowering creation and the Self. The time-frames of the four fixed signs take place where we find the major Pagan fire-holidays, still celebrated world-wide as various "Festivals of Lights." These festivals, known for example as Imbolc, Beltaine, Lammas, and Samhain, marked occasions when the rising and setting of the Pleiades were observed, providing a time-clock for the growing and harvest cycle.

The winged human represents Aquarius, spanning the time-frame of the Celtic lunar month of Willow, or Saille. Willow is a lunar tree, closely identified with tides, flood plains, water flow, breast milk, birthing and with women's menstrual cycles. It is a tree sacred to midwifes. The water-bearer is the more familiar zodiacal image for this time-frame (roughly February). The zodiacal glyph for Aquarius is the sign for waves. In the microcosm of the human body, Aquarius mystically corresponds to the circulatory system. The Pagan festival marked in Willow moon is Imbolc, with initiatory significance of midwifery and fostering.

The Babylonians called the month they associated with Aquarius *Shabatu*, meaning "the Curse of the Rain"; the Akkadians called the sign *Ku-ur-ku*, meaning "the Seat of the Flowing Waters." The Rune associated with this time frame is Sowelu, signifying female light of sun or moon. The water which the water bearer pours from the urn is the water of consciousness. "It is the power of the intuitive mind which is embodied by Aquarius . . . Aquarius is perfected by this understanding of the oneness of mankind [*sic*] . . . The water is alive and pregnant with ideas which can be useful to humanity . . ."[239]

> Aquarius occupies the primary position in a region of the heavens known in Euphratean astronomy as the "Sea." This name is derived from the abundance of constellations in this celestial neighbourhood which are associated with water. If we proceed in an easterly direction from the Sea-Goat, we will

come upon the Water-Bearer, followed by Pisces the Fish. Northwest of Aquarius is Delphinus the Dolphin. Due south of Aquarius lies the Southern Fish, or Pisces Australis and on the southeast, below Pisces, swims Cetus the Whale. In addition, the starry river Eridnus winds its way past Cetus and empties itself into the huge constellation of Orion.[240]

The second Herald to speak is the phoenix, representing the fixed water sign of Scorpio. Like the phoenix, Scorpio embodies the ability to dive, crash and burn, then rise again from the ashes, resurrected and renewed. Traditionally, Scorpio has two animal forms: the scorpion and the eagle, signifying both the subterranean and ascended natures of Scorpio. Scorpion expresses the chthonic aspect of Scorpio, while the phoenix or eagle expresses the Scorpionic spirit which soars aloft. Another animal which has symbolised Scorpio historically is the serpent, which embodied this quality of transfiguration and renewal in that it sheds its skin.

Just as the snake sheds it skin so that a larger body may emerge, human beings shed the layers of their consciousness so that a larger (and finer) Self may be born. "Individuals who are in a conscious state of growth can look back upon the snake skins of personality they have already shed over the years. They can see that the person they were is no longer alive and that a new being stands in their place. All the cells in the physical body are completely renewed each seven years. If the consciousness of the person also renews itself by intercourse with the generating flow of Spirit, they can see themselves reincarnated in their own lifetime."[241]

The Akkadians called Scorpio Girtab, meaning the Stinger. To dwellers on the Euphrates, it was the symbol of darkness, for it brought with it the waning strength of the sun after the autumnal equinox. The ancient Egyptians, Hebrews, Arabs, Persians, Turks, Hindus, and Chinese all had a scorpion or snake figure in their zodiacs.[242]

Scorpius is one of the larger constellations, composed of notably large and bright stars. Its magnificent body and long, arched tail are almost lost in the multitude of stars of the Milky Way. The time-frame of Scorpio spans the first month of the Celtic lunar tree calendar: Birch, or Beith. Beith has the same significance of mystical death and rebirth, transfiguration and resurrection. "The practice of 'Birching,' or ceremoniously flogging with a Birch switch was used in Britain, and all across Europe and central Asia, to drive out regressive or decadent influences. This custom was followed in The Isle of Man well into this century, applied to criminals. Initiatory practices of the Siberian shamans include 'purification,' or ritual scourging with Birch rods. The Altaic shamans, too, would be cleansed by leaping through a Birch hoop, and were required to demonstrate the ability to climb the World Tree in the form of a Birch Pole."[243]

Asiatic shamans of Altai, Magyar, and Tartar tribes (as well as others) employed a Birch hoop to transform or "shape-shift" into and out of animal bodies. This explains the incidence in eastern European folk-tales of magical characters (or reconstituted shamans) causing wolves to pass through Birch hoops, that they have the ability to "turn back into men." The ability of Birch to "resurrect" the soul is reflected in these elements of folk and fairy tales.[244]

The rune for Birch is Berkano. "Berkano" means "Birch," and also gestation, nourishment, renewal — the seed in the earth awaiting the Spring. Anciently, Birch moon began at the Samhain Festival, marked by the first, last quarter moon after the Fall Equinox. A Celto/Romano calendrical compromise fixed its beginning date where we now find the first of November. In the human microcosm, Scorpio is said to rule the genitals. Scorpio and the Samhain Festival of death and rebirth (a shamanic underworld descent at the advent of winter) are directly across the year wheel from Beltaine's erotic festival of emergent sexuality, Springtime and new green life in the Celtic lunar month of Oak, in the fixed sign of Taurus. Mithraic mysteries portrayed this as the Sacred Bull, or Taurus, sacrificed by Mithras, in the Mithraic Rite, with a scorpion clasping the bull's genitals. Depicted thus, this set of symbols was a calendrical tableau. Esoteric Scorpio functions are as "the custodian of the inner temple which contains the secrets of creation."[245]

The Bard is next addressed by the Winged Lion. This Herald represents the fixed sign of Leo, which roughly spans the time-frame of the Celtic lunar month of Vine, or Muin, where we now find late July and the first two-thirds of August. The Celtic festival of Lammas occurs in Vine month, with its celebration of the early harvest, and early wine. Social well-being and celebration earmark this festival, with all good things of the earth being feted in abundance. The beneficent aspects of solar energy are prominent in the consciousness of Lammas revellers, in the life energy of green and growing things, in golden grain, and fermented beverages. This suits Leo's love of pomp and luxury, social organisation, pageantry and good times.

> The boldness inherent in the nature of people born under the sign of the Lion is not lost by its position in the heavens. Leo is a very bright and easily identifiable constellation. It lies between Cancer on the West and Virgo on the East and is best seen, in the Northern Hemisphere, in late winter and in early spring. The most recognizeable feature of the Lion is his mane, which looks like a huge inverted question mark or a giant sickle. The point of the question mark (the handle of the sickle) is Regulus, "il petto del lione ardente" of Dante's Paradiso, the heart of the lion. Regulus, meaning "little king," is actually a triple star (three suns appearing to the naked eye as one). Its colours are white and ultramarine.[246]

Astrologer Alan Oken says of this sign, "Leo can call forth the courageous and masterly Lord of the Jungle, or the cowardly pussycat who, like the lion in

The Wizard of Oz, needs a heart to animate him with the force of life . . . It is the heart, the central pulse of one's being, which is the part of the body ruled by the fifth sign."[247]

Leo is a solar sign, the planetary body associated with it is the sun, and it endows the ability to realise the collective Will. Central to any group, the collective will is the heart of any social organisation — families, tribes, clans, and city states. For thousands of years prior to the current aeon, this central-ising, solar power was identified with Goddesses —Arinna, Kybele, Amaterasu, Amma, Ana, Aine, Allalu, Lucina, Saule, Hathor, Bastet, Sekmet, the Gorgo (with her swastika, or sun-wheel, posture), and many others.[248] She was the genius of the Neolithic settlement — and, with Her sister the Moon, the in-spiration behind the birth of agriculture. Civilisation sprang up under the aegis of the Great Goddesses, who encompassed earth, sea and sky in their dominion, animating the interrelationships of moon, stars, solar orb, plan-etary bodies, and the Earth as matrix, or "mother." The woman was likely "keeper of the hearth" in Paleolithic society, as she certainly was later, in the Neolithic. As such, she was the guardian of the "Eternal Flame." The rites of the Vestas probably originated with this duty of priestesses as representatives of the solar goddess as the hearth, or "heart" of the family unit and clan-struc-ture.

Folk customs around the "Yule Log," at the Winter's Solstice, or the "Sun Wheel" at the summer solstice, still mark the traditions of the Eternal Flame. New family units lit their hearth from a coal from the bride's mother's hearth, and the first fire in the grate after the New Year had to be lit from a coal from the fire of the old year. In this manner, the sense of continuity of matrilineal generation was passed down among the keepers of the hearth, well into this century in most parts of Europe. These customs reflect the former belief in the collective well-being as a matricist concern, and the principle value of early, communally-structured civilisations.

The Rune associated with Vine moon is Mannaz, the Rune of humanity. It signifies relationship to one another, the Sacred Marriage consummated, the fruit of the union or Divine Child, androgyny, partnership and community.

Finally, the Winged Bull addresses the Bard. The bull represents the fixed earth sign of Taurus, and has done so since earliest times. The names of the Taurus Mountains, the Minotaur, and Tauropolis reflect the lineage of the veneration of the bull as a creature sacred to the Goddess. Osiris was "the Bull of Heaven," Tammuz was Innana's "Moon Bull," and the word "Minotaur" simply means "Moon Bull." The curved horns of the bull's head have long identified him with the lunar crescent in the poetic imagination of Bards, priest-esses, artists and shamans. The bull and cow have each represented both the moon and the sun over the millennia, as in Mithras' solar bull, and Hathor as solar Cow-Goddess. Bulls' heads, along with women's breasts, adorned the interiors of subterranean temples in Old Europe, and were a staple of Minoan

Journey of the Bard

decoration of sacred vessels and architecture. Marija Gimbutas documented the uncanny similarity of the bull's head and horns with the shape of the uterus, fallopian tubes and ovaries viewed from the front. This would have had profound magical significance, poetic resonances and visual metaphor constituting a powerful, magical, mantic device.

The time-frame of Taurus roughly coincides with the Celtic lunar month of Oak, or Duir. Duir is thought to derive from proto-Indo-European *duir*, which means "door." The esoteric attribute of Oak moon is that it represents a door, or portal, into the deepest, most magical recesses of Self. Also called "the Hinge of the Year," it stands at the midway point of the Celtic year, which begins at Samhain with Birch moon. Positioned directly across the wheel from Birch, Oak month encompasses the Festival of Beltaine.

While Samhain and the month of Birch begins the "dark half" of the Pagan year, Beltaine begins the "light half," as the gateway to summer. The "Oak King" is a Pagan solar figure who rules the summer, figured by ancient Celts to encompass the half-year from Beltaine to Samhain. The "Holly King" is like him in as much as they are both Light Gods, but different insomuch as Holly displays his light energy in the winter. He remains evergreen, sporting bright red berries, while his deciduous brother is leafless and bare. Their relationship is personified in the dynamic of Arthur (a solar God) and Lancelot (an Underworld Light God related to Lugh, Llew, Lucifer and Lohengrin) in their mutual love of, and conflict over, Guinevere (the Earth, and Sovereignty — related to Blodeuwedd, Llew's inconstant bride "made from flowers"). The Celtic lunar month of Holly follows directly upon the heels of Oak moon, corresponding to the Swan Knights and Swan Maidens of folklore, as well as the Dioscuri (the Divine Twins, Castor and Pollux, or Light and Dark, born from Leda's swan egg) and the sign of Gemini.

Even though the Bull has only his frontal segments, the constellation of Taurus is very rich in its stellar components. Taurus is ruled by the planet Venus . . . and this influence is apt indeed! Manilus calls Taurus "dives puellis" — "rich in maidens," for contained within its demibody are the Pleiades or Seven Sisters and the Hyades, the seven mythological daughters of Atlas and Aithra and half sisters of the Pleiades. The hyades form the great V of the Bull's face, the most noticeable feature of the V being the large reddish star Aldebaran. The latter is clearly visible to the naked eye, for it is three times brighter than Polaris, the North Star. It is often called the "Eye of the Bull."[249]

The Oak, as well as Taurus, signifies strength and endurance, as well as lineage and ancestry. The Festival of Beltaine commemorates the Celtic God, Beli or Bile, who is said to have landed on Irish shores on Beltaine. "Beltaine" means "Fires of Beli" or "Light of Beli." Belfires were lit in His honour at this festival, and at Summer's Solstice (or "Litha") when the tribe of Beli, the Tuatha dé Danaan or "People of Danu," were said to have completed their conquest and claimed sovereignty in their new land. Danu was Beli's divine wife, and they were symbolised in sacred union as the Oak tree of generation. In this configuration, they resemble the Phoenician (Canaanite) divine couple, Baal and Ashera, both individually and in union represented by the Tree of Life, and symbolised by a stylised pole or "tree" upon their altars. The Maypole is actually an image of the Tree of Life, with the spiralling ribbons symbolising the spiral flow of energy along the spine.

Danu and Beli were ancestral deities, endowing genetic continuity, tribal survival, protection, and ancient (genetic or ancestral) memory. Though once associated with the Willow tree and the moon, Beli (or Goidelic Bile: "sacred tree") and Danu later became associated with the Oak tree and the sun. Their most ancient ancestor was probably related to Belili, "the Sumerian White Goddess, Ishtar's predecessor, who was a goddess of trees as well as a Moon-goddess, Love-goddess, and Underworld-goddess."[250] The word "Druid" is thought to be related to *duir* and there is a strong connection between Druid and Oak: the words are related (for example, *drus* is the ancient Greek word for Oak) and the Oak is the tree most sacred to Druids.

The Rune for Oak is Dagaz, bringing breakthroughs, the interface of realities, the empowering flow between the inner and outer realities, paradox, emergence of new generation, and magical doorways. Oak moon and Taurus both signify deep roots, stability, structural integrity and firm foundations.

Part IV

Gwynedd:
The Way Back

Chapter XI

The Realm
Beyond
the Stars

A living crown
of highest branches
Branches bent to hold
a magnificent jewel
Jewelled within the art
of nature's weave
Woven like branches
crossing a winter moon
Moonbright workings
of the triple fates
Fated to give
the souls of the living
A living crown
of highest branches

THE THREE FATES AND THEIR SILVER WHEEL

My curiosity again spurred me to lift the wings I possessed in this realm of the Tree and to fly beyond it. I wanted to see what lay within the softly glowing pearl above. As my flight brought me closer to the sphere, I saw that it was densely woven of the energy drawn up on fibres from the crown of the tree. All the colours of light were spun tightly together to form a white iridescence like a luminous ball of wool. Its sheen was like mother of pearl or milky opal. As I entered the sphere a tingling caused by the densely packed energy ran through me. Finally I broke through the veils of energy into a little chamber.

The hall was white as if made of the moon, with pearly floors, walls and ceiling. In it were three shining women. I recognised the Whiteladies as they had appeared in their first manifestation of Maid, Matron, and Crone.

One sat at an ancient spinning wheel, taking the violet strands of prismatic energy from below, and spinning them into threads. The second woman wove these into a marvellous, multi-dimensional fabric, which tumbled off Her loom and flowed out into the Universe like a sparkling, prismatic veil. The third woman sat with a pair of scissors, trimming loose ends here and there.

The strands of energy shone with an ultraviolet aura when they came to the spinner's hands, but the threads that emerged from them shone scarlet. In the emerging threads could be seen all manner of forming realities, from tiny human lives to the births of aeons. The loom wove the threads into a fabric that shone with all the colours of the rainbow, though it appeared silver in its sum effect, just as a spider's web does. The busy trio looked up at me when I approached, without disturbing the flow of their work.

"My word, but you've travelled far since we met you in Falias, Bard, and now you've caught us at it. There's nothing to be done but give you a prize, I suppose," said the eldest of the three.

"We'll have to bestow a treasure, it appears," said the matronly one at the loom. "Travellers who discover us always want a treasure."

"We don't have time for treasures," said the youngest, never stopping Her spinning for a moment. "Besides, who can be in need of treasure when all the world's an oyster filled with pearls?"

"Quite so," said I, for I didn't want to be a nuisance. "I've no need of treasure, nor of prizes. Just — could you answer me one question? Where am I?"

"That's a good question though you'll get no answer," said the Crone. "You're in a place that's not a place, and a time that's not a time. We are the Creatrix you see. We create time and space. We spin, weave, and cut it, so we're outside it. It's probably best to forget you ever saw us thus employed. No one will ever believe you anyway, even if you do write a story about it. Best keep it to yourself, we think. Try not to dwell on it. Surely you can't want to know everything . . ."

"Tell you what," said the youngest, apparently feeling sorry for my less than glorious reception where, surely, very few had ever ventured, "go back down the tree like a good Bard, to the garden of Gwynedd where you belong. On your way, pick up a present from each of the three realms of Ceugant. Tell them we sent you. Now, off you go."

Somehow these instructions failed to live up to my rather exalted notion of my progress. After all, I now had wings and was seven feet tall. I would have thought they'd be more impressed. Nevertheless, being directed back to Gwynedd was secretly reassuring. It meant I wasn't dead. I could return to my humble but rather interesting life as a Bard forthwith.

"Yes. Well, thanks . . ." I said, uncertainly. It looked as though they'd already forgotten me. Just as I was about to fly away through the massing energy of their spherical chamber the matron called out, "Well met, Bard. Give our regards to any who might enjoy a good yarn."

I could still hear them cackling at their little joke as I alighted on an upper branch of the Tree. The Four Heralds were there and placed a crown of silver and gold, studded with amethysts, upon my head. The Angel said, "This belongs to you. It is the crown of your true nature."

I thanked them and flew on in descending spirals through the branches of the tree. The light turned blue, and soon I saw the Four Fabulous Beasts. The centaur placed a blue jewel, a star sapphire, upon my brow, saying, "This is the jewel of your true knowledge. Wear it in wisdom."

My wings disappeared as I took my leave of the Fabulous Beasts, and I was wondering how to descend further when the spiral stair reappeared, glimmering through the branches. I started climbing down, around and around, until I emerged in the lower branches. The Four Birds of Enchantment greeted me, giving me a platinum torque for my throat. Set in the ends were two, large, faceted aquamarines. The fine metal seemed to hum, like a multi-octave chime. The Raven addressed me, saying, "This is yours. It is the sound of your own soul's expression."

I thanked them and continued down the silver stair, into the trunk of the mighty tree. The music of the spheres faded as I descended. I had the sensation of falling into a familiar sense of myself, one I'd come to value highly. I felt the familiar medium of air, comfortable and warm. The world rushed up to meet me as I descended, almost cosy in its embrace. I had the idea it had missed me, though that seemed a fanciful notion — even after all my strange adventures.

At last, I stood in the Emerald Hall. The Emissaries were there, in their alcoves. I knew that I could call on their aid again, whenever I had need of it. The regions of the Tree were familiar to me now. There was no realm in which I may not travel, in any of the three worlds, forever more.

As I left the Glass Castle, I felt the sun on my face and knew I had returned to the world I knew. Though it was no longer one to which I was confined by my limited perception of it, it was still the one I loved best, the one from which all others are gained. I went to the well in the garden and raised the bucket, taking a long drink from the dipper. When I returned the bucket to the depths and raised my head, the Glass Castle, the Tree, the well and the walled garden were gone.

I was back in the grove, where birds sang, squirrels ran in the trees, and small creatures rustled in the brush. The air was soft and mild, and a light breeze stirred the leaves. The drone of bees was a pleasant sound, amid the scents of many flowers. All was as I remembered it.

I couldn't tell if I'd been gone in the realms of the Tree for a year or a day, or even if it had merely been five minutes. I realised it would take a while for my perception of time to become reoriented. My experience, so recent, so fresh, was already turning into a lyric, a tale to tell at the very next opportunity.

I was eager for this opportunity, and for my life. It was the same old life I'd always had, yet was utterly new. I perceived it differently. I would never look on it the same way again.

Conclusion

Conclusion

In conclusion, there is not much to say. The Bard, inside you, in the stories our culture tells itself, in the collective zeitgeist, will tell the tales, keeping us all entranced and manifesting the dream we call reality. The only thing to know and to hold close is the realisation of how powerfully we contribute to, and partake of, this imagistic feast — and how directly this communion affects the lyrical expression we call the World.

At a certain level we are, ourselves, the creatrix portrayed by the three weavers at their loom. In closing, I can do no better than to quote a Bard of high repute:

> We may conclude our examination of these ancient Goddess forms by reference to the Morai, or Fates. They have a particular relevance to the dynamics of the magic circle of birth and death. Their number varied from two to four; although they are more generally recognised as a trinity. When only two are considered, as at Delphi, they are regarded respectively as the guardians of birth and death.
>
> In their triune form Klotho is the spinner of the thread of life; Lachesis measures the length that the thread is to be; and Atropos cuts it with her shears, bringing about physical death. They lived in a cave, in the inner worlds, from whence white water gushes — in one sense the waters of life, in another sense (and closely associated with it in its inner dynamics) moonlight.
>
> They can also be regarded as aspects of a simple primeval goddess, sitting at the centre of the circle, spinning the web of life in the worlds of form.[251]

— Gareth Knight

Notes

Introduction

1. Matthews (1987), 15.
2. Forrest (1992), 56.
3. Larsen (1976), 233.
4. Ibid., 11.
5. Eliade (1967), 173.
6. Ibid., 270.
7. Squire (1975), 31.
8. Green (1992), 211.
9. Campbell (1964), 262-68.
10. Squire (1975), 32.
11. Campbell (1981), 3-29.
12. Squire (1975), 32-34.
13. As an example of the acceptability of cultural genocide as a policy against indigenous peoples, in 1825, during the Irish potato famine, British dailies exulted that finding a Celt left alive in all of Ireland would soon be as rare an event as meeting a Native American on the streets of Manhattan.
14. An interesting example of this is the remnant of the culture of pre-patriarchal "Aryan" tribes still living in remote and isolated areas of the Himalayas. Here, ethnic "Aryans" and their primary societies have survived. It is as if groups who stayed at home, within the eternally renewed cycles of pasturing and agriculture, remained static in their beliefs. Unlike the great majority of their relatives, descent and inheritance is still traced through the female line. The differences between their culture and ours reveals much concerning the derivative social structure of the early Celts.
15. Mabbot and Rufus (1995), 2.
16. Green (1992), 22.
17. Squire (1975), 71.
18. Eliade (1967), 174.
19. Ibid., 127.
20. Huxley (1974), 257.
21. Starhawk (1982), 29.

Chapter I

22. Campbell (1981), 6.
23. Matthews (1987), 86.
24. Eliade (1967), 92.
25. Ibid., 98.
26. Matthews (1987), 131.

27. Ibid., 16.
28. Ibid., 18.
29. Ibid., 143.
30. Campbell (1981), 15.
31. Purce (1974), 29-30.
32. Ibid., 17.
33. Rees and Rees (1961), 187.

Chapter II

34. Matthews (1987), 110.
35. Ibid., 86.
36. Loomis (1977), 64.
37. Squire (1975), 304.
38. Matthews (1987), 14.
39. Ibid., 109.
40. Eliade (1967), 488-90.
41. Huxley (1974), 258.
42. Campbell (1981), 12.
43. Graves (1948), 397.

Chapter III

44. Eliade (1967), 412.
45. Ibid., 335.
46. Rees and Rees (1961), 193.
47. Ibid.
48. Eliade (1967), 476.
49. Ibid.
50. Eliade (1967), 484.
51. Ibid.
52. Walker (1983), 701.
53. Rees and Rees (1961), 187.
54. Skelton and Blackwood (1990), 18.
55. Ibid., 20.
56. Ibid., 22.

Chapter IV

57. Graves (1948), 65-66.
58. Rees and Rees (1961), 314-25.
59. Ibid., 343.
60. Ibid., 345.
61. Eliade (1967), 66, 159.
62. Squire (1975), 317.
63. Matthews (1987), 107.

64. Ibid., 366.
65. Eliade (1967), 41-42.
66. Patterson (1985), 197.
67. Matthews (1987), 48-49.
68. Matthews (1989), 250-251.
69. Rees and Rees (1961), 161.
70. Matthews (1992), 124.
71. Campbell (1988), 117-21.
72. Matthews (1987), 164.

Chapter V

73. Gimbutas (1989), 51-61.
74. Graves (1948), 314.
75. Ibid., 315.
76. Walker (1983), 111.
77. As reconstructed by Graves (1948), 42.
78. Matthews and Matthews (1988), 132.
79. Gimbutas (1989), 198-204.
80. See, for example, Degh (1965), 57-77.
81. Ibid., 76.
82. Eliade (1967), 477.
83. Ibid., 269.
84. Degh (1965), 70-71.
85. Graves (1948), 98.
86. Ibid., 439.
87. Ibid., 366.
88. Douglas and Slinger (1979), 171.
89. Graves (1948), 320.
90. Ibid., 229-30.
91. Matthews (1987), 143-44.
92. Graves (1948), 68.
93. Squire (1975), 61.
94. Ibid., 96.
95. Ibid., 136.
96. Ibid., 308-09.
97. Ibid., 326.
98. Matthews (1987), 172.
99. Ibid., 173.
100. Ibid., 147.
101. Ibid., 41-42.
102. Douglas and Slinger (1979), 131.
103. See, for example, Degh (1965), 280-82.
104. Ibid., 280.
105. Manning-Sanders (1972), 112.
106. Zipes (1992), 67.
107. Koch (1955), 6.

Chapter VI

108. Purce (1974), 11.
109. Ibid.
110. Ibid., 13.
111. Ibid., 11-12.
112. Ibid., 25.
113. Forrest (1992), 300.
114. Purce (1974), 25.
115. Matthews (1987), 164.
116. Matthews (1989), 4.
117. Ibid., 5.
118. Ibid., 25.
119. Chopra (1996), 83.
120. Campbell (1988), 210.
121. Ibid., 174.
122. Matthews (1989), 30.
123. Ibid., 216.
124. Kozocari, Owens, and North (1994), 175.
125. Chopra (1996), 83.
126. Kozocari, Owens, and North (1994), 6-7.
127. Knight (1985), 172.
128. Purce (1974), 67.
129. Ibid., 16.
130. Walker (1983), 967.
131. Ibid., 35.
132. Ibid., 36.
133. Ibid.
134. Ibid., 18-19.
135. Ibid.
136. Ibid., 18.
137. Purce (1974), 31.
138. Ibid.
139. Ibid., 17.
140. Koch (1955), 2.
141. Ibid., 19.
142. Ibid.
143. Ibid., 21.
144. Matthews (1987), 155.
145. Walker (1988), 31.
146. Patterson (1985), 192.

Chapter VII

147. Eliade (1967), 51.
148. Ibid., 76.
149. Ibid., 58.

150. Ibid., 89.
151. Ibid., 410.
152. Ibid., 478-79. The Witchcraft trials of fourteenth to seventeenth century Europe recorded many confessions of such mystical flights; for a recent analysis of these, see Ginzburg (1991).
153. Ibid., 407.
154. Ibid., 132.
155. Ibid., 133.
156. Ibid., 135.
157. Ibid., 138-39.
158. Ford (1977), 58.
159. Ibid., 71.
160. Brown (1959), 213-15.
161. Eliade (1967), 487-88.
162. Ibid., 488-89.
163. Ibid., 488.
164. Ibid., 490.
165. Starhawk (1979), 26.
166. Hozeski (1986), 89.
167. Eliade (1967), 173-74.
168. Ibid., 408.
169. Ibid., 174.
170. Starhawk (1979), 26.
171. Trapp (1973), 106-07.

Chapter VIII

172. Oken (1988), 40-41.
173. Purce (1974), 118.
174. Sykes (1993), 151.
175. Owens and Skelton (1996), 9.
176. Degh (1965), 285.
177. Eliade (1967), 177-80.
178. Ibid., 38.
179. Ibid., 402-03.
180. Ibid., 193.
181. Ibid., 196.
182. Ibid., 242.
183. Gimbutas (1989), 3-4.
184. Gimbutas (1974), 122, 135, 144.
185. Thompson, (1981), 112-13.
186. Manning-Sanders (1972), 7, 101, 146.
187. Eliade (1967), 448-49.
188. Zipes (1992), 562, 722, 725.
189. Crossley-Holland (1987), 42, 164.
190. Graves (1948), 227.
191. Ibid., 234.

192. Murray and Murray (1988), 18.
193. Graves (1948), 233.
194. Matthews and Matthews (1988), 53.
195. Ibid., 52-53.
196. Kozocari, Owens, and North (1994), 44-58.
197. Matthews and Matthews (1988), 140.
198. Ibid.
199. Ibid., 92.
200. Walker (1983), 411-12.
201. Hinckley (1963), 108.
202. Ibid., 84.
203. North (1987), 7.

Chapter IX

204. Kozocari, Owens and North (1994), 116-23.
205. Walker (1983), 963.
206. Matthews and Matthews (1988), 150.
207. Walker (1983), 963.
208. Ibid., 541.
209. For a magical application of this aspect of Centaurus, see Knight (1985), 70.
210. A traditional Wiccan invocation of sacred space   within a magic circle.
211. Walker (1983), 628.
212. Ibid., 1045.
213. Knight (1985), 65.
214. Walker (1988), 266.
215. Knight 1985), 57.
216. Graves (1955), 80.

Chapter X

217. Eliade (1967), 329.
218. Starhawk (1979), 25.
219. Douglas and Slinger (1979), 65.
220. Ibid.
221. Ibid.
222. Walker (1988), 234.
223. Ibid.
224. Nichols (1988), 351.
225. Ibid., 349.
226. von Franz (1967), 74.
227. Ibid., 350.
228. Jung (1969), 72.
229. Nichols (1980), 351.
230. "Among School Children," by Yeats (1967), 214.
231. Nichols (1980), 350.
232. Ibid., 353.

233. Ibid., 354.
234. Ibid., 362.
235. Schrödinger (1964), 21-22.
236. Squire (1975), 123-124.
237. Ibid., 356.
238. Walker (1983), 164.
239. Oken (1988), 150.
240. Ibid., 149.
241. Ibid., 120.
242. Ibid., 121.
243. Kozocari, Owens, and North (1994), 17.
244. Ibid., 19.
245. Oken (1988), 121.
246. Ibid., 92.
247. Ibid., 93.
248. Monaghan (1994), 191-244.
249. Oken (1988), 65.
250. Graves (1948), 58.

Conclusion

251. Knight (1985), 67.

Bibliography

Brown, Norman. 1959. *Life Against Death*. Middleton: Wesleyan University Press.

Campbell, Joseph. 1964. *Occidental Mythology*. New York: Viking Penguin.

——. 1981. "Peripheries of the Indo-European World," in *The Celtic Consciousness*. Edited by Robert O'Driscoll. New York: George Braziller.

Campbell, Joseph (with Bill Moyes). 1988. *The Power of Myth*. New York: Doubleday.

Chopra, Deepak. 1996. *The Way of the Wizard*. Chicago: Harmony Books.

Crossley-Holland, Kevin. 1987. *Northern Lights — Legends, Sagas, and Folk-tales*. London: Faber and Faber.

Degh, Linda. 1965. *Folktales of Hungary*. Chicago: University of Chicago Press.

Douglas, Nick and Penny Slinger. 1979. *The Secret Dakini Oracle*. New York: Destiny Books.

Eliade, Mircea. 1964. *Shamanism: Archaic Techniques of Ecstasy*. Boston: Princeton University Press.

Ford, Patrick. 1977. *The Mabinogion — And Other Medieval Welsh Tales*. Berkeley: University of California Press.

Forrest, Jodie. 1992. *The Rhymer and the Ravens*. Chapel Hill: Seven Paws Press.

Gimbutas, Marija. 1974. *The Goddesses and Gods of Old Europe: 7000-3500 B.C.* Berkeley: University of California Press.

——. 1989. *The Language of the Goddess*. San Francisco: Harper & Row.

Ginzburg, Carlo. 1991. *Ecstasies: Deciphering the Witches' Sabbat*. Translated by Raymond Rosenthal. Harmondsworth: Penguin Books.

Graves, Robert. 1948. *The White Goddess*. New York: Noonday Press.

——. 1955. *The Greek Myths: Volume I*. Harmondsworth: Penguin Books.

Green, Miranda. 1992. *Dictionary of Celtic Myth and Legend*. London: Thames & Hudson.

Hinckley, Richard. 1963. *Star-Names, Their Lore and Meaning*. New York: Dover Publications.

Hozeski, B. 1986. *Hildegard of Bingen's "Scivias."* Santa Fe: Bear & Company.

Huxley, Francis. 1974. *The Way of the Sacred*. London: Aldosbook.

Jung, C. G. 1969. *The Interpretation of Visions*. Dallas: Spring Publications.

Knight, Gareth. 1985. *The Rose Cross and the Goddess*. New York: Destiny Books.

Koch, Rudolph. 1955. *The Book of Signs*. New York: Dover Publications.

Kozocari, Jean, Yvonne Owens, and Jessica North. 1994. *The Witch's Book of Days*. Victoria: Beach Holme.

Larsen, Steven. 1976. *The Shaman's Doorway*. New York: Harper & Row.

Loomis, R. S. 1977. *Wales and the Arthurian Legend*. London: Folcroft Library.

Mabbot, J. and J. Rufus. 1995. *The Celtic Wheel of the Year*. County Tepperary: The Plug-In Office.

Manning-Sanders, Ruth. 1972. *The Three Witch Maidens*. London: Methuen.

Matthews, Caitlin. 1987. *Mabon and the Mysteries of Britain*. London: Arkana.

———. 1989. *Arthur and the Sovereignty of Britain*. London: Arkana.

———. 1992. *Ladies of the Lake*. London: Aquarian Press.

Matthews, John. 1990. *Gawain: Knight of the Goddess*. London: Aquarian Press.

Matthews, John and Caitlin Matthews. 1988. *The Aquarian Guide to British and Irish Mythology*. London: Aquarian Press.

Monaghan, Patricia. 1994. *O Mother Sun: A New View of the Cosmic Feminine*. Freedom: Crossing Press.

Murray, Liz and Colin Murray. 1988. *The Celtic Tree Oracle*. New York: St. Martin's Press.

Nichols, Sallie. 1980. *Jung and the Tarot: An Archetypal Journey*. York Beach: Samuel Weiser.

North, Jessica. 1987. *Runemal: The Ritual of Runeplay*. Victoria: Moonshadow.

Oken, Alan. 1988. *Alan Oken's Compete Astrology*. London: Bantam.

Owens, Yvonne and Alison Skelton. 1996. *The Festival of Oestre: The Wheel of the Witches, Series 2*. Victoria: Reference West.

Patterson, Nancy Lou. 1985. *Apple Staff and Silver Crown*. Toronto: Porcupine's Quill.

Purce, Jill. 1974. *The Mystic Spiral: Journey of the Soul*. London: Thames & Hudson.

Rees, Alwynn and Brinley Rees. 1961. *Celtic Heritage: Ancient Tradition in Ireland and Wales*. London: Thames & Hudson.

Schrödinger, Erwin. 1964. *My View of the World*. New York: Cambridge University Press.

Skelton, Robin and Margaret Blackwood. 1990. *Earth, Air, Fire, Water: The Goddess and Muse*. London: Arkana.

Squire, Charles. 1975. *Celtic Myth and Legend*. London: Newcastle Publishing.

Starhawk. 1979. *The Spiral dance*. San Francisco: Harper & Row.

———. 1982. *Dreaming the Dark*. Boston: Beacon Press.

Sykes, Homer. 1993. *Mysterious Britain*. London: Weidenfield and Nicolson.

Thompson, William. 1981. *The Time Falling Bodies Take to Light*. New York: St. Martin's Press.

Trapp, Jacob. 1973. *The Light of a Thousand Suns — Mystery, Awe, and Renewal in Religion*. New York: Harper & Row.

von Franz, Marie. 1967. *C. G. Jung: His Myth in Our Time*. New York: C. G. Jung Foundation.

Walker, Barbara. 1983. *The Woman's Encyclopedia of Myths and Secrets*. New York: Harper & Row.

————. 1988. *The Woman's Dictionary of Symbols and Sacred Objects*. San Francisco: Harper Collins.

Yeats, William. 1967. "Among School Children," in *The Collected Poems of W. B. Yeats*. New York: Macmillan.

Zipes, Jack. 1992. *The Complete Fairy Tales of the Brothers Grimm*. Expanded edition. New York: Bantam.